"For decades JoEllen has consistently tugged us back to the simple majesty of reading aloud great books with students and discussing them together. In this book, she offers everything you need to make this work a reality for you and your kids."

— Kate and Maggie Roberts, Authors and Guest Teachers

"In this important book, JoEllen McCarthy reminds us that the heart of read-aloud is in the community. Read-aloud routines have the power to support readers and create safe spaces for students to make sense of our world and more. JoEllen shares books and examples of the important ways that read-aloud in classrooms works to simultaneously grow readers' skills and to grow their hearts."

—Franki Sibberson, Teacher, Author, and NCTE Past-President

"The world needs this book NOW. JoEllen McCarthy masterfully weaves together reading and writing instruction through the lens of social emotional learning to help students understand themselves, each other, and the world. Using books as co-teachers, *Layers of Learning* guides readers to identify the why and recognize that 'literacy has the power to influence and change lives.' A timely book that identifies the most important lessons we may teach: connection, compassion and care. Literacy has the power to influence and change lives."

—Kristin Ziemke, Author and Innovation Specialist, Big Shoulders Fund

---

"*Layers of Learning* provides an amazing array of powerful picture books to connect hearts and learning. Through a teacher-friendly framework, JoEllen McCarthy invites us into ways we can blur the lines between our hearts, our heads, and our hands."

—John Schu, Scholastic Book Ambassador

"This wonderful book takes teachers by the hand and heart and leads them on a journey of connection to picture books, themselves, and their students of *any* age. Inspiring. Motivating. A reminder of the impact teachers have on kids' lives. This spectacular guide makes me long to teach again."

—Lynda Mullaly Hunt, *New York Times* bestselling author

JoEllen McCarthy's heart shines through each sentence with a focus on building community and finding our common humanity through story with a spotlight on the natural connections between reading and writing."

—Lester Laminack, Author and Professor Emeritus, Western Carolina University

―――――――

"*Layers of Learning* goes beyond lists of texts with JoEllen McCarthy's thoughtful curation of books and literacy activities that create and nurture communities of readers and writers. This is a must-read for all educators as it moves us to consider an intentional weaving of texts for discussions and ways to bring in community and family literacies into the classroom space. As a former middle grade teacher and now teacher educator, I was most moved by how the framework, books and extension activities bring together the lived experiences of all children, but especially those who find their humanity most relegated to the margins in schools. *Layers of Learning* amplifies these voices, from the authors and illustrators of books to the students as creators of their own stories in classrooms."

—Carla España, Author, Bank Street Graduate School of Education,
and Bilingual/TESOL Program, Instructor

―――――――

"*Layers of Learning* beats with energy, joy, passion, and love for reading. One of JoEllen McCarthy's most beloved gifts is her encyclopedic knowledge of books and, wow, she jam-packed this resource with titles and teaching ideas! *Layers of Learning* is a love letter to the power of community, built with books, and led by the care of children."

—Christopher Lehman, Founding Director of The Educator Collaborative

―――――――

"Picture books humanize us, making the world both simple and abstract at the same time. Layers of Learning gives multiple examples for doing this work. JoEllen's practical strategies as well as the ideological rationale behind them will be useful for teachers looking to refresh their ideas of what is possible through read-alouds while simultaneously making their teaching practice more equitable, representative, and humanistic."

—Julia Torres, Teacher Librarian, Denver Public Schools

LAYERS OF LEARNING

USING READ-ALOUDS
TO CONNECT LITERACY AND
CARING CONVERSATIONS

JoEllen McCarthy

Stenhouse
PUBLISHERS

Portsmouth, New Hampshire

Stenhouse Publishers
www.stenhouse.com

Acknowledgments for borrowed material begin on page 210.

Cover and interior illustrations © Kathryn Otoshi
Sun and apple icons courtesy of Vecteezy.com

Library of Congress Cataloging-in-Publication Data
Names: McCarthy, JoEllen, author.
Title: Layers of learning : using read-alouds to connect literacy and caring conversations / JoEllen McCarthy.
Identifiers: LCCN 2019043167 (print) | LCCN 2019043168 (ebook) |
    ISBN 9781625312914 (paperback) | ISBN 9781625312921 (ebook)
Subjects: LCSH: Oral reading. | Reading (Elementary) | Picture books
    for children—Educational aspects. | Affective education.
Classification: LCC LB1573.5 .M327 2020   (print) | LCC LB1573.5   (ebook) |
    DDC 372.45/2—dc23
LC record available at https://lccn.loc.gov/2019043167
LC ebook record available at https://lccn.loc.gov/2019043168

Cover design by Margaret Ringia Hart
Interior design and typesetting by Valerie Levy

Manufactured in the United States of America

PRINTED ON 30% PCW
RECYCLED PAPER

26 25 24 23 22 21 20   9 8 7 6 5 4 3 2 1

For my sonshines, Jack, Aidan, and Ryan, and my husband, Jack,
who teach me lessons about life and love every day

And for my family, thank you for being
my first and most cherished teachers

CONTENTS

PART I: LEARNING AS HEARTWORK

PART II: HEARTPRINT CONNECTIONS

8 EMPOWERMENT 140

CONNECTIONS

ACKNOWLEDGMENTS

"And what is the use of a book," thought Alice, "without pictures and conversations?"
—Lewis Carroll, *Alice's Adventures in Wonderland*

In my life, I've been lucky enough to find myself surrounded by conversations about books with colleagues, family, and friends who've been by my side over the years, connecting over stories, to help me learn more about teaching literacy and life lessons. These people have been my coteachers just as much as the books we've shared and have shaped my beliefs during our time together. This project evolved through countless conversations with them about the potential of read-alouds and the power of picture books, I will be forever grateful for the lessons they've taught me—lessons that continue to influence my life beyond the pages of a book.

To my colleagues at the Educator Collaborative, I appreciate the friendships we've formed and the mind-blowing level of ideas, research, and countless think tanks that have made me a stronger teacher and a better human being. #TheEdCollab is #PDLOVE.

Heather Rocco, I cherish the time we spend laughing and learning together. You're an amazing literacy leader and a wonderful friend.

Julia Torres, there is no one I'd rather build book stacks with. Your unconditional book love and commitment to disrupting learning continues to inspire me. Thank you for your friendship and support. I am honored that you were one of the first readers of this book.

To the countless educators I've been privileged to work with and learn from, thank you for inviting me to be a part of your learning communities. And, thank you for allowing me to share our stories.

To my Nerdy Book Club friends, thank you for your passion, energy, and unwavering commitment in celebrating books and readers. I appreciate each of the heartprint educators that make up this community of learners and the ripples of book love you send out into the world.

To the amazing teachers, students, and literacy leaders at Northern Parkway, there really aren't enough words. Thank you for giving me a home and for filling my heart and mind with so many ideas. My residency as a staff developer with you reminds me of the importance of learning together, and our collaborative coaching cycles have grown into friendships that I will always cherish. Special thanks go out to Dr. Bilal Polson, Dr. Sheila Jefferson-Isaac, Iraida Bodre, Roderick Peele, Adam Welt, Keith Hinnant, Alison Lange, Susan Paino, Ketty Hernandez, Cynthia Franco, Joy Renner, Janell Benny, and the extremely talented Erik Sumner. With each of you, #LearningIsJoyful.

Thank you to a very special group of educators and friends, Denise Toscano, Caroline Klein, and Jeni McCarthy. Having your rooms as lab sites and learning alongside you are always a pleasure. Your communities of learners are lucky to have you, and so am I.

So many heartprint authors have supported me over the years, and I'm grateful for all they have taught me. To Trudy Ludwig and Marissa Moss, thanks for inspiring me with the Common CARE standards. Jackie Woodson, your books continue to touch my heart and your work continues to remind me that authors and books can inspire change. To Georgia Heard, thank you for your guidance and for helping me navigate my teaching heart map. To Kwame Alexander, for sharing your *Playbook* with me. Thank you all. Your work and your words have taught me so many lessons about community, agency, respect, and empowerment. I am eternally grateful.

Regie Routman, I am in awe of all that you do. Thank you for taking the time in the early stages of this project to share your feedback; your insight and support were invaluable. Thank you, as well, for inspiring my residencies and helping me to read, write, and lead.

Kathryn Otoshi, thank you for your generosity, your friendship, and your beautiful hands. Your artistic vision helped bring the spirit of this project to life. You and your friendship mean the world to me.

I am grateful to the entire team at Stenhouse for helping to make this book a reality. Special thanks to Shannon St. Peter and Lynne Costa—your careful eyes on all the moving pieces of this project have helped in more ways than you know. Thank you for your support, energy, and enthusiasm for this work.

To my editor and friend, Terry Thompson, you truly are my More Knowledgeable Other. Thank you for believing in me, caring about me and this project, and encouraging me with your support, guiding questions, and precise word choice. Terry's TLC is felt in my heart and on every page.

And a huge thank you to the students and educators I have learned from on and off the pages who have contributed to this book. Thank you for sharing your voices, art, stories, hearts, and minds. This book would be incomplete without you.

Finally, heartfelt appreciation goes out to my family and friends who have supported me along the way. Thank you for your hugs, encouraging phone calls, and card game breaks—and for always reminding me that you care.

My heart, head, and hands are filled by the life lessons I have learned from each of you.

INTRODUCTION

Dear Readers,

We learn best when we feel safe, happy, and loved. From the moment our children step foot in our classrooms, we work to cultivate relationships grounded in care and trust that nourish the minds, hearts, and hands of our learning community. Those relationships matter—for teachers and students. Education may be the only profession that has the ability to influence lives so deeply. Yes, our work can leave lasting impressions, but so can books.

The role of literature in our classrooms goes far beyond its effect on academics. Reading regularly to students helps them develop a sense of belonging to a community of learners. Our read-aloud time together and conversations around books can help children acquire the necessary social-emotional learning skills, attitudes, and courage to promote self-care and compassion. Through books we not only nourish our reading and writing communities but also support the development of the whole child.

No tool is more powerful than the picture book, and this has shaped my beliefs and driven my practices beginning with my days as a student teacher at the Manhattan New School, through my years as a classroom teacher, and today as a staff developer. We can use read-alouds to celebrate new books, new ideas, and new possibilities that impact authentic life learning too. There's an immeasurable joy in sharing read-alouds, in seeing the smiles and the ripples of book love. From those first read-alouds in September to the books we share on the last day of school, we work tirelessly to find just the right book for just the right moment and surround ourselves and our students with quality literature. We trust the powerful connections created between books and readers.

When we use stories to invite complex questions and reflection, we see books as coteachers that inspire us to wonder, to see possibilities, and to illuminate the truths and sometimes the harsh realities about our world. As we read, our beliefs are affirmed, challenged, strengthened, or changed. The books we share can help shape this literacy landscape, from setting the stage for those getting-to-know-you conversations to those difficult conversations that can push us through discussions to be more caring, compassionate, and concerned community members. In her memoir *Becoming*, former First Lady Michelle Obama offers us an invitation: "Let's invite one another in. Maybe then we can begin to fear less, to make fewer wrong assumptions, to let go of the biases and stereotypes that unnecessarily divide us" (Obama 2018, 420). Books can bring us together in this way. Through read-alouds, we can teach our students about more than reading and writing and invite them into conversations that create spaces where they can start to understand one another better.

Countless researchers and educators have influenced my teaching and have informed my community of practice on the subject of caring in schools. I hope that this book will provide you with a balance of research and reasoning to support read-alouds, while offering insights into children's literature to help you and your students lead conversations beyond literacy to include layers of literacy and life connections, character education, and social-emotional support.

This book invites you to reflect on ways sharing picture books can empower all learners. In addition to promoting these important interactions with tons of ideas and recommendations, together, we'll explore stories, look through literacy snapshots, visit classrooms, and discover titles that sustain and strengthen whole-school communities.

Like all good teaching, our journey together will be about process, not product. I also hope this work will enhance your current practices. Use its framework and suggested ideas to help you find more connections between reading, writing, and life. Take the time you need to read and reflect. Use the conversations started in this book to enhance your ongoing reflection and collaboration with your professional community of learners. Look for opportunities to adopt or adapt the suggestions you'll find here to the work you are already doing. Since the most effective professional development experiences include time for reflective practice, we'll think beyond book lists to the various ways sharing texts can lift the quality of our reading and writing, change our conversations, and leave us feeling inspired. Books help us find a way of being as we celebrate stories, people, and practices that inspire all learners. Still, it's not just about which books we use, but how we use them. I hope that this book will help you read, reflect, and research the possibilities that lie within every text. I hope the vision and *visible* voice of students and teachers throughout this book will inspire your work. Perhaps you'll see something that causes you to nod in recognition, challenges you with a new way of thinking, or excites you with new ideas to try in your classroom.

This book has been years in the making, but it won't be complete without the experiences you and your students bring to its pages. Together, let's make every text we share and every move we make an invitation to learn about ourselves, others, and our world.

With hugs and book love,

Jo Ellen

PART I
LEARNING AS HEARTWORK

THE LITERACY CONNECTIONS TO COMMUNITY

Without a sense of caring, there can be no sense of community.
—Anthony J. D'Angelo, "An Ally's Promise"

THERE'S SOMETHING special about the routines and rituals the fresh start of each new school year brings. End-of-summer, beginning-of-school year errands. Back-to-school shopping, including fresh Sharpies, sacred new chart paper, carefully thought-out spaces and places, and of course amazing new books! It's really the most wonderful time of the year. You can almost see the Staples commercial, families dancing down the aisles with excitement. As educators we have even more reason to celebrate. New beginnings. New faces. New hopes. New dreams. New books. And opportunities for new smiles every year.

With each new start, building community is imperative. Every year we recommit to the mission of preparing kids for a wider, healthier conception of the world. That isn't always easy. And it doesn't happen overnight. But, as Debbie Miller says, "Real communities flourish when we bring together the voices, hearts, and souls of the people who inhabit them" (2016, 21). When that shared purpose focuses on building the literacy lives of those who learn in our communities, magic happens.

Though community, by definition, speaks to the coming together of a unified body of individuals with common interests, our school communities consist of unique individuals with a variety of different interests, backgrounds, and experiences. Still, I believe we can come together and nurture a sense of CommUNITY through story. Shared experiences through stories help us to celebrate, respect, and value what makes us unique while, at the same time, highlighting the commonalities we share as learners and as human beings.

To that end, read-alouds empower and strengthen our sense of community. When we read aloud and carry the messages from these communal experiences across our day, connecting our reading, writing, and thinking beyond the texts to include shared life lessons, we can have a more significant impact in shaping our community of learners. Every read-aloud gives us the opportunity for purposeful reflection and action, helping students manage emotions, navigate challenging times, prepare for a better tomorrow, and participate in a community of learners where all members are respected and valued. As we establish a sense of trust, a sense of belonging, a sense of purpose, the books we read and the stories we share affect how we relate to one another in our own classroom community and in our world. Books help lay this caring foundation and make it stronger with each additional layer—brick by brick, story by story.

SHARING STORIES, STRENGTHENING COMMUNITIES

Findings from the Collaborative for Academic, Social and Emotional Learning (CASEL) show that incorporating social and emotional learning contributes to greater success in school, careers, and life (Weissberg 2016). One way to make an enduring difference in the life of a child and build stronger learning communities is through positive, proactive character education. Many years ago I participated in a workshop led by Thomas Lickona, author of *Educating for Character: How Our Schools Can Teach Respect and Responsibility* (1991), and what stuck with me were his ideas around educating the whole child: through the head, the heart, and the hands. Lickona's theory complements the work of other thought leaders (Banks 1998; Charney 1992; Gay 2000/2018; Noddings 1984) when he emphasizes that, through the head, students may know the good; through the heart, they may care about the good; and through the hands, they may do the good. His beliefs centered around the impact of character education on caring and learning in schools touching minds, hearts, and hands.

Inspired by this, I've made it an ongoing practice to share books through read-alouds that, in addition to supporting our regular literacy learning, highlight the opportunity for knowing, feeling, and doing. Through carefully selected read-alouds, learners begin to understand (head) more about themselves and the community around them. This understanding translates to empathy (heart) and both, eventually with our guidance, translate to action (hands). We can take advantage of this virtuous cycle to create a complex chain of events that reinforces itself through a feedback loop. Each iteration of the cycle reinforcing the previous one. Know. Feel. Do.

We can find support for this work in the pages of a children's book. With powerful read-alouds that echo teaching as heartwork, we can balance academic and social-emotional growth to reach the whole child and the whole community. These social-emotional connections provide opportunities for layers of learning across all three areas of knowing, feeling, and doing.

This book aims to shift literacy instruction and social-emotional learning from *either-or* choices to responsive *yes-ands*. Literacy is about more than reading or writing, empathy or creativity, imagination or critical thinking. Just as it is essential to teach comprehension strategies, it is also essential to reflect on the multiple ways literacy instruction can integrate social, emotional, affective layers of learning. With purposeful planning, we can make our read-alouds do double— even triple—work. Know. Feel. Do.

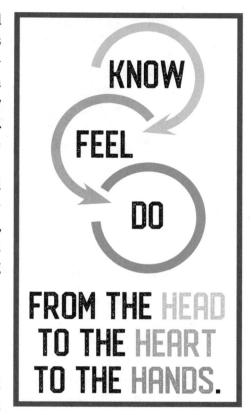

So, rather than thinking of social-emotional learning as isolated skills to add on to our already jam-packed days, we can explore read-alouds through a framework of thinking that layers reading, writing, and caring conversations. With the right read-alouds, we can nourish the reader, the writer, and the human in each of our students, feeding three birds with one hand.

THE HEARTWORK BOOKS DO

Books provide a lens into the world of others. They can also be the vehicle that drives conversations about diversity, inclusivity, equity, and respect for others and our world. When we share books that give all students voices and are mindful of a *curriculum of children*, we honor their experiences and the experiences of others. Through stories, we can affect kinder, caring, more compassionate learners who can in turn impact our world. And when we invite books to serve as coteachers in our classrooms, they offer a kindly gesture, opening doors and telling us to look for ourselves and welcome others.

In thriving learning communities, there are common *care* elements driven by stories, relationships, and opportunities to examine mindsets in new ways. We can use books to highlight these elements and help us examine how our attitudes and actions affect others. This shift from *me* to *we* supports our relationships and in turn impacts greater success in school and in life.

Children's picture books can help explain big ideas and complex emotional topics (i.e., identity, self-esteem, family dynamics, relationships, grief, loss, discrimination, power, privilege, equity), in a simple, straightforward way to young children, while older kids can appreciate their symbolism and multilayered meanings.

Since stories invite rather than impose, picture books can illustrate important life lessons and make a strong impact on your students and on their learning communities. As you look through the following examples, take a moment to reflect on how sharing these titles provides opportunities for big thinking in small spaces. And consider how a little book love can go a long way.

SELF-AWARENESS

To encourage awareness around personal preferences (and to illustrate the ageless power of picture books meant to be read and reread), I often share Timothy Young's *I Hate Picture Books!* (2013), where the narrator, a young boy named Max, is about to get rid of all the picture books he hates. In doing so, he is reminded of all the lessons he learned from the characters in those books, and he realizes he isn't ready to part with any of them. This reminder that we're never too old for a picture books is a great opportunity to discuss books that we cannot live without, books that have taught us life lessons, and books that teach us more about our world.

COLLABORATING WITH OTHERS

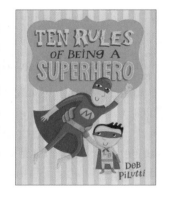

For an uplifting message about having collaborators in our work and the necessity of "sidekicks" to energize our learning journeys, look to Deb Pilutti's *Ten Rules of Being a Superhero* (2014). In this book, the narrator shares the rules for being a superhero. Discussions around this book often evolve into examining our individual strengths and challenges and, as we do so, strengthening our relationships with one another. Consider using this book as a springboard into "rules" for caring conversations, self-talk, and responsive classrooms.

SELF-MANAGEMENT AND DEALING WITH FEELINGS

When I want to address how moods can affect one's day, and also discuss changing emotions with lyrical language, I share *my cold plum lemon pie bluesy mood* by Tameka Fryer Brown (2013). In this old favorite, Jamie explores a variety of moods—"feeling and being kind of moods." This book offers a great way to check in on community concerns, to take the emotional temperature of a group, and to discuss mindsets. By sharing Jamie's story, we can explore the importance of managing emotions, as well as ways to deal with our own feelings and how to be mindful of others' feelings.

SOCIAL AWARENESS

In Jacqueline Woodson's *Each Kindness* (2012), Chloe and her friends exclude the new girl, Maya. They realize a little too late the importance of their actions and inactions and their ripple effects. By thinking about Maya's feelings, students and teachers can discuss the choices they make and the consequences of their actions as well as the importance of empathy, understanding, and relationships with others.

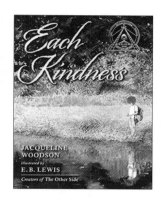

RESPONSIBLE DECISION MAKING

During a fire in *The Little Hummingbird* by Michael Nicoll Yahgulanaas (2010), all the animals flee the forest except the little hummingbird. The animals question how this little hummingbird and her little drops of water can make a difference. Rather than being overwhelmed or powerless, the little hummingbird demonstrates that we all have the ability to make a difference. The story can help explore the importance of identifying and solving problems, responsibility, and action.

Throughout this book, we'll continue to explore additional ways to use picture books to layer life lessons like these across your instructional day. A framework and suggested connections will inspire you to use read-alouds to blur the lines between lessons in reading, writing, and life. As you read, I invite you to think about how read-alouds can speak to the readers you work with every day. What are you and your students noticing? What community needs could be met through sharing books? And what titles will resonate best as ways to strengthen your students as readers, writers, thinkers, and caring community members? With that foundation, the rest of our journey together will be structured in three parts. The remainder of Part I will explore the importance of community and connections to both academic and social-emotional learning as it impacts literacy. We'll look at reasons and research for establishing caring communities of learners grounded in book love. Together, we'll explore the power of read-alouds and how to use books as coteachers to connect literacy and lifework across the day while complementing the work you are already doing. This section will provide an invitational approach to responsive teaching and caring in schools with practical, easy-to-adopt or -adapt ideas that merge research, authentic literature, and various classroom voices you can immediately apply in your classrooms.

In Part II, you'll find a variety of ideas tied to the Heartprint Framework, which illustrates ways to use books to educate the head (reading and writing connections), inspire the heart (socio-emotional connections to support empathy and understanding), and engage the hands (literacy snapshot takeaways to adopt or adapt). This section will include a collection of heartprint texts and sample connections (Chapters 5–8) that present teaching invitations specifically connected to the following CARE elements:

- Community
- Agency
- Respect
- Empowerment

Each chapter includes fifteen layered connections with a selection of optional teaching points that address academic standards along with invitations to connect affective elements in a variety of settings—whole-class, small-group, and one-to-one individual conversations—that support authentic experiences, investigations, and new understandings. The examples provided (based on my work alongside students and teachers) will help you tailor your instructional decisions around the anchor texts highlighted or, more important, inspire you to develop and customize lessons using your own heartprint books.

When we extend our work with read-alouds to strengthen connections between heads, hearts, and hands, we can address a real culture of care. Beyond bucket-filling, trait-of-the-week, and anti-bullying campaigns, learners need trusting, fair, and safe environments so that they feel comfortable engaging in learning challenges, taking academic risks, and acting as caring members of a classroom community. We can create those opportunities through the pages of a book.

THE POWER OF READ-ALOUDS ON AND OFF THE PAGE

Great literature doesn't tell us how to act, or what to think, or whom to become.
Rather, great literature offers us choices and insights into how we might act,
who we might become, and what we might think.
—Frank Serafini, *Reading Workshop 2.0*

READ-ALOUDS provide an unmistakable experience of hearts and minds coming together. When the conditions are just right, learning communities become connected and ignited by story—a circle of shared smiles and hearts beating to the same rhythm of words. You might see readers lean in longing to share more of a character's journey, hear fits of laughter, or notice nods of recognition for little secret messages. Read-alouds help learners share thoughts, dreams, fears, and cares and turn those moments into memories that connect us all, heartbeat to heartbeat.

The books we share during these read-alouds help strengthen a foundation for thinking and living together, nurturing our learning communities layer by layer, story by story. And, beyond these inter-personal connections, you'll find plenty of *concrete* evidence demonstrating the literacy benefits of read-alouds as well. Despite the ongoing reading wars, one thing everyone can agree on is the positive effects of read-alouds. Regie Routman (2018) states, "Read alouds are the indispensable first steps of reaching and teaching students" (199), and cognitive psychologist Daniel Willingham (2018) argues that read-alouds are the "lifeblood" in any literacy program, providing language opportunities for children to speak, listen, and write (on October 29, 2018). Read-alouds help students negotiate meaning before, during, and after the reading of texts (Burkins and Croft 2017; Clay 1991; Fountas and Pinnell 2006) and expose them to rich language, academic vocabulary, and phrased, fluent reading (Bennett-Armistead, Duke, and Moses 2007; Fountas and Pinnell 2006). Along with gains in vocabulary (Bennett-Armistead and Duke 2003), read-alouds affect pronunciation, add explanation and exposure to new and difficult words, expand comprehension, and help children develop word mastery (Calkins 2000; Fountas and Pinnell 2012; Whitehurst 2002). They also help children to "listen up" (Layne 2015), exposing them to literature above and beyond their independent reading levels and demonstrating complex ideas, vocabulary, and language patterns (Beck and McKeown 2001). Through rich read-alouds, students can explore multiple writing strategies about texts, text structures, language, vocabulary, grammar, spelling, and craft lessons. These connections are too good to be ignored, and with intentional, purposeful planning, using powerful read-alouds can expose students to quality texts that can directly influence their own reading, writing, and thinking.

As educators, it's essential that we make time for read-alouds throughout our teaching day to help serve the academic needs of our learners—reading with children, reading to children, and reading for children. Richard Allington and Rachel Gabriel (2012) outlined the academic and cognitive benefits of read-alouds as part of the six elements of effective instruction every child should experience every day. But read-alouds can also support the heartwork of teaching, nurturing an essential love of literature, a love of others, and a love of self—all while supporting the reading and writing skills needed for academic success.

Fueled by research like this, I've moved beyond theory and, through practice, have directly witnessed how read-alouds impact real classrooms to nurture and facilitate conversations about literacy and life connections. From my first days of teaching (way back when) and even today in my role as a staff developer, as I spend time working with children across the country, I continue to rely on read-alouds to:

Model a love of reading and writing
Introduce and familiarize readers and
    writers with authors, genres, and
    text structures
Lead to common language and
    connections over books
Teach kindness and compassion
Encourage empathy and awareness
    for self and others
Launch and introduce a new topic
Help make connections between
    what we read and what we write
Foster engagement
Create and nurture book bonds
Support social interactions
Bring stories and characters to life

Strengthen comprehension
Build background knowledge
Support deeper knowledge of craft:
    language, grammar
Facilitate development of second or
    multiple languages
Demonstrate fluency and voice
Lead to stronger vocabulary
Teach receptive language
Teach the beauty of story, words,
    language, and ideas
Facilitate joyful communities
    connected by shared reading
    experiences

You probably already use read-alouds to reinforce many of these benefits and to make connections to academic standards. Read-alouds can help launch a unit of study, provide background knowledge around a topic, kindle inquiry studies, introduce readers and writers to authors, and prompt further investigations about genres, text types, or structures. We can use read-alouds to support deeper knowledge of craft moves, such as language, grammar, wordplay, and ideas, or to model a specific reading or writing strategy.

Often, we refer to the same book again and again for multiple reasons. Perhaps on a first read, we'll call to mind a book's beautiful language, highlighting the impact of the writer's words on our ability to comprehend with deeper understanding as we discuss how those words affect our mental images. Later, during writing workshop, we might go back and read aloud the same selection to demonstrate how writers craft texts, exploring and discussing the author's use of rich, descriptive language; precise words; sensory details; or actions.

BOOKS AS COTEACHERS FOR LITERACY: READING AND WRITING CONNECTIONS

Figure 2.1

If you think back to a time you planned a literacy lesson using a picture book, chances are that you've already had a coteacher in your classroom. Each day, as I pack to visit teachers and students, I think about the learners I'll be working with as well as the coteachers (books) I'll be bringing to help me. One of my favorite coteachers is *Duck! Rabbit!*, the popular picture book adaptation of a classic optical illusion by Amy Krouse Rosenthal and illustrator Tom Lichtenheld (2009). Take a look (Figure 2.1).

What do you see? A duck or a rabbit? At first you might see a duck, but if you look hard enough and change your perspective a bit, you'll also see a rabbit. Can you see it? This dual image in *Duck! Rabbit!* serves as a powerful example of our ability to see the same thing through different viewpoints and

Figure 2.2

a nice reminder that we do the same when we use multiple lenses to address reading and writing through the same book. One day we might read a book aloud showcasing it through the lens of a reader and then revisit that same book at another time to focus on the text as a writer. Let's use this same dual perspective to take a look at Trudy Ludwig's *My Secret Bully* (2015) (Figure 2.2).

On the cover, we see two girls standing face to face. From a reader's angle, you'd likely begin by thinking about what's going on in your head as you look at the title and the pictures. What comes to mind? How do your life experience and background knowledge influence your inferences? Are you visualizing a bully that no one knows about? Are you connecting to someone who has acted as bystander, equating their inaction with being a secret bully? Do you recall a time when someone was secretly bullying someone else?

On the opening pages, Monica, the narrator, says, "Katie is my secret bully. A lot of people would be surprised to know this because they think she's my friend. And she does act like my friend . . . sometimes." Perhaps, as a reader, you're beginning to question how someone can be a friend and a bully at the same time. On the next page, we see a reference to "Mon-ICK-a" as her sometimes friend and secret bully calls her. This little added detail changes our interpretation, influencing the inferences we're making as readers, affecting the mood-driven fluency of the text, and perhaps calling to mind a time when someone was teasing, taunting, or excluding a so-called friend.

Those three words, *my secret bully*, take on new meaning with every turn of the page. As we read on, we continue to synthesize new details, expand or revise our inferences, focus on character traits, deepen our understanding of the book's theme, and much more.

Now let's revisit *My Secret Bully* using our lens as writers and think about how doing so can help us lift the level of our own writing. For example, the title, *My Secret Bully,* discloses a little bit of information to the reader, reminding us that, as writers, we think long and hard about our titles. Will it be a sneak peek to our piece? How might it thread back to the heart of our story? Will it elicit feelings in our readers, making them want to read more? We could also look closely at how Trudy Ludwig includes exact actions, dialogue, and inner monologue to create stronger images and strengthen ideas for her readers—and how we might do the same when we write personal narratives about an experience with a friend or a family member.

As you look through the books in your classroom using both lenses, you'll likely notice lots of ways each text can inspire you as a reader or a writer in this same way. If we want students to evolve as literacy learners, we need to "emphasize the reciprocal processes that nourish each other" (Routman 2018, 169). It is undeniable. <u>Reading influences writing and writing influences reading.</u> <u>Rather than separate the two, we can capitalize on the inherent reading-writing connections displayed in the following chart to make the most of the read-alouds we share and, just as important, to make the most of our day.</u>

AS A READER . . .	AS A WRITER . . .
Readers set a purpose for reading and consider the author's purpose to shape or deepen understanding of a text.	Writers consider purpose and audience and reflect that plan to address their intended readers.
Readers access and use prior knowledge as an entry point and use that information and understanding to discern more about a text.	Writers write about what they know and care about and look for ideas and inspiration from their experiences, wonderings, and interests.
Readers make connections among texts to support their thinking, noticing similarities in text types, text structures, topics, story elements, and other patterns.	Writers connect ideas, events, and images to develop their writing and build meaning across the text.

AS A READER . . .	AS A WRITER . . .
Readers ask questions to monitor their comprehension, to clarify, and to expand meaning.	Writers ask and answer questions to develop their ideas, drive their research, or anticipate readers' wonderings.
Readers make inferences to interpret texts based on words, images, information, and background knowledge.	Writers often imply with text and images clues to support meaning.
Readers create mental images, considering moods, action, and sensory details to support understanding texts.	Writers use words, images, and phrases to create a picture for the reader.
Readers filter information and organize ideas to determine importance.	Writers include information, facts, and details that highlight what's most important for readers.
Readers summarize and synthesize known and new information to interpret texts and expand their thinking.	Writers disclose ideas and intentions cumulatively in ways that help their readers merge new understandings.
Readers think about text structures to gain information based on the organization and patterns found in a text.	Writers collect and categorize information to organize the presentation of their facts and ideas.
Readers think about the impact of grammar, conventions, sentence length, and mechanics on comprehension, fluency, and voice.	Writers make intentional decisions using conventions of grammar, mechanics, and sentence length to impact voice and message to the reader.
Readers analyze and critique texts recognizing facts, opinions, and an author's bias (stance) to think more critically about a text.	Writers express individual feelings, opinions, beliefs, and values through their use of craft, topic, and style.

This reciprocal rethinking applies not only to how we view texts but also to how we use them to differentiate based on the needs of our students. Reflective practice is key. As you select your read-alouds, ask yourself: *What does my class need in this moment? What specific reading strategies or craft moves in writing could this book showcase for my students? How could this particular book act as a coteacher for this group of readers, writers, or thinkers?* Know your why. Try this. Host a BYOB (bring your own book) meeting and work with your peers to practice considering books from the two perspectives of reading and writing. Choose several titles from your read-aloud stack. Use the first three columns of the chart in Figure 2.3 to list all the possible reading strategies each title inspires and all the qualities of writing it exemplifies. Now, take a moment to reflect on what you've noticed and the benefits of using the same book to teach a variety of reading and writing skills and strategies.

TITLE AUTHOR ILLUSTRATOR	NOTICINGS AS A READER	NOTICINGS AS A WRITER	NOTICINGS FOR LIFE LESSONS

Figure 2.3 Heartprint Connections: Using Books as Coteachers

Figure 2.4 During our professional development sessions and our BYOB (bring your own book) meetings, we go through stacks of picture books to discuss the various ways we might use them. Ask your students to share their noticings in their own stacks.

BOOKS AS COTEACHERS FOR LIFEWORK: LAYERING LITERACY LESSONS WITH SOCIAL-EMOTIONAL CONNECTIONS

Reading is good for the brain and the heart. As we capitalize on read-alouds as coteachers to connect reading and writing, we can easily add a layer to address cognitive and affective strategies too (Figure 2.3). Scientists have studied the brain's capacity to empathize and found that we easily connect to others through stories. In his research, psychologist Raymond Mar (2018) found that children as young as age three begin to understand what characters in stories are feeling and thinking. Reading aloud has been proven to have sustained impact on positive behaviors as well as attention span and may also influence a child's ability to control and handle emotions (Klass 2018). In elementary schools and in middle schools, read-alouds have also been proven to impact cultural sensitivity (Verden 2012). Books have been found to influence our emotions while encouraging empathy and positively affecting our attitudes toward others (Maunders and Montgomery 2015; Oatley 2011). They have and will always play a pivotal role in helping to explore concepts, characters, conflicts, and compassion.

As we continue to consider powerful children's books alongside the academic needs of our learners, we can go beyond craft lessons for reading and writing, and utilize literature to model prosocial attitudes effectively and build emotional behaviors like self-management, social awareness, and responsible decision making, to create and maintain a culture of respect within a school learning community. With every read-aloud, we have an opportunity to expand our hearts and minds and deepen our humanity. Feelings can be validated, shared, and explored with new insights. Read-alouds can be "an oral vaccine for literacy" (Trelease 2019) that can be just the kind of medicine many students may need. Stories can provide a healthy dose of laughter, tears, and learning together. With books as coteachers for life lessons, we layer on another perspective to the complex conversations we're already having about reading and writing to include social-emotional connections.

With that in mind, let's take another look at *My Secret Bully* (Ludwig 2015). Monica is the target of relationally aggressive acts such as intentional exclusion, the silent treatment, gossip, and humiliation. This form of emotional bullying, explains Ludwig in the endnotes, is often hidden among friendship groups. Ludwig gives us a lot to think about, providing several entry points for children to discuss how often they experience bullying in schools, what degrees of bullying they're aware of, and what it means to be a bystander. Reading aloud powerful picture books such as *My Secret Bully* invites opportunities for reflection in the safety of student-led discussions. These conversations often affect opinions and actions within and outside of our classrooms. As you reflect on these additional social-emotional layers, we can add to the thinking we started in Figure 2.3 to consider the various ways books can serve as coteachers to connect reading and writing while, at the same time, offering an additional layer of life lessons:

AS A READER . . .	AS A WRITER . . .	AS A LIFE LEARNER . . .
Readers set a purpose for reading and consider the author's purpose to shape or deepen understanding of a text.	Writers consider purpose and audience and reflect that plan to address their intended readers.	Learners consider personal connections and the impact of a message's purpose, weighing it against their own opinions, beliefs, and values.
Readers access and use prior knowledge as an entry point and use that information and understanding to discern more about a text.	Writers write about what they know and care about and look for ideas and inspiration from their experiences, wonderings, and interests.	Learners use past experiences for reflection and transference to real-life situations.
Readers make connections among texts to support their thinking, noticing similarities in text types, text structures, topics, story elements, and, other patterns.	Writers connect ideas, events, and images to develop their writing and to build meaning across the text.	Learners connect ideas, perspectives, events and images to inform responsible, empathetic interactions and decision making.

AS A READER...	AS A WRITER...	AS A LIFE LEARNER...
Readers ask questions to monitor their comprehension, to clarify, and to expand meaning..	Writers ask and answer questions to develop their ideas, drive their research, or anticipate readers' wonderings.	Learners ask questions, challenge thinking, and seek other perspectives and opinions to affirm or alter viewpoints.
Readers make inferences to interpret texts based on words, images, information, and background knowledge.	Writers often imply with text and images clues to support meaning.	Learners reflect on experiences and information and apply them in their lives to understand themselves and others better.
Readers create mental images, considering moods, action, and sensory details to support understanding texts.	Writers use words, images, and phrases to create a picture for the reader.	Learners use words, images, and phrases to imagine situations, question realities, express their perspective, and expand their understanding of the world.
Readers filter information and organize ideas to determine importance.	Writers include information, facts, and details that highlight what's most important for readers.	Learners consider information and multiple viewpoints to access ideas and consider effects of authentic and relevant information.
Readers summarize and synthesize known and new information to interpret texts and expand their thinking.	Writers disclose ideas and intentions cumulatively in ways that help their readers merge new understandings.	Learners reflect and consider the overall effects and behaviors of emotions, thoughts, and multiple viewpoints that impact and influence behaviors of themselves and others.
Readers think about text structures to gain information based on the organization and patterns found in a text.	Writers collect and categorize information to organize the presentation of their facts and ideas.	Learners make constructive, intentional decisions to express their thoughts, behaviors, and emotions in various life situations.

(continues)

(continued)

AS A READER . . .	AS A WRITER . . .	AS A LIFE LEARNER . . .
Readers think about the impact of grammar, conventions, sentence length, and mechanics on comprehension, fluency, and voice.	Writers make intentional decisions using conventions of grammar, mechanics, and sentence length to impact voice and message to the reader.	Learners consider emotions and meaning connected to texts and messages.
Readers analyze and critique texts recognizing facts, opinions, and an author's bias (stance) to think more critically about a text.	Writers express individual feelings, opinions, beliefs, and values through their use of craft, topic, and style.	Learners consider details and form opinions based on perspectives, positions, and voices to strengthen and/or revise their thinking or stance on a subject.

Beyond the images on and off the pages of a book, everyone views the world differently. How does our personal set of filters, beliefs, and experiences impact the way we see the world and interact with others? And how can our experience with books make us more aware in a way that helps us learn from the views and experiences of others? Being open and listening with these questions in mind, we can read to know more, feel more, and do more. The books we share can help our learning communities gain emotional intelligence and empathy. Through literacy, we can show students how to live in the world. When our lessons layer in the heartwork of social-emotional learning, our work goes beyond reading and writing strategies to extend conversations to what books can teach us about life, nurturing learners *affectively* as well.

Whether it's fiction or nonfiction, all texts provide opportunities for readers to ask and answer questions about life. As we strengthen our understanding of theme and author's purpose, we can also strengthen our understanding of what it means to be compassionate citizens. Let's use our read-alouds as part of a virtuous cycle that includes critical reading, thinking, and talking to strengthen our connections as life learners.

HEARTPRINT BOOKS: THE FOUNDATION OF LITERACY AND LIFE CONNECTIONS

In an attempt to celebrate this power of books as coteachers for reading, writing, and life lessons, I've spent many years (and dollars!) searching for texts that best illustrate the connected nature and overlapping relationship between minds, hearts, and hands. These *heartprint books*, as I call them, leave footprints on our hearts and lasting impressions on our learning communities. I can think of no better reason for us to read aloud every day. When we invest in books, we invest in kids—an investment that is ageless and priceless.

CHOOSING HEARTPRINT BOOKS

When you go to select heartprint books for your classroom, you'll want to choose titles carefully. As you do, it's helpful to stay mindful of Louise Rosenblatt's (1978) transactional theory. As an educational researcher, Rosenblatt's work revolutionized reading instruction. Those "ink spots on paper," Rosenblatt argued, become meaningful symbols that connect us with books through our intellectual and emotional contexts (2005, 62). In other words, reading is a complex process that includes a reciprocal exchange between the text and the reader, so our job is to facilitate conversations where learners can share multiple perspectives about the meaning they transact from texts. The reader writes the story.

With this transactional theory in mind, heartprint books can and should help us teach in ways that honor the lives, cultures, languages, and histories of every reader and writer in our classrooms (Souto-Manning and Martell 2016). When we choose well, relationships and communities evolve through collaborative teaching—learning experiences and heartfelt responses to stories. This response-based approach to sharing books empowers all learners involved—teachers and students—while planting seeds for conversations that will grow over time. It also requires an investment in books that speak to learning communities at just the right time, in just the right ways.

When you think about the qualities of exemplary heartprint books, consider texts that provide an invitation to notice something about reading or writing and life:

- Texts that students can relate to in learning about themselves, others, and our world
- Texts that are sure to mirror (Bishop 1990) the lives of students in class as well as serve to reflect a deeper understanding of varied cultures and experiences
- Texts with relatable, multidimensional characters that hook the reader and portray realistic, humanistic emotions
- Texts that explore a variety of voices and stories that examine choices, characters, communities, and conflicts and empower others to do the same
- Texts with rich language
- Texts that serve as models for craft lessons in writing and comprehension lessons in reading
- Texts to examine the impact of illustrations and artistic techniques
- Texts that can influence acts of justice and support compassionate members of a learning community
- Texts that feel right and necessary in the moment because of current events, situations, or complex issues in our world
- Texts that simply touch hearts in an indescribable way

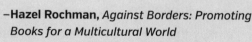

Books can make a difference in dispelling prejudice and building community: not with role models and recipes, not with noble messages, but with stories that make us imagine the lives of others.

–**Hazel Rochman,** *Against Borders: Promoting Books for a Multicultural World*

READING AS LIFEWORK

As you select your heartprint texts and reflect on noticings, you'll also want to remember that books are important influencers in who we become and on what biases we do or do not harbor (Nel 2017). In 2018, only 23 percent of books published featured nonwhite children (Cooperative Children's Book Center 2018) and only 7 percent were by nonwhite creators (Corrie 2018). It's essential that we stay mindful of the texts we select and reflect on the messages they share. Are we discussing issues of diversity, equity, and inclusion? Do the books we highlight reflect the students we work with? Are they true reflections of the world? (See Figure 2.5.)

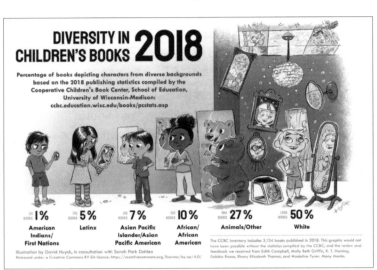

Teachers often ask for a specific book recommendation or a list of the best books to use in this heartwork, but like our students, books are always changing. Selecting texts is a complex process, because our kids are complex (as is our world). The idea is to focus *beyond the book* and to look for texts that serve your students best. It's not about

Figure 2.5

that book but instead about *books that* support children with conversations, strategies, and lessons about reading, writing, and life. Luckily for us, there are amazing books being published every day.

Now, go back to the chart from Figure 2.3 that you started earlier to explore reading and writing connections across your read-aloud stack. Use this fourth column to think about how those same titles can offer invitations for additional life lessons. Use the final column on your chart to make notes about social-emotional concepts you could layer in with each book's corresponding academic conversations. As you reread the text, what notions come to mind that might plant seeds for deeper conversations? Is there a theme or a message from the author? Are there issues to examine further? Perhaps there are some character actions or inactions that might be worth exploring. Is there an event or dialogue within the text that can support further connections, cares, and concerns? Whose voice is represented and whose is missing? What do the illustrations say? Not say? What open-ended questions does the text bring to mind that would support students' inquiries and caring perspectives? What opportunities to explore identity, culture, gender roles, religion, power, and privilege do you notice? Look for entry points that will engage your learners in critical explorations of the texts from simple noticings to more complex conversations.

More important than the texts you choose, though, is the line of thinking around your choice. Understanding the why behind your selections will fine-tune your search for those *just-right* read-alouds. Even as you make selections, stay flexible about your decisions and constantly reevaluate them based on your intentions (Ray 2006). Engage in research, investigations, and ongoing inquiries about read-alouds. Participate in conversations, workshops, webinars, and conferences. Seek out literacy leaders, mentors, and edufriends to discuss and share titles and tips for read-alouds. Talk with one another about books. And, most important, think about your students, and find texts that pair with their needs. Knowing books is important, but knowing your students will direct your book selection and guide you as you support their conversations around the stories you share. Together, all of these impact our communities' transactions with the text.

SHOW ME, HELP ME, LET ME: BOOKS AS OUR COTEACHERS

You may want to start with a simple book that addresses feelings. Recall *my cold plum lemon pie bluesy mood* by Tameka Fryer Brown (2013), with illustrations by Shane Evans. This story can serve as a multilayered heartprint book to illustrate descriptive language (writing), to emphasize inferences about emotions (reading), and to explore mindsets and moods with students (life lessons). In the text, the narrator, Jamie, explores what colors he connects to his moods. For example, listening to music puts him in a purple kind of mood, but when he is teased by his two bossy older brothers, he is in a gray, gloomy kind of mood.

As I shared this read-aloud in Miss Fils' fourth-grade class, I saw smiles and nods of recognition. We talked about colors and the emotions they evoked. Lively debates ensued. Deandre quickly declared red as his anger "because red is what most people would say reflected anger." Deandre also agreed with the author's description of blue being "a cool, okay-time-with-myself mood." Miranda argued that blue is not cool nor happy; for her, blue is angry. She explained her connection to her fear of the ocean waves and the rough surf as a source of dread for her every summer. Each student made the case for the color they thought reflected their "happy." Clearly, there was no correct answer. Eventually, we sought out other books that demonstrated the impact of colors to evoke emotions, examining different interpretations of feelings through color and artwork. Some of those titles included *Yesterday I Had the Blues* (Frame 2008), *The Color Monster* (Llenas 2016), *In My Heart: A Book of Feelings* (Witek 2014), *A Paintbrush for Paco* (Kyle 2018), *Golden Domes and Silver Lanterns: A Muslim Book of Colors* (Khan 2015)—and even a book of colors expressed through the use of braille and imagery, *The Black Book of Colors* (Cottin 2008). Over time, we revisited *my cold plum lemon pie bluesy mood* again and again for discussions and lessons about word choice for more descriptive images, vocabulary to connect ideas and images, visualization, character traits, language to show feelings, and powerful student-led conversations about our ever-changing moods and emotions.

When we teach with books, we're never alone. We can always turn to our bookshelves to find new coteachers and—looking through the lenses of reading, writing, and life—we can use these texts to spark conversations, to nourish hearts and minds, and to empower our learning communities with the life lessons we find there. Teaching through this Heartprint Framework (see Chapter 3 for further details on this framework) allows us to make affective connections to the work we already do in our classrooms by complementing existing units of study, literacy standards, and learning goals. Our read-alouds can act as anchor texts to expand beyond the parallel strategies of reading and writing to lift the level of our work. Rather than struggle to "fit it all in" we can look for opportunities to purposefully connect the books we share to both academic and social-emotional learning: What can this book teach us about writing? What have we noticed this book teaches us about reading? What life lesson conversations can it inspire in our community meetings and responsive classrooms? Whether we're mining mentor texts for craft lessons, reading strategies, or life lessons, read-alouds energize the heartwork we do—spreading ripples of book love that extend off the pages to inspire imitation, inspiration, and emulation. Picture books are a constant source of this possibility. And, as our coteachers, they support living, breathing units of study created for children, with children, and alongside children.

THE HEARTPRINT FRAMEWORK

Mentor texts are more than just craft coaches for writers—
they can also offer inspiration and life lessons.
—Georgia Heard, *Finding the Heart of Nonfiction*

WE WANT all students, whether in reading, writing, or art, to use their voices to create change. When we help children acquire the necessary social-emotional learning skills to promote compassion and self-care, we support not only reading and writing communities but also learning as lifework. As we move forward in our efforts to layer affective and academic learning, this chapter will focus our lens on specific ways the Heartprint Framework can support this goal.

The Heartprint Framework includes CARE-focused, social-emotional connections built around a heartprint read-aloud and grounded in student-led conversations. Instruction within the framework is anchored in the following foundational beliefs:

- Teachers are caregivers who use knowledge of students to make informed decisions that impact inclusive, caring communities beyond the four classroom walls.
- Academic and affective standards are best explored together across all our teaching and learning—educating the minds, hearts, and hands of all learners.
- Authors and illustrators serve as recruiters to help kids see the importance of caring about our world, and, using books as coteachers, we can focus on methods and mindsets to be responsive and adaptive educators.
- Conversations can inspire new ways of seeing, thinking, and being. We empower ourselves and others through listening, speaking, sharing ideas, asking questions, and collaborating to encourage more social responsibility.
- Learning is a celebration, and ongoing, joyful learning includes a partnership of school and family community members who work to connect the lives of our students through shared stories and a culture of literacy.

These principles have driven my practices and continue to evolve from my work with passionate educators and students who continue to shape my beliefs as we learn more about this work every day. Responsive educators are constantly reflecting, sharing ideas, and adjusting their teaching to be more empathetic and mindful of the whole child and their community of learners. Teachers engaged in this heartwork focus on the ways that people and practices contribute to a caring school culture, connecting literacy lessons to build and strengthen community all year long. In preparation to dive deeper into the structures and routines found in the Heartprint Framework, let's take a look at environments that include the vision and *visible* voice of a community of learners where all members feel welcome to share their affective sides—because every student, every smile, matters.

ESTABLISHING CARING LEARNING ENVIRONMENTS

Let's take a moment to visit Northern Parkway, a school that has been open since 1923 and is overflowing with history, heart, and stories. If you walk the halls on any given morning, it's clear the community is dedicated to educating the whole child. You might hear the laughter of the youngest learners passing the prekindergarten corridor, or perhaps you catch a whiff of cinnamon and know that Ms. Erica is serving up her buttery rich, sweet French toast in the cafeteria. If you travel to the back of the building, you'll pass through the weather-protected awning lined with student artwork and quotes to live by and find walls dedicated to the study and celebration of artists and activists. The school embraces its students' cultures as vehicles for learning with schoolwide literacy and cultural celebrations all year long. Every inch of space, all the halls and walls, are filled with images of artwork created with, by, and for children in celebration of their voices and authentic learning. All aspects of their reading and writing are focused on empowering students, with a dual emphasis on literacy that also has the power to influence and change lives. Environments like this encourage students to take risks, to open their minds, and to share their voices. Take a look at this piece from a fifth-grade poetry slam, which was written and performed by Kirah:

> Society thinks that people
> have to be a certain way
> girls are supposed to look like this
> boys are supposed to look like that
>
> and if you don't
> society can look at you
> with a sour face
> well I've got something to say
>
> the thing called "Society" can go away
> we are all amazing
> in our own kind of way
> Wear what you want to wear
> Say what you want to say
> It's okay
> I'm not going to judge you
> So be yourself
> That's what I have to say
>
> Kirah

Thinking and writing like this doesn't happen in a vacuum. It happens when teachers work to create an environment that honors student voice and encourages them to use that voice to affect social changes both in their school lives and outside of school. It manifests itself in rooms that reflect literacy and learning connected to agency, advocacy, and caring relationships.

Further down the hall, in Mr. Peele's fifth-grade classroom, the first thing that might catch your eye is the rug area—a designated spot for this community of readers and writers to gather. You'll see students have access to an array of book titles, celebrating choices and never-ending to-be-read stacks. The baskets are overflowing with books that have been sorted and organized with the students who inhabit this reading zone in mind. You'll see children choosing books, books being recommended, and books based on interests, identities, passions, topics, cultures, history, and more. Such "reading zones," as Nancie Atwell (2014) would describe them, help to shape students into more passionate, habitual, critical readers who are exposed to a diversity of words, ideas, events, people, and places (Figures 3.1a and 3.1b).

Figure 3.1a Baskets of books in this classroom library were sorted and named by the students. Some of the labels include *Books We Love Right Now, Favorite Series, Need to Know Now, My Life, The Great Beyond, Ahhhh! All About Me, Running on Words,* and *True to Life.*

Figure 3.1b

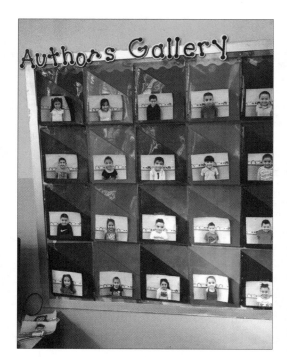

Figure 3.2 Authors' gallery in a kindergarten classroom where students proudly display their writing.

The bookshelves are overflowing with coteaching heartprint books, like Jacqueline Woodson's *Harbor Me* (2018), Kathryn Otoshi's *Beautiful Hands* (2015), and Sheetal Sheth's *Always Anjali* (2018). Look closely and you'll notice posters and messages that speak positive reminders to its residents like "Read Woke" or "Your future is created by what you do today, not tomorrow."

In the primary classrooms, you will find a chart of names with photos and initial letters by color to help students from day one to get to know their friends' names and their letter sounds. You'll see word walls in multiple languages and a corner display, also known as the authors' gallery, to celebrate the work of young writers all year long (Figure 3.2).

Results from the Holistic Evidence and Design Project (Barrett et al. 2015) showed that well-designed spaces and places boost academic performance. In addition, there are clear links between physical environment and emotional and cognitive functions (Immordino-Yang and Damasio 2007). With this in mind, bulletin boards are used for instructional purposes, and the halls and walls celebrate teaching and learning. Along the back of the room, you'll see a wall covered with artifacts, favorite quotes, and

Figure 3.3 In this third-grade room, you'll find a display, or goals wall, to celebrate what students are reading and goals they are currently working on to encourage a mindset that we are always learning.

powerful life lessons that show tracks of students' thinking and the connective messages found in heartprint books they've shared during the school year.

Well-designed spaces and experiences that support affective connections to learning aren't unique to Northern Parkway. I have seen the impact of learning environments in schools across the country, where literacy landscapes like these illustrate messages of authentic, relevant literacy work and, at the same time, reflect the lives of the students who live there. In this book, we will travel together to celebrate the rooms and the work of those learners.

STUDENT-LED MEETINGS

Building communities isn't just about the environments we create. It's also about the conversations that connect us to one another, establishing relationships that respect our uniqueness and encourage us to be caring members of our learning communities. To support this, the Heartprint Framework sets aside time each day for a student-led community meeting. These meetings begin with conversations about what's happening in our lives, in the world, and in our community. We incorporate time for compliments and celebrations before turning our attention to concerns that we need to address, because community is about sharing our hardships as well as our joys (Christensen 2009).

Which is why we move on to exploring a read-aloud along with our thoughts and connections before extending the topic and closing the meeting. These read-alouds are a critical component of the framework because they establish a common connection while guiding the type of thinking and conversations that support this heartwork of learning. There is a reciprocal relationship between emotional and instructional support (Curby, Rimm-Kaufman, and Abry 2013), and carefully chosen literature can impact our relationships and empower us to challenge ideas or accept new realities, pushing us to grow page by page, story by story. Though many of the initial conversations focus on feelings, we can connect this same book to reading and writing behaviors in our literacy block later in the day or week. In this way, the same book can be used to support reading and writing lessons as we discussed in Chapter 2, as well as our work as life learners. But in the student-led meeting, our priority focus is establishing caring connections in our learning community.

Figure 3.4

Charlotte is overwhelmed by the noises of the busy world all around her like sounds from her neighborhood and apartment, as well as school noises like clanging bells and trays that clatter and crash in the lunchroom. Luckily, she finds comfort under a tree where she calms her breathing and her mind, discovering a "quiet place" she can return to as needed.

For example, at the beginning of the year, you might decide to focus on a student-led meeting that centers on exploring learning environments and preferences, by inviting a conversation around Deborah Sosin's *Charlotte and the Quiet Place* (2015; Figure 3.4).

Like Charlotte, it is essential to be mindful of our moods and acknowledge the events and experiences that influence our state of being. This powerful book invites conversations about mindfulness and awareness of the learning environment that best suits us as learners. Sharing it in student-led meetings is a great way to kick off self-reflective conversations around concepts: *When might you feel overwhelmed? Where do you do your best work? What do you need in your own spaces and places to find comfort, to feel confidence, and to be your best self? Where do you like to read or write or think? How might we calm ourselves when things are overwhelming us? Who might we turn to? What might we try?*

Read-alouds from thought-provoking books such as *Charlotte and the Quiet Place* often lead to further heartprint connections across our lives and learning days. After sharing it to explore learning preferences, you might extend the conversation to raise awareness and respect for moods. Perhaps use it to model ways students can self-monitor their moods and recognize how their feelings might impact their interactions, focus, and learning throughout the day. Carefully chosen literature offers multiple opportunities to layer literacy and life lessons.

Figure 3.5 Spaces and places that bring joy, like reading in the coveted laundry basket, help learners do their best thinking.

GETTING STARTED WITH STUDENT-LED MEETINGS

As you begin your work with student-led conversations in the Heartprint Framework and as you think about how books can guide these conversations, you may notice a need for some structural supports that help students reflect and focus through thoughtful, active listening. To help with this, you could share a text such as *Listen* by Holly McGhee, with illustrations by Pascal Lemaître (2019), which invites readers to use all of their senses and, most important, to use their hearts to connect and engage with others and our world (Figure 3.6).

> *Teaching involves helping learners to create cultures that nurture engaged, persistent, collaborative, responsible and caring minds.*
>
> –Peter H. Johnston, Gay Ivey, and Amy Faulkner, "Talking in Class"

After reading the book aloud, have students reflect on what they notice. *What does it mean to listen? What does it look like, feel like, and sound like when we truly listen?* Through collaborative conversations, invite students to think about agreements for how you'll listen to one another and

Figure 3.6

interact in your student-led meetings throughout the year. You may need to take some time to teach these skills and give lots of opportunities for practice and guidance. Model and demonstrate ways to talk and listen in your gatherings. Once the community establishes agreed upon routines for this type of active listening, consider posting their agreements on an anchor chart as a reminder (see Figure 3.7).

Figure 3.7 Post an anchor chart to remind learners of your agreements for speaking and listening routines in student-led conversations.

To practice this, consider starting your community gatherings with a quick greeting that invites students to share a comment or compliment about someone or something in a positive way:

Something I like about . . .

Something I look forward to today . . .

One thing that is going well . . .

One thing I am excited about . . .

Then, through your kid watching and observations, give feedback that clarifies the expectations for the kinds of conversations and routines that will support your students, so they can eventually take the lead in thinking, talking, and reflecting on books. Sit down, lean in, and listen.

> *Teaching children how to listen and respond to each other in respectful, thoughtful ways helps to foster new relationships and caring communities.*
>
> –Debbie Miller, *Reading with Meaning*

Remember that we want our students to share from their hearts. The ultimate goal is for them to have authentic, student-led conversations where they can explore how to think, not what to think. Depending on the needs of your learning community, you may find it necessary to offer further practice in these initial meetings to support the types of interactions required for effective student-led conversations:

- Set up rituals for turn-and-talk partners.
- Use signals like smiles and nods in recognition of the speaker.
- Take turns respectfully.
- Use an agreed-upon method to help navigate when speakers want to share.
- Know how to listen and when to talk (or not talk).
- Ask clarifying questions.
- Restate and/or add your own thoughts to an idea.

Once your listening and sharing norms are beginning to take place, the following routines may also help you further facilitate your student-led meetings. Note that these structures are by no means a script to follow. As always, stay flexible and adjust the process to fit the group you're working with. Responsive, adaptive educators know their *why* and use it to direct how they'll nurture the varying needs of their learners. Your scaffolding will support routines and rituals with kids leading the way.

Gathering

Invite students to find a comfortable spot to gather for these conversations. Circle up, if you like. If needed, decide as a group how your room arrangement will allow for community gathering. For instance, students could move to a particular section in your room, adjust chairs, or reorganize to reflect and support a sense of community.

Figure 3.8 To help primary students practice active listening, consider starting out with a book pass routine, which allows each student to share connections about the book in turn while the others practice listening and responding.

Greeting

Student-led meetings depend on our collaborative conversations and personal connections. Create a special routine to signal your meeting time or to schedule a consistent time students can look forward to. Perhaps you'll decide to meet first thing every morning. Perhaps you'll meet after lunch. Craft a schedule that fits your day, your routines, and your students. Decide on a greeting to welcome and settle the group for your community gathering such as welcoming each other by name or commenting on how things are going.

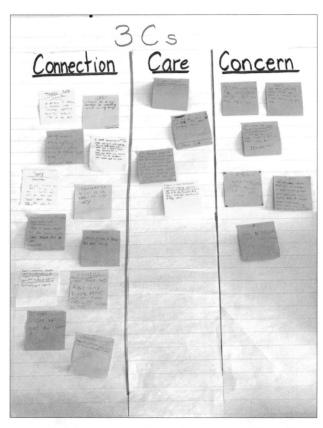

Figure 3.9 In this example, students use the Three Cs, by jotting their ideas on sticky notes as a way to launch their conversations.

Guiding

Share the meeting's heartprint read-aloud and facilitate student conversations around it. Refer to your read-aloud to encourage connections and responses about theme, messages, or wonderings. One way to structure this part of the meeting is to use the Three Cs—connections, cares, and concerns (see Figures 3.9 and 3.10), prompting with questions: *What connections are you making to the text? What does this text have you caring most about? What concerns do you have about the information, story, characters, events, or problems in the text?* For instance, after revisiting Trudy Ludwig's *My Secret Bully* (2015), a group of fourth-grade students shared their thoughts guided by the Three Cs, offering a variety of connections to text, self, or others. For *connections,* several children discussed how they related to "a time when" someone treated them in a similar way, while others shared times when a family member, sibling, friend, or other experienced hurtful behaviors. In response to *cares,* students reflected on the characters that were being mistreated and expressed their thoughts in support of Monica and Sarah, who were being hurt by Katie, someone who was supposed to be their friend. For *concerns,* they echoed worries about some bigger issues they noticed, such as patterns of behaviors associated with bullying and hurtful behaviors from so-called friends. Students made inferences about Sarah who was unable to stand up for Katie and wondered whether maybe she had once been bullied by Katie too. In addition, the group was deeply concerned by Katie's lack of consequence (which, by the way, is addressed in Ludwig's companion book, *Confessions of a Former Bully* [2010]). Be sure to model this type of reflection and give lots of time for students to explore their thinking and prepare to share them out. Through modeling, rehearsal, and practice sharing thought-provoking connections, cares, and concerns, we can lift the level of student conversations.

CONNECTIONS	CARES	CONCERNS
Share direct, text-based responses and connections they sparked . . . <ul><li>to art and illustration</li><li>to thoughts about characters</li><li>to problems and challenges</li><li>to words, ideas, or messages</li><li>to self</li><li>to other texts</li></ul>	Share affirmative feelings of support, appreciation, recognition, or respect that show caring . . . <ul><li>for a particular situation or an event</li><li>about a character or subject</li><li>in relation to new understandings or different perspectives</li><li>for an idea or opinion</li></ul>	Share concerns the book brings to mind . . . <ul><li>issues</li><li>thoughts</li><li>fears or worries</li><li>wonderings</li><li>confusions</li></ul>

Figure 3.10 As you consider ways to extend conversations in your student-led meetings, invite learners to reflect on any connections, cares, or concerns prompted by the heartprint read-aloud.

Giving Thinking Time

As you build your community of learners and practice active listening, you'll want to establish routines that reflect the needs of your students. Some students may need additional time to think before they're ready to share. One way you can include more wait time is to incorporate thought prompts: *What are you thinking? Wondering? Imagining? Feeling?* Students may stop to chat or stop to jot their thinking before they are invited to share out. If needed, partners can share thoughts, rehearse ideas, or consider questions together, before opening the conversation to the whole group. Of course, students need to know it's okay to listen and not talk until they are ready.

Growing Ideas

Your heartprint read-alouds will inspire a variety of possibilities for reflection and sharing ideas. Students' discoveries will grow over time as they extend and revise what they are thinking both individually and as a community. After a read-aloud, it's helpful to do a lot of kid watching. This is a great time to observe and reflect on your students' interactions so you can determine the next right steps that will inspire them to go deeper in their thinking and exploration.

Throughout this book, you'll find lots of instructional strategies to help you facilitate rich, structured conversations among your students—as a whole class, in small groups, or with partners. Being productive members of student-led meetings requires that community members contribute thoughts and questions; identify accurate, relevant information; respond to and develop what others have said; make comparisons and contrast ideas; and analyze and synthesize a variety of viewpoints. If we establish routines that provide success within a simple structure, our students eventually develop habits of mind and heart to work independently and to think critically about every book as an invitation to learn more about being members of a caring community.

INVITING DEEPER CONVERSATIONS

When we talk about heartprint texts with children in student-led meetings, we try to make connections about what matters to them. We need to get past what Cris Tovani (2004) calls, the "so what" connections so students can engage in more meaningful conversations. What lessons have they found hidden in the text? How can they stretch their thinking to grow beyond the story to the story's impact in their own lives? What cares and concerns does the text stir for them personally? There is no greater fuel for this work than the personal connections our students make. The key, however, is to help students see the difference between surface-level connections and deep, meaningful work. It takes time and relationships to make this happen.

Our invitational approach to *thinking about* and *beyond the text* (Fountas and Pinell 2006) is what helps lift the level of our discussions. To support our community conversations, we guide students with open-ended questions. For instance, to help them process texts as a group, we might prompt discussions with wonder statements that support bigger thinking:

I wonder . . .

I wonder why . . .

I wonder if . . .

I wonder how . . .

I wonder who . . .

I wonder what . . .

We can also encourage opinions and perspectives, probing for expanded thinking and supporting learners as they revise and stretch their connections. After reading a line or exploring an image, we might ask for clarification:

What are you thinking?

What are you noticing?

What are you questioning?

What do you want to know more about?

What are you feeling?

What makes you say that?

Can you say more?

Prompts and questions remind students to slow down to look for deeper meaning. When we talk with one another, we often clarify our own thinking and come to appreciate other perspectives and ideas. When questions encourage our students to notice, to reflect, and to evaluate texts, we create opportunities for deeper thinking to evolve. We let the books and the kids do the work.

> Questions are like keys. The right question, asked at the right time, will open a door to something you don't yet know, something you haven't yet realized, or something you haven't even considered about others and about yourself.
>
> –James E. Ryan, *Wait, What? And Life's Other Essential Questions*

We want our student-led meetings to empower readers, writers, and critical thinkers. We want our conversations to push them to rethink and revise their thoughts based on new interpretations and noticings. We want students to challenge ideas, not search for agreements or right answers. To do this, we invite a variety of perspectives that come from thinking together and thinking across texts. *How might the text echo students' experiences and understandings? How might the text provide insight into the experience of others? What implicit or explicit messages about ourselves and others are being shared?* With the right conditions and encouragement, student talk around texts can allow for authentic, meaningful, necessary interactions.

INVITING READING AND WRITING CONNECTIONS

Remember that the Heartprint Framework makes room for and encourages reading and writing connections. After sharing a read-aloud in your student-led meeting, let it ripple through your academic conversations by revisiting it throughout the day or week, connecting it directly to your reading and writing instruction. Using excerpts from your shared texts, go back to explore specific reading and writing strategies that will support the needs of your individual students. In this way, you can feed three birds with one hand—reading, writing, and the heart.

The possibilities to layer and connect heartprint read-alouds to your literacy lessons are endless. After discussing moods and learning preferences in your student-led meeting, you can return again to *Charlotte and the Quiet Place* (Sosin 2015) to look specifically at the way the book supports your reading and writing instruction. Notice how Sosin and illustrator Sara Woolley craft their writing using specific word choices or the way their engaging photos and story line support fluent phrasing and mood-driven expression.

Over time, you and your students will begin to notice the considerable overlap between literacy and life, and your student-led conversations will become deeper as you

- Connect to personal experiences that you empathize with characters
- Notice how certain characters are portrayed, thinking about how they are like or unlike us
- Look closely at actions, dialogue, and decisions characters make and reflect on their effects
- Pay attention to illustrations in a text and think about who is represented and who isn't

- Notice when characters, places, or events are shown from a single perspective
- Question the author or illustrator and how their choices impact the reader's interpretations
- Use texts to reflect on how the author and or illustrator's own experiences may have influenced the text and or images
- Think about the heart of the story, message, and big idea
- Revisit critical scenes, events, and ideas revealed to uncover themes and life lessons
- Notice larger issues within a text
- Analyze characters' struggles and connect them to social issues
- Pair informational texts with fiction selections to look more critically at social issues
- Use informational texts to think about bias, stance, and opinions of the author
- Notice that talking about these ideas can be tricky at times and recognize the importance of keeping an open mind
- Consider why an author might use certain literary devices, such as flashback, quotes, dialogue, or another writing technique, to help to convey ideas or present stances on social issues
- Compare and contrast how texts in the same genre approach similar themes and topics
- Realize that texts can address multiple issues that can leave imprints on our hearts and minds

Read-alouds enable us to help our students grow as readers, writers, and thinkers. With books as coteachers, the Heartprint Framework is crucial to the work we do, because it provides a structure that gives intentional, purposeful connections across layers of literacy and life lessons. When it comes to bonding together over books, every story matters. Every book has the potential to leave a long-lasting mark. Immerse students in literature and powerful stories that build community and impact our children as readers, writers, *and* people.

THE ELEMENTS OF CARE
Planning with the Heartprint Framework

CHAPTER 4

*The main aim in education should be to produce
competent, caring, and lovable people.*

—Nel Noddings, *The Challenge to Care in Schools*

NEL NODDINGS'S (The Challenge to Care in Schools 2015) work extends the traditional view of learning, arguing that it's not about what or how much we know about a particular subject, but what we do with it. Have we become better people because of it? Have we grown from it? Have we used it to make our world a better place? If you're already doing work around responsive classrooms, this thinking likely rings familiar. Responsive educators are encouraged to do three things: to know, to care, and to act. But knowledge means nothing without care (Gay 2010; Noddings 1984). Both Nel Noddings and Geneva Gay have discussed the difference between caring *about* and caring *for others* and the impact this level of intention has on our actions. When caring *for* students is at the heart of what we do, our teaching empowers them to be engaged, self-directed learners who think about their work and the impact it sends out beyond the four walls of their classroom. Caring *for* is empathy at work. Seeds of empathy are planted with every book we read. Over the years, as my work in bringing more heartprint books into the classroom has evolved, I've found it helpful to organize my thinking around a set of affective principles that influence empathic learning communities. These principles, detailed in the following elements of CARE, are the foundational components of the Heartprint Framework, which includes methods and mindsets to support:

- **Community**: An environment where all members are valued as individuals and as a group to support and actively construct learning.
- **Agency**: A mindset where all students identify as agents of their own learning, thinking, and actions.
- **Respect**: An opportunity to recognize and value all aspects of the learning process, including relationships with self and others.

■ **Empowerment**: Finding ways for all students to be strengthened by their connections to self and others through reading, writing, and speaking. Celebrating every child, every day.

The elements of CARE are a merger of practice and theory grounded in children's books to help us rethink the notion of school work as caring *for* our learning communities. Geneva Gay (2010) reminds us that "while 'caring about' conveys feelings of concern for one's state of being, 'caring for' is active engagement in doing something to positively affect it" (58). Folding life lessons into our reading and writing instruction is an actionable step we can take that can significantly impact our goal of caring for all learners. Literacy life lessons, then, become natural extensions of our academic work as well as the conversations we're having about mindset, relationships, motivation, and responsive classroom communities.

BUILDING ON THE ELEMENTS OF CARE THROUGH HEARTPRINT CONNECTIONS

In Part II of this book, you will find suggested resources that include a brief introduction to an anchor heartprint text, followed by a series of possibilites for connecting its theme. Each one is an opportunity to layer conversations across reading, writing, and life lessons. Through real classroom examples that illustrate the elements of CARE in action, each collection of connected texts and ideas demonstrates options for extending the virtuous cycle made possible with a powerful read-aloud.

To streamline all of this, you will find repeated elements to support your efforts in reaching students' heads (reading and writing strategies and skills), hearts (affective standards), and hands (extension ideas to adopt or adapt) along with some alternative anchor titles, which you can use to replace the suggested text with a selection that feels most appropriate for you and your students or share to continue the conversations. These elements are organized to support your thinking as you plan the best way to use the showcased heartprint books to complement your teaching and address the needs of your students.

Heartprint Layers Tied to an Element of CARE

Each heartprint connection centers around a specific element of CARE—*Community, Agency, Respect,* or *Empowerment.* This element grounds the selected heartprint texts and drives the classroom conversations. The element of CARE listed is the basis for *why* each text was chosen and the *what* that drives its possibilities for exploration. Instruction should be planned in response to the needs of the class (Avery 2002) and based on responsive teaching, so it's important to keep in mind that the ideas presented can enhance any minilesson as an invitation, not a mandate.

Heartprint Book

Each connection centers on an anchor text chosen to drive conversations that emphasize its correlating CARE element, while evaluating—and, perhaps, renegotiating—interpretations of equity, diversity, and unity. Selected heartprint texts are suggestions that have worked well for me in classrooms across the country with a variety of students across various age levels. As you peruse these heartprint titles, you'll likely notice plenty of overlap across the CARE elements. For instance, *We're All Wonders* (Chapter 7) could just as easily be featured under "Agency" as it is under "Respect" and, depending on where your students take the conversation, might be just as applicable for discussions about "Community" and "Empowerment." This is intentional. These connections are just samples of ways you *might* position books for study and discussion, but be flexible. If a heartprint title resonates more for you and your learners under a different CARE element, go for it!

About the Book

Each connection also includes a quick summary of the heartprint text and how it applies to its element of CARE. This discussion will give you a more detailed idea of what the anchor text is about so you can think forward in planning or choose a different text, if needed, to replace that selection or extend the conversation further.

Life Layers: Invitations to Share Connections, Cares, and Concerns

This brief explanation gives the rationale behind the book, its heartprint connection, why it was chosen, and how it connects to its correlating CARE element. The information provided here supports reflections for connecting your conversations to social-emotional themes and inspiring a culture of kindness, community, and character that goes beyond the pages of this book and deeper than any academic standard. This section offers discussion possibilities to invite students' voices by sharing their Three Cs—connections, cares, and concerns—stirred by the read-aloud and its connected conversations as well as optional prompts for consideration such as *How would you feel?* and *What would you do?*

Literacy Layers: Possibilities to Nurture Our Readers and Writers

The literacy layers sections include several teaching points and connected ideas for layering in reading and writing, as well as listening and speaking. These options are deliberately broad to allow for organic conversations, but feel free to customize them, as needed, to align more closely with your instructional goals and your students' needs. The heartprint anchor books can enhance any unit of study (such as reading workshop lessons, writing workshop goals, book club themes, author studies), or stand alone to support students as readers, writers, and thinkers.

Literacy Snapshots: Ideas to Adopt or Adapt

Literacy snapshots provide even more opportunities to extend your conversations and may include writing, art, anchor charts, group work, class discussion prompts, or guided questions inspired by the heartprint books and the CARE elements behind them. The ideas shared offer classroom examples of visible and invisible extensions beyond the anchor book, including conversations about classroom culture, the literate environment, and halls and walls that teach, that can engage learning communities and further celebrate the transparency of literacy and life in action.

Continuing Conversations: Additional Heartprint Connections

No set of texts will be the best match for every reader. As readers, we come to a text with our own interpretations. Therefore, the heartprint texts that anchor each element of CARE are chosen with room for innovation and interpretation. Each connection also includes a collection of additional texts to provide you with optional pathways to explore the elements of CARE that correlate with a universal theme presented.

Continuing Connections: More Layers for Learning Together

As you read and explore these connections, share your experiences with the Heartprint Framework along with your own unique ideas and book recommendations on social media with #LayersofLearning for others to adopt or adapt.

Along the way, you'll see additional possibilities for continuing to explore reading and writing or extend student-led conversations. These are designated with specific icons—book, video, computer—for easy reference. Some examples include meaningful quotes, links to videos, internet resources, interviews, presentations, or additional literacy snapshots. This feature will help you connect, collaborate, and expand on the ideas presented.

As you consider this component, I hope to specifically invite coaches, administrators, and all learners to be part of this work. So, this section often includes professional resources to go deeper to impact your professional learning culture. These ideas can add to coaching or professional book study conversations as you reflect on teaching and learning together.

Throughout all of this, you'll likely notice visible examples of spaces and places where every student's voice is valued. Think of these as an invitation to envision what's possible. What validates what you already do? What gives you food for thought? How might you adopt or adapt similar ideas using the Heartprint Framework across your day? In this way, you can choose and select read-alouds to add to your own playbook.

Beyond Book Lists

As I organized the heartprint connections in this book, I struggled with the pitfalls and dangers of including a list of titles. I worried that an excitement to dig in to such a captivating collection of children's books might override the importance of the conversations they can promote. But I also know that not every educator reading this book is a bookaholic, and you might need some help finding effective titles as you get started with this work. I've tried to strike a balance. The suggested heartprint books can complement existing units of study, character education planning, book-of-the-month interactions, or stand alone to support joyful read-alouds. They can influence a range of strategies to comprehend, interpret, evaluate, and appreciate the possibilities for reading, writing, and thinking about life lessons. As you move forward with your purposeful planning, to support your students, I encourage you to consider the benefits of curating your own book collection while reflecting on the limitations of a contrived book list.

BUILD BOOK COLLECTIONS THAT . . .	BEWARE OF BOOK LISTS THAT . . .
• provide vision for what's possible • enable and empower choices • encourage collaborative conversations • expand points of view • support questioning • invite input from staff and students • build on students' interests, passions, and needs • give access to various text types, formats, structures, and genres • showcase books with universal themes • reflect multicultural and intercultural representation • avoid the dangers of a single story • increase awareness of marginalized topics and voices • allow for differentiation to grow knowledge of texts and resources • affirm a variety of identities: ability, sexual orientation, gender economic status, religion, race	• take the place of inquiry, investigation, and understanding • create dependency • are one size fits all • get created in isolation without input or reflections from your community • are driven by a narrow curriculum (holidays, calendars, heroes) • are dictated or mandated • censor books • discriminate or perpetuate stereotypes • are built to focus on only one form or structure • overwhelm teachers with programmatic expectations • aren't reassessed and reevaluated regularly

As with my daily visits to classrooms, my recommendations are here to help serve as examples and as guidance, not as required texts or book lists. My vision does not, of course, imply the only application for the selected suggested texts. It's merely a collection of ideas that have worked well for me along with samples to inspire you to think more deeply about using the texts you have in your room. It's not about using *that* book or *that* author. Just as it's not only about the text, the art, or reading and writing. It's all connected.

As we work, it's important to continually refine the routines and materials we use in our classrooms and think about why we use them. I am learning every day. I continue to read professional texts and articles, attend conferences, and participate in chats and think tanks around these ideas. If you have prescribed units of study or curriculum mandates, think about new methods, new moves, and new titles to add to your toolbox. Collaboration is the key to everything. Surround yourself with colleagues who will help you grow in your practice. Read. Read some more. Reflect. Connect with your librarians. Visit your favorite library or local bookstore. Join a chat online about books. Talk with friends. Try out these ideas. See what happens when you blur the lines of reading, writing, and life lessons and select read-alouds that fall under the umbrella of the elements of CARE. Find those texts that you trust will touch your students' hearts, minds, and hands. As mentor and literacy expert Shelley Harwayne taught me long ago, surround children with the finest literature and handle those children and that literature with care.

Our heartprint conversations grow over time, and with every shared reading experience, they get stronger, reflecting students' thinking and learning *beyond the books*. In exploring literacy lessons and layering in the elements of CARE, we can use stories to invite complex questions about ourselves, others, and our world. No script necessary. Instead, we are led by our *curriculum of children*. When we establish inviting conditions for this work in our communities, we can let real reading and real voices *guide* the conversations and the learning.

PART II
HEARTPRINT CONNECTIONS

COMMUNITY
AGENCY
RESPECT
EMPOWERMENT

*The key to community is the acceptance—in fact
the celebration—of our individual and cultural differences.*
—M. Scott Peck, *The Different Drum*

CREATING CLASSROOMS communities where students feel safe, loved, and cared for is all part of the heartwork of teaching. In the heartprint connections you'll find in this chapter, we start small, moving from understanding our students' names, likes, and dislikes, to getting to know more about their experiences. We begin by inviting our children to express who they are and how they learn best, trusting that we'll learn plenty about them through thoughtful conversations and reflections on heartprint texts. *How are we alike? How are we different? What makes us unique?* In this section, you'll find some great titles to help you create a space for discussions like these to help your community of learners get to know themselves and one another. The stories of our names, families, cultures, and traditions are unique yet universal. Stories affirm who we are and where we are from and connect us and our community. By starting the year honoring our students' stories, we help them be the best they can be and begin to grow as a community of learners. As Linda Rief (2006) reminds us, students need read-alouds because they "will make them think and feel something about themselves and make them pay more attention to the world" (185). Through discussions grounded in texts that connect us, we can explore and celebrate who we are and who we wish to become.

The following community connections also make room for the essential task of finding out what best suits our students' needs, which may include quiet reading nooks for some or busy buddy chats for others. Our students need the communities they inhabit to reflect their best learning environment. Keep in mind that this will not look the same for every child. Being sprawled out on the floor with a book could be one student's heaven and another's nightmare. Are we inviting children in to work collaboratively but also giving them space to process alone? Are we providing a variety of options that demonstrate we care about ways to learn together, as a group, and as individuals?

When our schools and classrooms establish a culture of care, there is an expectation that our learning communities become safe places to make mistakes, experiment, try new things, and wonder about the world around us. Inclusive, caring communities also recognize and embrace culture and identity as a vehicle for learning. Identity is our life story, and it is being written each day.

The single most important thing we can show our children is that we care. Real learning flourishes in safe, caring communities. By working with others, listening to their ideas, sharing our thoughts, and finding ways to connect and extend knowledge, we learn and grow as a community together. In these classrooms, the environment is shaped with respect for our social, emotional, civic, and intellectual interactions. All learners—including teachers, students, and families—can work together to contribute to this type of caring environment. When students are welcomed, appreciated, and valued as members of a learning community, they will thrive.

This chapter includes community-driven connections to stir conversations about identity, learning styles, environment, and appreciation for the contributions and cultures of others. Each heartprint book is specifically suggested to help you set the stage for caring learning communities, including ways to nurture identity, character, and understanding and acceptance for all.

CELEBRATING NAMES AND IDENTITIES with *ALWAYS ANJALI*

HEARTPRINT BOOK: *Always Anjali* by Sheetal Sheth, illustrated by Jessica Blank

ABOUT THE BOOK: Anjali, a young Indian American girl, faces a challenge when she can't find a nameplate with her unique name, which makes her feel different because of her name and background. When she shares her concerns with her family, she learns more about the beautiful cultural traditions, connections, and story behind her name.

LIFE LAYERS ♡ INVITATIONS TO SHARE CONNECTIONS, CARES, AND CONCERNS

Individuals work and learn best in communities where they can celebrate their authentic selves. Learning the stories of our names is one of the first steps on our journey to grow together as a community of learners. As individuals and as a community, we come to appreciate and value the stories we have to share all year long.

Discussion Possibilities

- Have students discuss the story behind their names and how that story can reveal more about who they are, their backgrounds, family, culture, and traditions.
- Encourage students to consider how names might define who we are as individuals and the role our own names play in our identities.
- Guide learners in discussing Anjali's negative experiences with her name, considering her response to the situations, people, and events in the story.
- Plan for students to share the story of their names. Be prepared for conversations that might include those who wish they could change their names. Encourage others to discuss what they like or dislike about their names and explain why.

LITERACY CONNECTIONS 📖 POSSIBILITIES FOR NURTURING OUR READERS AND WRITERS

Based on the needs of your students and their instructional goals, consider the following possibilities for layering in reading and writing connections to complement your workshop, small-group, or individual conversations.

As a Reader	As a Writer
Using Prior Knowledge	**Writing About Our Experiences**
Readers use prior knowledge and pay close attention to how a character is feeling by examining picture clues, facial expressions, and words. You might lead students in a discussion about how Jessica Blank's images and Sheetal Sheth's words illustrate Anjali's feelings.	Writers create narratives to show true account stories of their lives, feelings, and emotions. As you discuss how Sheetal Sheth used her own life to inspire this story, your writers may be inspired to share their own stories about those times they experienced strong emotions or feelings (positive or negative).
Making Inferences	**Showing Rather Than Telling**
Readers notice how a writer reveals characters through feelings, traits, motivations, actions, and dialogue to support inferences. Reflect on lines that reveal more about Anjali, as when she "blinks back tears."	Writers use images and words to clarify and express meaning to help readers connect ideas in texts and with their own life experiences. Notice how Sheetal Sheth included dialogue to show how Zachary repeatedly taunted Anjali by calling her "Peanut Butter An-Jelly." Invite students to reflect on ways they could add to their pictures and/or words to show more about a character's feelings.
Synthesizing	**Using Writers as Mentors for Revision**
Readers learn about others by thinking critically to gain empathy and make connections from their own lives and the lives of others. Consider how readers might gain new understanding based on texts involving a different point of view and perspective. Anjali's mother provides readers the opportunity to think more deeply about the importance of family, traditions, and culture behind one's name.	Writers select specific pictures, words, and well-chosen details to strengthen ideas and merge new understandings. Sheth created several scenes to illustrate Anjali's frustrations. Consider Sheth's decisions to show emotion and intonation through bold font, capital letters, and repetitive letters to stress how Anjali felt about her name: **"I HAAATE IT!"** Inspire your writers to revise a piece of their writing trying new tags, fonts, or word choices.

LITERACY SNAPSHOTS IDEAS TO ADOPT OR ADAPT

My name is Isis.
I don't like my name.
I don't like it because in the news
    it's bad.
My dad gave me my name.
My mom has the same name.
My name means a powerful female
    goddess from Egypt.

Students can write, illustrate, share, and honor the stories of their names.

Younger students can study letter sounds associated with their names while celebrating the stories of their own unique names.

CONTINUING CONVERSATIONS 📖 ADDITIONAL HEARTPRINT CONNECTIONS

Alma and How She Got Her Name by Juana Martinez-Neal

Your students will enjoy this heartwarming book about a young girl with six names! Read it in English or in Spanish to celebrate the origin of your students' names. This book is a great addition to conversations around family, names, cultures, and traditions.

The Favorite Daughter by Allen Say

Allen Say takes his daughter's personal experience and challenges with her unique name to create a universal story that celebrates pride in one's heritage.

My Name Is Aviva by Lesléa Newman and illustrated by Ag Jatkowska

This story celebrates the Jewish rituals surrounding name traditions. Often, newborns are given a name to honor a recently deceased loved one. Sometimes, the newborn will be given the same name as that deceased individual's name, a first initial connected to their name, or a gender-specific variation. Read to share and expand on various cultures and traditions in students' family name stories.

CONTINUING CONNECTIONS MORE LAYERS FOR LEARNING TOGETHER

Invite staff members to explore the power of relationships with students and getting to know them beyond their names using Donald Grave's work from *The Energy to Teach* (2001) to create a chart that helps staff members identify individual students' names, their likes, and their dislikes.

Try this: People Bingo is a fun way to learn about your students. Using a traditional bingo board structure, prepare a game with interesting information in each box. For example, *loves to read, has a favorite illustrator,* or *speaks more than one language.* Then have community members fill in the boxes by finding peers with each characteristic and asking them to share something unique about their name. This can be a great way for students to learn one another's names while getting to know the members of their learning community better.

STANDING OUT AND FITTING IN with *MARISOL MCDONALD DOESN'T MATCH/MARISOL MCDONALD NO COMBINA*

HEARTPRINT BOOK: *Marisol McDonald Doesn't Match / Marisol McDonald no combina by Monica Brown, illustrated by Sara Palacios*

ABOUT THE BOOK: Marisol is a soccer-loving, Peruvian Scottish American girl who celebrates and embraces her unique and wonderful self. She loves things that don't match and is especially proud of her mixed heritage. She prefers peanut butter and jelly burritos, wears green polka dots with purple stripes, and wonders why so many of her classmates are concerned with "matching things."

LIFE LAYERS ♥ INVITATIONS TO SHARE CONNECTIONS, CARES, AND CONCERNS

Students who recognize the beauty in our differences learn how to embrace and celebrate diversity in our community and in our world. *Marisol McDonald Doesn't Match/Marisol McDonald no combina* can encourage students to embrace the unique qualities that make each of us who we are as individuals and as members of a learning community.

Discussion Possibilities

- Encourage students to discuss the dangers of judging or labeling individuals and/or groups based on what they look like, act like, or wear.
- Discuss any inferences your students have as they consider the friends that suggest Marisol change her ways to be more like them.
- Propose that readers explore what Marisol's ability to express herself reveals about her character and her self-esteem.
- Encourage learners to reflect on the author's note and consider how Monica Brown's life experiences influenced her decisions in writing *Marisol McDonald Doesn't Match.*
- Guide students, depending on their readiness, to discuss additional aspects of their identities (e.g., ethnicity, gender, race, class, religion, ability), how these shape who they are, and which ones they have strong feelings about.

LITERACY CONNECTIONS POSSIBILITIES FOR NURTURING OUR READERS AND WRITERS

Based on the needs of your students and their instructional goals, consider the following possibilities for layering in reading and writing connections to complement your workshop, small-group, or individual conversations.

As a Reader	As a Writer
Making Inferences Readers read closely to analyze what the text says implicitly and explicitly and to make logical inferences using details to support their thinking. Students might discuss how Marisol's friends' challenging her to match can lead students to infer messages or themes from the story that connect to important issues in people's lives today.	**Strengthening Writing Ideas** Writers use various techniques to show voice and point of view. Like Monica Brown, your students can talk to their readers, using speech or thought bubbles, or additional dialogue to show emotions and inner thoughts.
Synthesizing Readers compare story elements—connecting them with their previous understanding—to develop new understandings as their thoughts are affirmed or changed. Readers may consider how Marisol changes as they integrate new information and apply new perspectives as the story unfolds.	**Establishing a Voice** Writers try to help the reader see through the eyes of a character in a piece. Marisol's voice helps readers have a strong connection to her. Notice how Monica Brown writes using first person in both English and Spanish. Invite your students to consider how voice reflects a character's unique attributes and influences the reader's interpretation.
Maintaining Fluency Readers read with intention—pausing, slowing down, or speeding up based on the clues given in the text, noticing punctuation marks, font changes, and dialogue that influence their reading. Students may revisit various lines in this text and in their own texts to practice making their voice show (Marisol's) strength and emotions.	**Analyzing Craft and Word Choices** Writers use words to describe feelings and use font changes to reflect the mood and emotions of a character. Your writers could create a noticings chart to collect model craft moves and word choices Monica Brown uses to lift the level of their own writing.

LITERACY SNAPSHOTS IDEAS TO ADOPT OR ADAPT

Students can use photos, drawings, or writing to celebrate the best part of themselves. You can adapt or adopt this idea to explore characters in books as well.

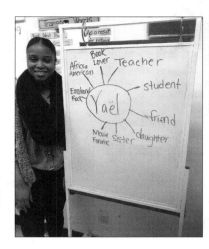

Students and teachers can reflect personal traits and get to know one another by creating individual identity webs with words that describe who they are, such as the one shown, created by fourth-grade teacher, Yael Fils..

CONTINUING CONVERSATIONS ADDITIONAL HEARTPRINT CONNECTIONS

Not Quite Narwhal by Jessie Sima

Kelp is a young unicorn living with a family of narwhals and struggling with identity. Through a series of events, he finds a way to fit in and stand out at the same time. This sweet story highlights the many ways to embrace and respect our differences.

The Best Part of Me: Children Talk About Their Bodies in Pictures and Words by Wendy Ewald

This collection of photos and poems compiled by award-winning photographer Wendy Ewald showcases our unique qualities. These poems can inspire writers to reflect and celebrate positive body image and self-esteem and encourage creativity and confidence.

Stand Tall, Molly Lou Melon by Patty Lovell, illustrated by David Catrow

Molly Lou is not afraid to be herself. She lives by her loving grandmother's advice: to stand tall, smile big, and be proud of who you are. The playful artwork and illustrations can also teach important life lessons about self-acceptance as well as how we treat others.

CONTINUING CONNECTIONS MORE LAYERS FOR LEARNING TOGETHER

Explore or revisit Facing History, a great resource for teachers where you can register for a free educator account to get updates and find current events, teaching strategies, lessons, videos, and much more centered on building community by "facing history and facing ourselves." Check out their identity charts link and explore identity webs with your students and colleagues that will lead to discussions about the many factors that shape who we are.

SPACES AND PLACES with *CHARLOTTE AND THE QUIET PLACE*

HEARTPRINT BOOK: *Charlotte and the Quiet Place* by Debbie Sosin, illustrated by Sara Woolley

ABOUT THE BOOK: A young girl struggles to find peace and quiet among the noises that surround her at school, at home, and in her noisy city of New York.

LIFE LAYERS ♥ INVITATIONS TO SHARE CONNECTIONS, CARES, AND CONCERNS

Charlotte and the Quiet Place can help lead conversations about individual learning styles as well as identifying the spaces and places that are our best learning environments. Communities can also reflect on aspects of mindfulness, as many children and adults struggle with what can be an overstimulating world.

Discussion Possibilities

- Facilitate conversations with students about the many different needs and moods that can affect one's day.
- Encourage students to discuss the various environments they feel most comfortable in for work or for play.
- Support students as they reflect on what they might need for their best learning environments and encourage them to express their individual needs as they change. Discuss the systems you may have in place in your room or building (for example, flexible seating, book nooks, writing tables, standing desks, or quiet corners).
- Discuss your students' support systems as options for help during times when they might become overwhelmed like Charlotte.
- Guide students, depending on their readiness, to explore the emotional connections to learning environments and how collaboration and communication help them advocate for their most productive learning environments

LITERACY CONNECTIONS POSSIBILITIES FOR NURTURING OUR READERS AND WRITERS

Based on the needs of your students and their instructional goals, consider the following possibilities for layering in reading and writing connections to complement your workshop, small-group, or individual conversations.

As a Reader	As a Writer
Exploring Fluency Readers use fluency as the bridge to comprehension. After reading *Charlotte and the Quiet Place*, you might explore the impact Debbie Sosin's font choice, words, and punctuation and Sara Woolley's illustrations have on fluency. Inspire your readers to search for examples in other books to notice how those clues impact their reading for fluency and comprehension.	**Exploring Figurative Language** Writers use alliteration, onomatopoeia, and other techniques to add "sound" to their pieces. Notice Debbie Sosin's examples of alliteration, such as "the TV bellows and blares" or "the steam radiator hisses, whistles and whines." Invite your students to reflect on additional lines that reveal imagery or sensory details and encourage them to consider including figurative language in a piece of their own writing.
Inferring and Discussing the Impact of Setting Readers read and think about the impact of setting in a story. Discuss the ways Charlotte's location impacts her problem (e.g., how she responds to the noises in her environment). Students can share additional observations and new understandings based on what the settings throughout the book reveal about Charlotte, and apply to their own reading.	**Analyzing Craft, Structure, and Word Choice** Writers play with word choice, font, and punctuation for emphasis that guides the reader to read intentionally. Your students may notice how Sosin leaves clues for her readers about how Charlotte is feeling with bold font and larger print to suggest she is screaming.
Reading to Determine Importance Readers identify multiple events that impact how a character changes in a story. Encourage students to reread and recount details that hint at Charlotte's character development, thinking about and how she changed over time.	**Drafting and Revising** Authors and illustrators use words and images to strengthen an idea. Notice how illustrator Sara Woolley uses specific images to match the words that show Charlotte practicing her breathing and mindfulness. Encourage students to find places in their own writing where they can add texts and or images to clarify an idea and help the readers create a stronger image.

LITERACY SNAPSHOTS IDEAS TO ADOPT OR ADAPT

Invite students to try out several spots in your classroom to figure out where they learn and work best. In response to the excitement over their favorite *Fortnite* video game, a community built do-it-yourself cozy nooks and called it "Fortday" reading areas.

Suggest your students write or draw about their favorite learning spots at home, in school, or in your classroom community. Christopher wrote about his reading life and shared his love for reading in a laundry basket.

CONTINUING CONVERSATIONS 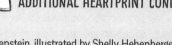 ADDITIONAL HEARTPRINT CONNECTIONS

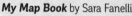

Visiting Feelings by Lauren J. Rubenstein, illustrated by Shelly Hehenberger

This book invites readers to explore all kinds of emotions with a sense of mindfulness and acceptance. This heartprint book takes a close look at having feelings and emotions without judgment.

My Map Book by Sara Fanelli

Beyond the exploration of maps, this book is a way to connect community, story, and self-expression. You'll also notice lots of opportunities to connect to concepts like mapping one's heart and mapping writing territories to nurture and share stories.

Please, Louise by Toni Morrison and her son, Slade

This ode to reading is dedicated to librarians. Through simple texts about overcoming fear through new knowledge, using one's imagination, and falling in love with story, its hidden lessons speak to the transformative power of a good book. Read to share ways we can find real or imagined solace in books and learn through them as "loyal friends helping you to explore."

CONTINUING CONNECTIONS MORE LAYERS FOR LEARNING TOGETHER

Consider creating a space in your building to promote quiet reading or a room to "chill." Some schools are implementing sensory rooms, literacy lounges, and additional areas to provide opportunities for individuals when quiet spaces are needed to decompress and reenergize.

CONNECTING MINDS AND MOODS WITH *DANIEL'S GOOD DAY*

HEARTPRINT BOOK: *Daniel's Good Day* by Micha Archer

ABOUT THE BOOK: In this companion to *Daniel Finds a Poem*, we get to walk with Daniel through his neighborhood. Daniel continues to find poetry in his everyday life as he searches for the answer to what makes "a good day."

LIFE LAYERS ♥ INVITATIONS TO SHARE CONNECTIONS, CARES, AND CONCERNS

We can explore the interconnected circles of our community, including families and neighbors and the roles they play in our own circles of care. A perfect pairing for your student-led meetings, *Daniel's Good Day* can help facilitate conversations and reflections on how the day is going and what defines a "good day."

Discussion Possibilities

- Suggest ways your students could expand on the definition of "a good day" with examples from the story and from their own lives.
- Help students, as they consider the responses from Daniel's neighbors, to reflect on how each neighbor's thoughts echo what they value and what brings them joy.
- Lead students in celebrating the concepts of diversity in communities by discussing noticings, wonderings, and inferences about who is and is not represented in Daniel's community and neighborhood.
- Help students read and reflect on observations *Daniel's Good Day* prompts about community, family, and neighborhoods.
- Encourage students to consider how one's physical, emotional, or socioeconomic status can affect the concept of a "good day."

LITERACY CONNECTIONS POSSIBILITIES FOR NURTURING OUR READERS AND WRITERS

Based on the needs of your students and their instructional goals, consider the following possibilities for layering in reading and writing connections to complement your workshop, small-group, or individual conversations.

As a Reader	As a Writer
Making Inferences Readers use texts and images to enhance understanding of story elements based on illustrations and observations. Students can explore the illustrations in *Daniel's Good Day* to make inferences about Daniel's urban neighborhood.	**Revising Texts and Adding Details** Writers make observations and add written words, phrases, or speech bubbles to connect to illustrations and to extend ideas. As you discuss the interactive dialogue Micha Archer includes between Daniel and his neighbors, your writers may think about places in their own writing to go back, revise, and add dialogue in a similar way.
Analyzing Texts Readers think critically about how ideas are connected, including ways they connect back to the title. After reading *Daniel's Good Day*, discuss the varied interpretations of a good day. Consider the ways different characters' personalities, professions, and perspectives shape their opinion and contribute to the overall message from the author.	**Writing to Connect and Organize Ideas** Writers use texts and illustrations to tell a story or to extend meaning across pages, choosing words to show logical, sequential order. Invite your students to select a piece of their own writing and consider ways they could make the sequence of events stronger using words or images to show the passing of time, as Micha Archer does in *Daniel's Good Day*.
Writing About Reading Readers write in response to reading, using structures such as *I see, I think, I wonder . . .* Students may respond through drawing or writing to make connections from the text to what their "good day" would be like.	**Writing Opinions and Analyzing Texts** Writers share their opinions using information, experience, and evidence from texts. As your students reflect on *Daniel's Good Day*, encourage students to notice and expand on the ideas of intangible ways to have a good day. Perhaps your students could write about life lessons found within each neighbor's response.

LITERACY SNAPSHOTS IDEAS TO ADOPT OR ADAPT

Invite students to share what makes a good day for them. Students can share through storytelling, drawing, and writing to express things throughout their day that cause them to smile or bring them happiness.

Create a CARE calendar where students come up with ideas to connect good deeds within their school community. Students can sign up for a day of the week to visit a classroom to facilitate a read-aloud or offer peer support for buddy reading or writing. Consider pairing upper-grade students with buddies from lower-grade classrooms.

CONTINUING CONVERSATIONS ADDITIONAL HEARTPRINT CONNECTIONS

My Blue Is Happy by Jessica Young, illustrated by Catia Chen

Our community is strengthened by our interactions with one another. In this book, Jessica Young and Catia Chen explore an ode to colors and all of the emotions they can evoke. This book prompts a nice invitation to connect our feelings using metaphors to deepen our understanding.

my cold plum lemon pie bluesy mood by Tameka Fryer Brown, illustrated by Shane W. Evans

Help students reflect on and express their various moods by reading this book about a boy who identifies his moods and moments with colors. This is a great mentor text to explore writing free verse as well as metaphors, rhyme, and rhythm.

My Papi Has a Motorcycle by Isabel Quintero, illustrated by Zeke Peña

Connect the love of family and neighborhood as you share a special moment and a special ride between a father and his daughter. For Daisy Ramona, the best part of her day is when she gets to ride on her papi's motorcycle. Travel along with them and see what makes their day, their bond, and their community special. Share Quintero's sweet memoir to add to your discussion of family moments, community, and appreciation for both.

CONTINUING CONNECTIONS MORE LAYERS FOR LEARNING TOGETHER

Using Maslow's hierarchy of needs and positive psychology, *Take Time for You: Self-Care Action Plan for Teachers* by Tina Boogren (2018) looks at the importance of self-care. Sometimes we need to take care of ourselves so we can take care of our students. Read and reflect on ways you can implement self-care as part of your grade-level meetings, faculty meetings, or a professional development focus.

Try this: Our emotions play a huge role in our presence. In Chapter 3, "The Heartprint Framework," we looked at the impact of physical and emotional environments on student learning, but this is also important for adults. Try implementing time to check in as needed at professional development meetings too. Perhaps you can start your meetings using a physical sign or have teachers discuss moods on a continuum to connect to the parallels of mood and engagement when they work with children.

CHALLENGES AND OPPORTUNITIES with *BRAVE*

HEARTPRINT BOOK: *Brave* by Stacy McAnulty, illustrated by Joanne Lew-Vriethoff

ABOUT THE BOOK: Written like in a series of list poems, *Brave* gives an array of examples that encourage readers to hold onto their unique qualities and passions and to have the confidence to be who they are! The accompanying images show multiple interpretations for what it means to be brave.

LIFE LAYERS ♥ INVITATIONS TO SHARE CONNECTIONS, CARES, AND CONCERNS

All children are unique and yet the same: they have passions, talents, likes, dislikes, and face challenges. *Brave* can encourage students to celebrate identity and individual potential while defying stereotypes.

Discussion Possibilities

- Have readers consider what it means to be brave.
- Guide students in reflecting on the many ways we all have been called on to be brave.
- Encourage students to discuss what words or images they would use to describe their varied strengths and challenges.
- Support students as they share feelings about a time when they were brave or helped another person to be brave.
- Extend the conversation about what it means to be brave by having students explore and question assumptions about other words, such as *strength, bravery, battles,* and *heroes.*

LITERACY CONNECTIONS 👦👧 POSSIBILITIES FOR NURTURING OUR READERS AND WRITERS

Based on the needs of your students and their instructional goals, consider the following possibilities for layering in reading and writing connections to complement your workshop, small-group, or individual conversations.

As a Reader	As a Writer
Synthesizing Readers read to find the messages and big ideas the author wants us to learn. Explore the ways that Stacy McAnulty uses wide-ranging ideas and images to help students extend their thoughts and conversations about the lessons *Brave* teaches.	**Analyzing Texts** Writers use repetition of words or phrases to strengthen a message. Notice how Stacy McAnulty and Joanne Lew-Vrietoff use a repetition of phrases and connected images to illustrate what it means to be brave. Reflect on the possible ways students could write about a topic of their own choice using multiple examples or images to help illustrate an idea.
Making Connections Readers can make connections between personal experiences and a text to better understand what they are reading about. Facilitate conversations to explore your students' connections to the images and ideas in *Brave.*	**Exploring Word Choice** Writers enrich vocabulary by experimenting and playing with words. Stacy McAnulty explores the layers of meaning for the word *brave.* Students might try creating a list poem to explore what it means to be brave or other common words used to describe character traits.
Analyzing and Critiquing Texts Readers interpret words, phrases, and images used by an author. Consider re-reading the images in *Brave* to explore details and the inferences they invoke that shape the meaning of the text. Students may discuss what the images say and how they add to the ideas and information.	**Critiquing Texts** Writers express their opinions, beliefs, and values through what they include and by what they don't include in their texts. Students may respond in writing to express their opinions and preferences after reading a text, giving rationales and examples for their thoughts.

LITERACY SNAPSHOTS IDEAS TO ADOPT OR ADAPT

Create an anchor chart or bulletin board to celebrate a trait such as brave (or another character trait.) Try including words in multiple languages to represent a variety of cultures and include diverse learners of all ages.

Set up time for students to work with partners to interview one another about the many ways we can define words and actions, such as brave or different. They can discuss how they connect to the story and to each other.

CONTINUING CONVERSATIONS 📖 ADDITIONAL HEARTPRINT CONNECTIONS

Cute as an Axolotl by Jess Keating, illustrated by David DeGrand

This playful informational photo-essay explores what it means to be a "cute" animal and can be an important vehicle to discuss the subjective, tricky nature of words and labels.

Beautiful by Stacy McAnulty, illustrated by Joanne Lew-Vriethoff

This companion text to *Brave* has a similar structure and illustration style. It makes a great addition to your conversation about how we can interpret words, actions, and ideas through multiple meanings and perspectives.

I Am Peace: A Book of Mindfulness by Susan Verde, illustrated by Peter H. Reynolds

In this book, a worried child learns to find peace through empathy, imagination, and presence. *I Am Peace* is part of a series of books with messages that can lead to discussions about peace, kindness, and compassion in and among our community of learners.

CONTINUING CONNECTIONS MORE LAYERS FOR LEARNING TOGETHER

In *A Mindset for Learning: Teaching the Traits of joyful Independent Growth*, Christine Hertz and Kristi Mraz (2015) explore the ways mindsets affect children's learning. Their work on how we teach habits of mind, what we say, and the ways we interact with students can have tremendous impact on attitudes, motivation, readiness, and beliefs.

INSIDE AND OUTSIDE FAMILIES WITH *A FAMILY IS A FAMILY IS A FAMILY*

HEARTPRINT BOOK: *A Family Is a Family Is a Family* by Sara O'Leary, illustrated by Qin Leng

ABOUT THE BOOK: The book begins with a teacher asking, *What makes families special?* The result is a heartwarming collection of joyful families that come in all shapes and sizes.

LIFE LAYERS ♥ INVITATIONS TO SHARE CONNECTIONS, CARES, AND CONCERNS

This book celebrates the beauty of families and varying family structures. It also serves as a vehicle to explore the school community as a type of family, encouraging students to view school as a safe place to call home, full of nurturing relationships and individuals who care about—and for—one another.

Discussion Possibilities

- Encourage students to celebrate the unique and wonderful families in the book and in your class community as they reflect on the many definitions of what makes a family.
- Inspire readers to share information about what makes up their own family.
- Look for opportunities to discuss the dangers of assumptions, stereotypes, and single stories while inviting greater awareness of the beauty and variety found in multiple family structures.
- Demonstrate how learners may explore ways to take pride in their individual families while respecting others.
- Discuss the ways being part of a learning community is like being part of a family.
- Plan your discussions about families. Celebrate and recognize all families and be sensitive to those students for whom the word *family* may not have a pleasant connotation.

LITERACY CONNECTIONS 👥 POSSIBILITIES FOR NURTURING OUR READERS AND WRITERS

Based on the needs of your students and their instructional goals, consider the following possibilities for layering in reading and writing connections to complement your workshop, small-group, or individual conversations.

As a Reader	As a Writer
Analyzing Texts Readers read and reflect on the significance of titles to notice symbolism or multiple meanings. Consider how the title *A Family Is a Family Is a Family* influences the implicit and explicit messages in this text.	**Developing and Strengthening Writing Ideas** When writing about experiences, writers make decisions to include specific details that help their readers understand their ideas. With students, highlight the small moments depicted in images and ideas in *A Family Is a Family Is a Family* that convey the importance of love in families of all shapes and sizes. Discuss how the feelings associated with those moments might inspire their own narrative or memoir about family from their lives.
Making Connections Readers make connections from texts and express new understandings that result from vicarious experiences in reading fiction. Students could select examples from the families depicted in the book to reflect on what ways they are similar and in what ways they are different.	**Writing Arguments** Writers respond in writing to demonstrate their understanding and interpretation of a text. Discuss how reading *A Family Is a Family Is a Family* might encourage students to write about arguments they can make about family, society, or identity to support or critique this text.
Evaluating Illustrations Readers notice how illustrations and graphics can reflect the theme or a writer's tone. Invite students to select and share their thoughts about images that best contribute to their interpretations of the book.	**Analyzing Craft** Writers share details in their writing that provide deeper insights into their characters' emotions and motivations. Notice how Sara O'Leary uses emotive lines such as "Before I was born, I grew in her heart" or "Because I live with my grandmother, people sometimes think she's my mother. She's not. She's my everything." Students could study these and other similar text as models to inspire them to use language to add deeper meaning in their own pieces.

LITERACY SNAPSHOTS IDEAS TO ADOPT OR ADAPT

Invite all members of the community to come the classroom to talk about books, to read aloud, to be a surprise guest reader, to share reading tips, or to just celebrate book love!

Host a family workshop or family literacy night on the power of read-alouds at home and at school.

CONTINUING CONVERSATIONS ADDITIONAL HEARTPRINT CONNECTIONS

Bringing Asha Home by Uma Krishnaswami, illustrated by Jamel Akib

This heartprint story explores familial love and adoption. At the same time, it gives readers an opportunity to learn about, and celebrate Rakhi, a Hindu holiday special to siblings.

Love Is a Family by Roma Downey, illustrated by Justine Gasquet

This book is another celebration of how families come in all shapes and sizes. A young girl doesn't want to go to the school Family Night alone with her mom. Sometimes she wishes she had a different kind of family. When she goes to the event, she sees all kinds of families, and she realizes the beauty and diversity of families.

Poems to Dream Together/Poemas Para Soñar Juntos by Francisco X. Alarcón, illustrated by Paula Barragagán

This brief bilingual (English/Spanish) collection includes poems that celebrate communities, families, and the connections among all living things along with lots of opportunities for conversations about life lessons on and off the pages.

CONTINUING CONNECTIONS MORE LAYERS FOR LEARNING TOGETHER

 Beyond the Bake Sale: The Essential Guide to Family/School Partnerships, a professional resource from Anne T. Henderson et al. (2007), shares lots of ideas for taking parent/school connections and collaboration deeper.

 Try this: Host a family university ed-camp style. Invite all family and community caregivers in for a day of collaborative conversations on social–emotional learning. Choose a heartprint text to read and discuss or host book talks with attendees that model connecting books and social-emotional learning with families.

FACES THAT MAKE UP OUR COMMUNITY WITH *I AM AMERICA*

HEARTPRINT BOOK: *I Am America* by Charles R. Smith Jr.

ABOUT THE BOOK: Poet and photographer Charles R. Smith Jr. created this photo-essay picture book that celebrates the many faces of America. Each page speaks to individuality and inclusion.

LIFE LAYERS ♥ INVITATIONS TO SHARE CONNECTIONS, CARES, AND CONCERNS

Readers use books as an invitation to learn about themselves, others, and their world. Through photos and verse, this wonderful picture book honors the diversity that makes America, America. Readers will find lots of inspiration to discuss the variety of people who collectively represent America. *I Am America* can inspire students to reflect on bigger issues as they explore the people, photos, and messages included in this photo-essay.

Discussion Possibilities

■ Have readers explore the way Charles R. Smith Jr. uses the refrain "I am America" to capture the "beautiful mosaic" that includes people from all backgrounds, cultures, races, and religions.

■ Take some time to extend the conversation around the ways we can honor all identities and recognize the beauty in our diverse America.

■ Have students lead discussions about who they are, including their cultures and traditions. They may choose to use patterns from *I Am America* as talking points.

■ Remind students, depending on their readiness, to read with a critical lens and to think carefully about the voices or identities represented in—and missing from—the book.

LITERACY CONNECTIONS 👥 POSSIBILITIES FOR NURTURING OUR READERS AND WRITERS

Based on the needs of your students and their instructional goals, consider the following possibilities for layering in reading and writing connections to complement your workshop, small-group, or individual conversations.

As a Reader	As a Writer
Analyzing Texts Readers learn from content presented in diverse media formats and understand that illustrations or photographs add to the ideas and information in a text. Have students think about how the images, photo-essay, and poetry in *I Am America* impact their thinking on a literal and an inferential level.	**Drafting Ideas and Writing in Response to Reading** Writers can reflect on their reading by selecting a line or a phrase and extending its message. Invite students to draw a sketch, write a poem, or add their own thoughts to expand on a line from *I Am America*.
Inferring As readers consider ways texts and photos inspire inferences across the text, they could create a T-chart to identify specific lines from *I Am America* alongside the ideas they inferred from them: "I am candy cane sticks" or "I am a new branch sprouting in my majestic family tree."	**Developing and Strengthening Writing Ideas** Writers can borrow ideas from mentor authors. Charles R. Smith Jr. uses intentional repetition of words and phrases in *I Am America*. Students may want to try creating a poem or essay using the same phrase about their own life. *I am . . .*
Writing About Reading Readers express their thinking about the books they read, citing text evidence to support their ideas. After reading *I Am America*, students might respond by answering the question, *What connections can you make from this book to your community and to your world?*	**Gathering Relevant Information from Multiple Sources** Writers write about the important information and concepts found in one text and connect it to information and concepts in other texts. Using the phrase "I am America. I am proud." Suggest students look for connections that expand on this theme using other texts or in current events.

LITERACY SNAPSHOTS IDEAS TO ADOPT OR ADAPT

Connect students with writing mentor authors by inviting an author or illustrator to visit in person or virtually. These students listen intently as Charles R. Smith Jr., author of *I Am America*, shares his process and inspires them through his experiences.

As students discuss their heartprint texts, consider sitting outside of the circle to observe, taking notes and collecting ideas for future ways to support your readers, writers, and thinkers.

CONTINUING CONVERSATIONS 📖 ADDITIONAL HEARTPRINT CONNECTIONS

One Green Apple by Eve Bunting, illustrated by Ted Lewin

In *One Green Apple*, readers walk in the shoes of a character who is new to this country and new to a school. This is a great text to explore how we can learn from others and expand our own knowledge of language, culture, and experience. This heartprint book is a powerful reminder that smiles, laughter, and kindness are universal languages.

 Blue Sky White Stars by Sarvinder Naberhaus, illustrated by Kadir Nelson

This gorgeous picture book is a tribute to the American flag. Through breathtaking illustrations by award-winning author Kadir Nelson, readers explore symbols that represent America's history, landscape, and people. The themes presented are a wonderful opportunity to reflect on community as a class and globally.

Window by Julia Denos, illustrated by E. B. Goodale

Windows takes readers through a neighborhood offering glimpses into other people's lives, encouraging human connections and a celebration of the places and communities that we call home.

CONTINUING CONNECTIONS MORE LAYERS FOR LEARNING TOGETHER

Watch Charles R. Smith Jr. inspire wordplay and poetry love in this YouTube clip. Then invite your students to create their own videos (Flipgrid, Padlet, iMovie) to celebrate what makes them unique and special using the driving phrase "I am . . . "

HONORING WHO WE ARE with *WHERE ARE YOU FROM?*

HEARTPRINT BOOK: *Where Are You From?* Yamile Saied Méndez, illustrated by Jaime Kim

ABOUT THE BOOK: When a young multiracial girl is repeatedly asked where she is from, her wise grandfather, Abuelo, teaches her that the answer lies inside her heart. *Where Are You From?* is a celebration of heritage, family, ancestry, and pride in all of the above.

LIFE LAYERS ♥ INVITATIONS TO SHARE CONNECTIONS, CARES, AND CONCERNS

This is a powerful book with themes of self-acceptance, family, and love to prompt discussions around identity. The story is a vehicle for pondering our many backgrounds and how our heritage reflects who we are and where we are from. It also invites complex discussions around the bias in the question, *Where are you from?*

Discussion Possibilities

- ■ Learners might explore what the author's message reveals about identity, belonging, acceptance, and love from family and from others.
- ■ Suggest students think more about the narrator's abuelo. Encourage them to reflect on those family members and/or individuals who might be important in their own lives.
- ■ Discuss the ways others can help enhance and strengthen our school families and communities.

LITERACY CONNECTIONS 👥 POSSIBILITIES FOR NURTURING OUR READERS AND WRITERS

Based on the needs of your students and their instructional goals, consider the following possibilities for layering in reading and writing connections to complement your workshop, small-group, or individual conversations.

As a Reader	As a Writer
Inferring	**Drafting Ideas**
Readers analyze pictures and words to develop ideas about what they have read. Readers may notice and discuss the word choices, figurative language, and images in *Where Are You From?* that add to their understanding and reveal more about the message from the Yamile Saied Méndez.	Writers use observations about places, people, and experiences to share ideas that are close to their hearts. Using places of significance that spur strong memories, writers could create a list of writing territories—what Nancie Atwell (1998) and Georgia Heard (2016) would describe as places from your life and your heart that inspire your stories.
Synthesizing	**Exploring Figurative Language**
Readers ask themselves about the illustrator's and author's intended message or messages. Students may consider what Méndez and Kim may have wanted their readers to think about or learn as the story progresses.	Writers use metaphors to strengthen ideas and images. Writers can study the way Yamile Saied Méndez's words pair with the powerful illustrations from Jaime Kim. Encourage students to take a closer look to explore what Abuelo means when he points to his heart and says, "You're from here, my love and the love of all those before us."
Questioning the Text	**Exploring Word Choice**
Readers have opinions and consider issues of identity, power, and bias in texts. Invite your students to reflect on the author's decision to include the question "Where she's from, where she's really from?" and share their wonderings.	Writers consider personal, cultural, and other connections to word meanings. Words or phrases can have special meaning for writers, such as "Abuelo" for Yamile Saied Méndez and her narrator. Suggest students consider ways to include words that have special meaning in their own writing.

LITERACY SNAPSHOTS IDEAS TO ADOPT OR ADAPT

To illustrate the collective importance of each member of a community, students can create a collage of hands coming together to show we are each unique and beautiful individually—but together we are a masterpiece.

To inspire further conversation or writing, you might share George Ella Lyon's poem "Where I'm From" and ask students to observe how she includes poetic language, similes, and metaphors that move away from a geographic "place" to describe origins in a more heartfelt way. Students can create list poems that follow the pattern *I'm from . . .*

```
I am from
  the Irish sea
  with eyes green
    like the grass
and the four leaf clovers
  I am from
    blue skies
        and
      farm lands
When I'm sad
   my eyes are gray like
    the Blarney stone
But when my heart is happy
   They shine brighter.
```

CONTINUING CONVERSATIONS 📖 ADDITIONAL HEARTPRINT CONNECTIONS

The Map of Good Memories by Fran Nuño, illustrated by Zusanna Celej, translated by Jon Brokenbrow

This book offers another look at writing territories as inspiration for students to write about memories and moments found in various places. The themes included can also deepen the conversation around the plight of refugees who are forced to flee their homes.

Home Is a Window by Stephanie Parsley Ledyard, illustrated by Chris Sasaki

This book is an exploration of what home is and can mean to others. The art and images expand on the definition of home and share a powerful message about finding comfort in familiar things as well as ways to explore feelings associated with new experiences. You'll find this heartprint book helpful for conversations about changes of any kind.

My Diary from Here to There/Mi diario de aquí hasta allá by Amada Irma Pérez, illustrated by Maya Christina Gonzalez

Written through diary (in both English and Spanish) format, a young girl writes about her fears, concerns, and dreams. This book is based on the author's own experience with her family's immigration to America.

CONTINUING CONNECTIONS MORE LAYERS FOR LEARNING TOGETHER

Georgia Heard's *Heart Maps: Helping Students Create and Craft Authentic Writing* (2016) continues to inspire teachers as they help learners curate ideas for writing. Her latest thinking looks at ways to get writers to "ache with caring" about writing across all genres. You will find lots of ways to engage your students as they practice mapping writing territories and finding story ideas that come from those places and people they care most about.

UNIVERSAL LOVE WITH *THE LITTLE RED STROLLER*

HEARTPRINT BOOK: *The Little Red Stroller* by Joshua Furst, illustrated by Katy Wu

ABOUT THE BOOK: When little Luna is born, she is given a brand-new little red stroller. When Luna outgrows her stroller, we see it get passed on from family to family. Readers will discover the loving families that make up this community and see the red stroller come full circle when full-grown Luna needs one of her own.

LIFE LAYERS ♡ INVITATIONS TO SHARE CONNECTIONS, CARES, AND CONCERNS

The Little Red Stroller depicts the variety of people who make up our communities and will invite conversations about family, community, and the power of giving among both. This simple book shares a universal message that reflects the impact of kindness, caring, and helping others.

Discussion Possibilities

- Invite students to share their noticings and wonderings about the various families and family structures depicted by Joshua Furst and Katy Wu.
- Encourage students to share their observations about the settings and familiar spots they often explore or places they like to travel to.
- Reflect on the helpers in your community and your school and how they care for and help others.
- Have students think about what opportunities exist for giving and sharing in your community.
- Help students think about different kinds of gifts by considering these questions: What intangible gifts can we give others? In what ways can we use our time as a gift? Our talents? Our words? Ask students to discuss what they could share as a "gift" with others.

LITERACY CONNECTIONS 👥 POSSIBILITIES FOR NURTURING OUR READERS AND WRITERS

Based on the needs of your students and their instructional goals, consider the following possibilities for layering in reading and writing connections to complement your workshop, small-group, or individual conversations.

As a Reader	As a Writer
Monitoring Sentence Fluency Readers notice sentence length and adjust their reading to reflect feelings with intonation and pausing. As you read, students may notice the way that the text depicts the stroller's travels. Help them think about where you pause in your reading and where you speed up. Readers can discuss clues they notice from authors that lead to these fluency decisions.	**Analyzing Craft** Writers make use of dialogue to show feelings and emotions often repeating a word or a phrase to emphasize and idea. Joshua Furst includes dialogue that repeats among the family members who share the little red stroller. "You should have my . . . And so they did." Invite students to investigate other texts where writers choose a repeated phrase as a craft move for emphasis.
Analyzing Text Structures Readers notice the chronological order of a story through sequence words and time-order phrases to understand the passing of time in texts. Students can reflect on the ways Joshua Furst suggests the passing of time with phrases like "A long time ago," "On weekends," and "One day . . ."	**Developing Ideas** Writers use sequence words and phrases to slow down a moment, show the passing of time and sequence of events such as "A long time ago," "On weekends," "One day . . . ," and "Later that morning." Suggest students find a piece of their own writing where they can try adding sequence words, signals, or phrases to show the passing of time.
Writing About Reading Readers talk about what they've learned about characters and problems in a story and support their thinking using text evidence and inferences. Students might discuss their inferences about giving to others and provide examples about its ripple effects.	**Exploring Sentence Fluency** Writers connect ideas using words to link, to show agreements, to demonstrate contrasts, and more. Notice the repeated use of conjunctions such as *but, so, and* in the *Little Red Stroller:* "But I'm too big for it now." or "And so, they did." Explore this pattern with students and suggest they discuss ways they might try using similar patterns in their own writing.

LITERACY SNAPSHOTS IDEAS TO ADOPT OR ADAPT

Invite other classrooms to participate in *We've Been Booked!*, an activity where classes anonymously gift other classrooms with a book. The receiving class passes the book along to another group to continue the gifting, spreading book love with the whole school community of readers. #GetBooked!

Create a bulletin board that invites communities to reflect on caring and kindness, like this display that encourages community members to plant seeds of kindness through thoughts, words, and deeds.

CONTINUING CONVERSATIONS ADDITIONAL HEARTPRINT CONNECTIONS

What Is Given from the Heart by Patricia C. McKissack, illustrated by April Harrison

A heartwarming celebration of loving, giving, and appreciating all that you have, this book inspires conversations about tangible and intangible giving and sends a powerful message about how what is given from the heart reaches the heart.

Love to Mamá: A Tribute to Mothers by Pat Mora, illustrated by Paula S. Barragán M.

More than a tribute to mothers, this collection of art and poetry was written by Latinx individuals as a celebration of love and feelings connected to family. Readers see a sense of pride and honor for family with a celebration of community and cultural heritage, and may be encouraged to share and write poetry with the people they love the most.

All My Treasures: A Book of Joy by Jo Witek, illustrated by Christine Roussey

When a young girl receives a porcelain box as a gift from her grandmother, she must sort through the things she loves best to decide what she'll store in this treasure chest. As she reflects on the "things" that bring her joy, readers will notice the intangible pleasures included in her everyday, joyful moments. In addition to being an engaging read, Jo Witek's books are a great inspiration for writing ideas, and the die-cut illustrations make for extra playful moments of exploration and wonder.

CONTINUING CONNECTIONS MORE LAYERS FOR LEARNING TOGETHER

In *Life in a Crowded Place: Making a Learning Community*, Ralph Peterson (1992) invites teachers to take an in-depth look at growing collaborative learning communities with ideas that focus on routines and rituals to support thriving communities.

Try this: Give your faculty room a do-it-yourself makeover with new purpose. As a way to extend your staff's professional development and collaboration, consider repurposing your staff room as a "literacy lounge" where school community members can celebrate learning and access professional resources. Consider adding a professional corner with resources, articles, and *new* children's books. Invite teachers to post ideas that have impacted their students' literacy learning and classroom communities. Create space for a bulletin board (or hashtag for virtual displays) for staff members to capture and showcase their own literacy snapshots.

NEW BEGINNINGS WITH *THE DAY YOU BEGIN*

HEARTPRINT BOOK: *The Day You Begin* by Jacqueline Woodson, illustrated by Rafael López

ABOUT THE BOOK: At the start of school, a young girl faces her fear of new beginnings—a new school with new people and new experiences. Through stories, she finds the courage to connect with others and recognizes how common experiences can bring us all closer together.

LIFE LAYERS ♥ INVITATIONS TO SHARE CONNECTIONS, CARES, AND CONCERNS

All community members should be encouraged to find their voices and share their stories. This book was inspired by a poem from Woodson's poetic memoir, *Brown Girl Dreaming*, about her grandfather who was the only black student in an all-white school. In *The Day You Begin*, Woodson offers another heartprint book that will empower readers to celebrate the differences between the people we interact with in our school community and all over our world.

Discussion Possibilities

- ■ Request that students share some of their own new beginnings (school, firsts, and other memories). Be sensitive to conversations that could provoke strong positive and negative emotions connected to those memories.
- ■ Facilitate student discussions about the characters they meet in *The Day You Begin* and reflections on the ways they each felt different. Children may relate to fears such as starting a new school or new grade, making new friends, learning new languages, and trying to adjust to a variety of new social situations. Invite your students to share perspectives as they reflect on similar experiences they've had.
- ■ Reflect on the ways sharing our differences can help us grow as a community of learners.

LITERACY CONNECTIONS POSSIBILITIES FOR NURTURING OUR READERS AND WRITERS

Based on the needs of your students and their instructional goals, consider the following possibilities for layering in reading and writing connections to complement your workshop, small-group, or individual conversations.

As a Reader	As a Writer
Synthesizing Readers reflect on new ways of thinking as they react to events and challenges characters face in stories. Students could discuss how it must feel to be a new student in a classroom and what it's like to make a new student feel welcome. As an example, revisit Angelina's and Rigoberto's concerns.	**Drafting and Developing Ideas** Writers develop small moments from seed ideas, expanding on a moment using a sequence of connected events, dialogue, inner thoughts, and sensory details. Suggest students find a piece they are writing and look for places to add dialogue or a character's inner thoughts that reveal the emotion of the moment.
Making Connections Readers make connections between personal experiences and texts. Consider how Jacqueline Woodson alludes to the many ways someone can feel different or alone. Expand on the ideas Woodson includes to make her characters or situations appear like "the only one who" stands out.	**Exploring Point of View** Writers think about perspectives and the impact of the narrator. Notice how readers get insight into Angelina's feelings as she tells her story directly. As you discuss point of view, your writers may be inspired to change the narrator from first person (I) to third person (they) in a piece they are working on and see how it impacts the story.
Analyzing Texts Readers analyze and evaluate texts through a variety of lenses and perspectives. As you revisit the text, suggest your students think about the impact of points of view. Students might consider how Angelina, Rigoberto, or any of the other characters feel in a scene by analyzing the situation from their perspectives.	**Analyzing Craft** Writers learn to write by noticing the decisions writers and illustrators make. As your students continue to reflect on the craft moves Woodson includes, invite them to think about how illustrator Rafael López's intentional techniques might inspire them to add illustrations to support to their own narratives.

LITERACY SNAPSHOTS IDEAS TO ADOPT OR ADAPT

As students review and celebrate texts they love, invite them to curate award-winning lists (modeled after the ALA Youth Media Awards) or to create their own categories that celebrate community, identity, family, and much more. Here, primary students vote in a mock Caldecott contest to support their favorite illustrated books of the year.

Create a list of ideas to nourish your community of learners, such as ways we can support our friends, encourage our reading and writing partners, and share ideas that help us grow together.

CONTINUING CONVERSATIONS 📖 ADDITIONAL HEARTPRINT CONNECTIONS

School's First Day of School by Adam Rex, illustrated by Christian Robinson

This book includes a look at school firsts through the perspective and point of view of the school building. You can use it to study personification or to discuss feelings, fears, and excitement about starting something new.

All Are Welcome by Alexandra Penfold, illustrated by Suzanne Kaufman

Take a glimpse through this book and celebrate schools where everyone is encouraged, supported, and welcomed as valuable members of a learning community.

Zero by Kathryn Otoshi

Zero has a powerful message in a simple picture book that teaches social skills, helps build community, and explores finding value in ourselves and others. (If your students enjoy this book, check out *Zero*'s companion texts, *One* and *Two*.)

CONTINUING CONNECTIONS MORE LAYERS FOR LEARNING TOGETHER

Your students will enjoy meeting author Jacqueline Woodson in this author video. She shares a little about who she is and how she finds "ideas in the air." Woodson will inspire writers as she discusses how ideas can be found everywhere.

In 2018, Jacqueline Woodson was selected by the nonprofit Every Child a Reader to serve as the sixth National Ambassador for Young People's Literature. During her tenure, she encouraged readers to consider the equation: Reading = Hope × Change. You can find many resources to engage, inspire, and encourage readers by visiting everychildareader.net.

RECOGNIZING OUR STRENGTHS WITH *PIPSQUEAKS, SLOWPOKES, AND STINKERS*

HEARTPRINT BOOK: *Pipsqueaks, Slowpokes, and Stinkers: Celebrating Animal Underdogs* by Melissa Stewart, illustrated by Stephanie Laberis

ABOUT THE BOOK: Readers learn about animal underdogs and their interesting survival traits while exploring surprising facts that make each animal unique and contribute to their survival. Author Melissa Stewart uses animals to help highlight that what others see as a weakness may actually be a strength.

LIFE LAYERS ♥ INVITATIONS TO SHARE CONNECTIONS, CARES, AND CONCERNS

Melissa Stewart offers learners a powerful message about understanding and celebrating differences that extends beyond the animal kingdom. This is a great read to encourage pride for those qualities that make each of us unique, especially characteristics that make us stand out.

Discussion Possibilities

- Have partners share thoughts about perceptions and new ideas learned. Suggest students discuss what surprised them the most.
- Recommend that learners describe their own strengths or challenges.
- Consider what it means to be an underdog and who decides what makes someone an underdog.
- Support students as they reflect on ways they can speak up or help others who might be seen as underdogs.
- Suggest groups extend conversations about the misunderstandings found in the text to similar misunderstandings they notice beyond the animal world.
- Invite students to explore other traits sometimes mistakenly thought of as weaknesses.
- Open possibilities for more complex conversations about the impacts of privilege and power, depending on the maturity of your learners.

LITERACY CONNECTIONS 📖👦 POSSIBILITIES FOR NURTURING OUR READERS AND WRITERS

Based on the needs of your students and their instructional goals, consider the following possibilities for layering in reading and writing connections to complement your workshop, small-group, or individual conversations.

As a Reader	As a Writer
Exploring Key Ideas and Details Readers analyze, infer, and draw conclusions about persuasive texts and provide evidence to support their analysis. Students might share their noticings, questions, and inferences about how an animal's size in the book impacts whether it gets "respect."	**Researching to Build Knowledge and Supporting a Claim** Writers research and gather information to support claims with evidence. Melissa Stewart includes additional back matter with information about the underdogs she highlights. Suggest ways students could try including fun facts, back matter, or research to support claims they are making in a text they're writing.
Critiquing Texts Readers grow ideas to evaluate and integrate information provided by pictures, illustrations, and words in the text. Students can describe how pictures may or may not add to their understanding of what the author has written, using text evidence for rationale and examples.	**Gathering Relevant Information** Writers collect details and make choices about which facts to include and what information will best support their claims. With students, explore the variety of ways researchers collect information and discuss how taking notes can become a part of their informational writing process.
Analyzing for Point of View and Purpose Readers consider different points of view and analyze the author's purpose, citing evidence from text to support their inferences. Suggest students consider the ways Melissa Stewart's text and Stephanie Laberis's illustrations reveal their stance on the subject of animal underdogs.	**Writing from Sources** Writers choose subject matter they want to learn more about and gather information from a variety of different texts, including digital resources, to learn more about a concept. Help students explore your classroom, campus, or neighborhood library as places to find inspiration and support for their research writing.

LITERACY SNAPSHOTS IDEAS TO ADOPT OR ADAPT

Have writers go on a hunt to locate information about things that make them go "Wow!" In narrative writing, invite students to think about their personal *wows*—things that make them unique and special.

Melissa Stewart is an incredibly connected author who shares her writing and research process through kid-friendly information as well as accessible educator resources on her website ("Celebrate Science" at Melissa-Stewart.com). You can hear directly from Melissa in videos and find an array of joyful nonfiction strategies.

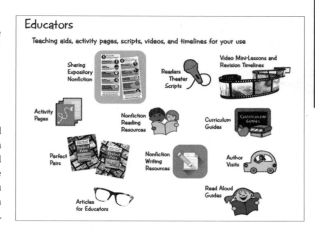

CONTINUING CONVERSATIONS ADDITIONAL HEARTPRINT CONNECTIONS

Better Together: Creating Community in an Uncertain World by Nikki Tate

In this photo-rich text from Nikki Tate, readers will explore the social structures that make up community. This book is filled with a variety of resources and ideas to encourage the many ways we can come together to inspire change, understand ourselves, and strengthen our communities.

Animals Nobody Loves by Seymour Simon

Seymour Simon celebrates the attributes of another group of often misunderstood animals reputed as the ugliest, meanest, or most dangerous of their kind. This is another interesting, informational text to inspire further reading, writing, and thinking. It's also a great conversation starter about how our perceptions and opinions often affect the way we view others.

Biggest, Strongest, Fastest by Steve Jenkins

This engaging book with appealing text structures serves as a model for writers and readers. Through Jenkins's artwork and book design, readers learn about the animals that hold all kinds of records as the biggest, the strongest, and the fastest. With lots of comparisons and relatable examples that help readers gain a greater understanding about these fascinating facts, *Biggest, Strongest, Fastest* will extend your community's conversations around finding and celebrating your passions.

CONTINUING CONNECTIONS MORE LAYERS FOR LEARNING TOGETHER

Check out more ways to celebrate science and children's literature from Melissa Stewart and Nancy Chesley. In *Perfect Pairs, Grades K–2* (2014) and *Perfect Pairs, Grades 5* (2016), you'll find a great collection of paired fiction and informational picture book titles to discuss science standards and celebrate joyful learning!

MEANINGFUL PLACES IN OUR COMMUNITY wɪᴛʜ *ON MY BLOCK*

HEARTPRINT BOOK: *On My Block: Stories and Paintings by Fifteen Artists* edited by Dana Goldberg

ABOUT THE BOOK: This collection of short text is a tribute to neighborhoods everywhere, presented through the work of a variety of exceptional artists from all around the world. It is a celebration of the variety of places, blocks, streets, and countries that make up who we are.

LIFE LAYERS ♥ INVITATIONS TO SHARE CONNECTIONS, CARES, AND CONCERNS

On My Block can open possibilities to celebrate community through art and words. This heartprint book will encourage readers to investigate the influence of art in our world as well as places that are special to us.

Discussion Possibilities

- Lead students in discussions about places that hold special memories (e.g., their neighborhood, their block, their school).
- Facilitate conversations about how the artists' neighborhood communities influenced their art and who they've become.
- Discuss how where we grow up and what we do there can shape our memories and our interests. Ask students to consider how the experiences in our neighborhoods or communities define us.
- Suggest students discuss how the spaces and places in their community reflect who they are and what they are like.

LITERACY CONNECTIONS POSSIBILITIES FOR NURTURING OUR READERS AND WRITERS

Based on the needs of your students and their instructional goals, consider the following possibilities for layering in reading and writing connections to complement your workshop, small-group, or individual conversations.

As a Reader	As a Writer
Analyzing/Inferring Readers infer how writers and illustrators highlight important places and objects to communicate ideas and memories. For example, students can discuss inferences they made about the significance of the "park-park" to Cbabi Bayoc's life and art or what Cecilia Álvarez implies when she writes about how her abuelita's garden grew in places it "wasn't supposed to." Ask your students to look for evidence that reveals the impact of settings in the books they are reading.	**Developing Ideas** Writers pair significant topics with illustrations, symbols, or titles to enhance the body of the text. An artist's reference to a specific place from their childhood memories can be an effective model for writers. Ask your writers to think about a place and all that it symbolizes. Inspired by the stories or paintings in *On My Block*, invite writers to draw, sketch, or write about what comes to mind.
Critiquing Readers express tastes and preferences in art, information, and ideas as they analyze and share opinions of text and accompanying illustrations. Invite students to select an artist featured in *On My Block* to explore further. Consider how their art complements the text. Readers can share opinions, noticings, or wonderings about the images the artist included.	**Organizing Ideas** Writers use features such as text boxes, illustrations, captions, titles, subheadings, and clarifying definitions to extend information for their readers. Students can search for examples and discuss how each entry in *On My Block* has an additional commentary from the author or illustrator. Writers may want to reflect on ideas they could add or additional thoughts they might include to give their readers insight into their process.
Exploring Vocabulary Readers recognize that texts describe a variety of places, people, and customs using beautiful but unfamiliar language. When this happens, readers use context to explain the meaning of those words.	**Exploring Word Choice** Writers use a range of words, images, and colors to describe a setting and to convey an intended mood or effect. Similarly, the artists shared memories made in special places to them in *On My Block*. Writers could revisit a description of a place in their writing to revise for mood and tone.

LITERACY SNAPSHOTS IDEAS TO ADOPT OR ADAPT

Celebrate culture and communities. Hispanic Heritage in the Arts recognizes the ongoing contributions from various artists, authors, and illustrators while modeling the importance of showing pride in one's heritage.

Host a schoolwide celebration like this Harlem Renaissance program with connected projects, including reading, writing, and artistic exploration of individuals, communities, and history.

CONTINUING CONVERSATIONS 📖 ADDITIONAL HEARTPRINT CONNECTIONS

Amazing Places by Lee Bennett Hopkins, illustrated by Chris Soentpiet and Christy Hale

This collection of original poems by multiple authors encourages an appreciation for the variety of historical, environmental, and cultural heritages found among the many people and places across the United States.

All Around Us by Xelena Gonzalez, illustrated by Adriana M. Garcia

All Around Us affirms the interconnections of family and community as well as the circular nature of life's beginnings and endings. Told through the lens of the author's indigenous heritage, this heartprint book can also support conversations about traditions with birth and death.

Home by Carson Ellis

Using simple text and art, this book explores the many places people call home. Your readers will want to revisit again and again. Carson Ellis has crafted an homage to the variety of ways the idea of home can be considered and invites readers to explore the many possibilities of home.

CONTINUING CONNECTIONS MORE LAYERS FOR LEARNING TOGETHER

As you reflect on your home-school communities, what are the essential elements of your caring community? Consider sharing the ways you honor and engage families inside and outside of school contexts. Curate a list of your principles of practice. In what additional ways can you create opportunities to invite community members to share their unique experiences, cultural practices and expertise to enhance your teaching and learning communities?

Work with students to create a time line, photo-essay, or map of your school community to acknowledge those spaces and places that hold meaning to them. Display it to plant seeds for stories, acquaint students and staff with one another, or provide a resource about your community.

SHARING WITHIN A COMMUNITY WITH *THANK YOU, OMU!*

HEARTPRINT BOOK: *Thank You, Omu!* by Oge Mora

ABOUT THE BOOK: *Thank You, Omu!* is Oge Mora's story of giving and community. *Omu*, the Igbo word for "queen," was a term of endearment for the author's grandmother, the matriarch of the neighborhood. As Omu prepares her "scrumptious" stew, the scent drifts throughout the neighborhood. Many neighbors are led by the smell to visit Omu who unselfishly shares her meal.

LIFE LAYERS ♡ INVITATIONS TO SHARE CONNECTIONS, CARES, AND CONCERNS

Oge Mora includes a nod to traditions and names founded in her Nigerian culture. The story reflects a community in an unnamed city with a powerful female role model and provides opportunities to reflect on the importance of sharing, the value of community, and the impact of caring for one another.

Discussion Possibilities

- Invite students to share their connections about Omu and her neighbors. Support students as they reflect on gender, race, age, and professions.
- Raise a question about what it means to be giving like Omu. Think about the ways one can be generous by giving their time, talents, words, thoughts, or deeds to others.
- Suggest students reflect on neighbors (or individuals in school communities) they can count on who care for them and who they care for.
- Discuss the ways Omu could inspire others. Ask students to reflect on things they can do to "give" more in their communities.
- Ask students to consider whether all community members are as welcoming as Omu. Discuss why or why not.

LITERACY CONNECTIONS 👥 POSSIBILITIES FOR NURTURING OUR READERS AND WRITERS

Based on the needs of your students and their instructional goals, consider the following possibilities for layering in reading and writing connections to complement your workshop, small-group, or individual conversations.

As a Reader	As a Writer
Recognizing Messages and Themes Readers recognize how events connect to impact the meaning and resolution of a text's problem. Omu cooks all day only to give away her "scrumptious" stew. Learners can reflect on this ending to think about how its message relates to bigger issues of relevance to their world.	**Developing Ideas** Writers develop story plot using multiple events to communicate relevant, interesting, and vivid information. Oge Mora shared memories of her grandmother, which evolved into a beautiful story that celebrates community and giving. Suggest students revisit a text they are writing to search for the heart of their story. Support students as they revise plot events to build on a big idea they want their readers to take away
Inferring About Character Readers make inferences about characters using clues such as what they say, think, or do. Readers can also think about characters' reactions to what others say, think, or do. For example, highlighting phrases like "her heart was full of happiness and love" can lead to a discussion about how Omu was feeling after her neighbors enjoyed her stew.	**Writing Idea Development** Writers use illustrations or words to create mental images that demonstrate various elements in their writing, such as setting, character traits, plot, problem, or solution. Encourage your writers to consider adding sensory details to further illustrate the setting of a piece they are writing.
Analyzing Texts Readers analyze texts to affirm, challenge, or change their thoughts. As Omu's neighbors return, they are no longer there to ask but instead "are here to give." Students might discuss how their original thinking about the neighbors may have changed based on the neighbors' actions toward the end of the story.	**Writing Conclusions** Students can discuss how Oge Mora chose to conclude her tale and think about other ways writers end pieces. Students can create a noticings chart to explore and collect multiple examples of conclusions they can find from other heartprint books. Then encourage writers to play with a variety of endings in their own writing: ending with a stated lesson, a reflective question, or a strong feeling.

LITERACY SNAPSHOTS IDEAS TO ADOPT OR ADAPT

Celebrate an attitude of gratitude with your community. Post a chart or graffiti wall and invite everyone to leave notes of appreciation for different members of their community.

Students can leave thank you notes to show gratitude for staff or friends that work around the building. This learning community expresses special appreciation for the cafeteria staff.

CONTINUING CONVERSATIONS ADDITIONAL HEARTPRINT CONNECTIONS

A Sick Day for Amos McGee by Philip C. Stead, illustrated by Erin E. Stead

When zookeeper Amos McGee is too sick to make it to work, his worried animal friends leave the zoo and travel to his home to look after him. This book offers a nice reflection on the reciprocal nature of loving, caring friends.

The Big Umbrella by Amy June Bates, illustrated by Juniper Bates

Through multiple metaphors, this book supports deeper explorations of impactful topics, such as immigration and politics, and can be another addition to your classroom library to reflect on inclusive, welcoming communities.

A Bus Called Heaven by Bob Graham

A neighborhood comes together to clean up an abandoned, broken-down bus. Through their collaborative, caring efforts, community members unite in hearts and action. Don't be surprised if this book inspires classroom conversations about possible community service projects.

CONTINUING CONNECTIONS MORE LAYERS FOR LEARNING TOGETHER

 Consider sharing this animated video about the science of gratitude with your student or professional learning community. Discuss the importance of keeping an attitude of gratitude and how this can impact the way we interact in our communities.

 Acknowledge the community helpers in your building. Host a meet and greet by inviting helpful staff members (e.g., teachers, office staff, cafeteria staff, custodians, special area teams) to visit your classroom and participate as special guests in your morning meetings or as guest readers for your read-aloud time.

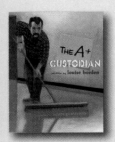

APPRECIATING OUR SCHOOL COMMUNITY with *THE A+ CUSTODIAN*

HEARTPRINT BOOK: *The A+ Custodian* by Louise Borden, illustrated by Adam Gustavson

ABOUT THE BOOK: A school plans a surprise celebration to honor and show their appreciation for a well-loved custodian. Author Louise Borden based this story on a school visit to edufriends in Dublin, Ohio.

LIFE LAYERS ♥ INVITATIONS TO SHARE CONNECTIONS, CARES, AND CONCERNS

This heartprint book provides an opportunity to focus on appreciating the wonderful support staff in school communities who work hard to make our schools special. On a larger scale, *The A+ Custodian* will prompt deeper discussions of gratitude and valuing the contributions of all the members that make up our school communities.

Discussion Possibilities

- Lead a discussion in which students reflect on what they appreciate about school community members.
- Facilitate conversations on the ways we can help make each other's work easier by pitching in and doing our best. Encourage students to discuss ways they can share responsibilities to improve their communities and their spaces.
- Discuss how students can and do show appreciation for their friends and classmates.
- Help students generate ideas for how they might show gratitude in their learning community.

LITERACY CONNECTIONS POSSIBILITIES FOR NURTURING OUR READERS AND WRITERS

Based on the needs of your students and their instructional goals, consider the following possibilities for layering in reading and writing connections to complement your workshop, small-group, or individual conversations.

As a Reader	As a Writer
Making Connections Readers make connections between texts and personal experiences to understand and apply an author's message to their own lives. These connections are strengthened by ideas presented in the text. For instance, in *The A+ Custodian*, Mr. Carillo says, "The whole building is my classroom." Students might discuss the personal meaning they place on this statement or share additional connections to lines that personalize characters and their experiences.	**Developing Ideas** Writers use evidence from personal experience to support insights and opinions gained from fiction or nonfiction texts. Louise Borden based this story on a school visit. Writers can discuss how they use their own experiences to inspire their writing. Remind students to find inspiration from what they care a lot about or from what they want to teach their readers about.
Inferring Character Traits Readers pay attention to descriptions to infer more about characters. Mr. Carillo "always beamed like a father" shows his pride in the students' work. Readers can explore what this says about his relationship with the children at his school and discuss other personal descriptions of Mr. Carillo along with the inferences they prompt about him.	**Analyzing Ideas and Information** Writers recognize and use models found in texts, such as craft moves, word choice, and style, to lift the level of their own writing. To show the level of support and gratitude for Mr. Carillo, the writer intentionally included a run-on list with ellipses to illustrate all of the messages that were left for him and the places they were left. Reflect on the ways your students could use ellipses in their own writing to extend a thought or an idea.
Analyzing Ideas and Information Readers use pictures, words, and information to interpret texts and make meaning. Discuss how the author of *The A+ Custodian* uses images of sticky notes and one-word messages to reveal how much the community cares for Mr. Carillo.	**Writing in Response to Reading** In the book, the "early birds" plotted to surprise the custodian, Mr. Carillo, with a banner to show their appreciation. Inspired by this, students might choose to express gratitude through multiple written formats. Invite students to think about an idea to show gratitude and how they might express that appreciation in writing (e.g., a banner, sticky note, letter, poem, card) and share it with someone you they admire.

LITERACY SNAPSHOTS IDEAS TO ADOPT OR ADAPT

Celebrate and share acts of kindness around the school. Students can keep a bulletin board with sticky notes nearby to identify the acts of kindness they've witnessed throughout the school that show they care for one another.

Plan a celebration to thank members of your school family (e.g., custodian, librarian, cafeteria staff). Create thank you cards, make positive posts, or leave special notes to show gratitude to those who help make your school community special.

CONTINUING CONVERSATIONS 📖 ADDITIONAL HEARTPRINT CONNECTIONS

Thank You, Mr. Falker by Patricia Polacco

This book is an autobiographical story about Mr. Falker, who helped the author overcome her challenges when she was learning to read. Patricia Polacco wrote and illustrated this book to show her appreciation for a life-altering teacher. Her experiences are a great launching point to start discussions about the power of teachers, family, and community members who have made or continue to make a difference.

My Teacher by James Ransome

James Ransome wrote and illustrated this story in admiration for his teacher and for all teachers who inspire their students. Add this book to conversations that reflect on the gifts of those individuals who go above and beyond to help others achieve their goals.

A Letter to My Teacher by Deborah Hopkinson, illustrated by Nancy Carpenter

A Letter to My Teacher is written as a thank you letter, with an up-close look at the impact of the care and hard work of a dedicated teacher.

CONTINUING CONNECTIONS MORE LAYERS FOR LEARNING TOGETHER

Try this: Invite your school community to connect with an author or an illustrator they love. Reach out to share appreciation, comments, and gratitude via Twitter or social media. If possible, set up visits virtually or in person to extend the conversations. You can get started with a few authors and illustrators from the titles found in this connection:

- *@LouiseBorden*
- *@Deborahopkinson*
- *@PatriciaPolacco*
- *@NancyCarpentr*

HONORING INDIVIDUALS IN COMMUNITIES WITH *ONLY ONE YOU*

HEARTPRINT BOOK: *Only One You* by Linda Kranz

ABOUT THE BOOK: Through vibrant art and words, a fish family passes along advice on how to navigate the world. On each page, they share their experiences and wisdom on how to be true to yourself and make the world a better place by just being "you."

LIFE LAYERS ♥ INVITATIONS TO SHARE CONNECTIONS, CARES, AND CONCERNS

This inspirational book encourages readers to make the world a better place and inspires multiple opportunities to reflect on the value of being true to yourself. *Only One You* is another celebration of all that is possible when we are not afraid to express who we are and what we believe in through our ideas, our actions, and our words.

Discussion Possibilities

- Revisit the text to look for clues about the title and reflect on the messages the author may want the reader to know and understand.
- Instruct students to explore the messages and life lessons shared by Linda Kranz.
- Invite students to think about those individuals who they consider to be wise in their own lives or in their community.
- Encourage students to share "wise" messages they recall receiving from friends, families, or teachers.

LITERACY CONNECTIONS POSSIBILITIES FOR NURTURING OUR READERS AND WRITERS

Based on the needs of your students and their instructional goals, consider the following possibilities for layering in reading and writing connections to complement your workshop, small-group, or individual conversations.

As a Reader	As a Writer
Analyzing Texts Readers reflect on the tone of a book, including its use of colors, graphics, images, and text to impact mood. Consider how the placement of text and use of illustrations (e.g., prominent words on painted rocks) impact your understanding of individuality in *Only One You.*	**Analyzing Craft** Writers notice ideas, patterns, and style in a text and borrow them to emulate writing they admire. Using *Only One You* as a model, students might choose to create a book of advice to share their knowledge and experience.
Monitoring for Deeper Meaning Readers reread to reflect and deepen understanding, exploring patterns, repetition, and ideas that reinforce messages throughout a text. Notice how Linda Kranz directs the reader and Adri on every page. Students can revisit her use of repetition to discuss its impact on the message of individuality.	**Writing in Response to Reading** Writers use specific lines, words found in texts, or text structures to inspire their own ideas. Students might select a particular lines from *Only One You*—"Always be on the lookout for a new friend." "Blend in when you need to. Stand out when you have the chance."—to add their thoughts to extend an idea.
Thinking About the Text Readers think about word meaning and reflect on how specific phrases contribute to and clarify a text. Students might reflect on words Linda Kranz uses and discuss how the playful poetic language creates a meaningful pattern for the readers.	**Organizing for Conclusions** Writers reread and reflect on their writing by revising and reorganizing to clarify a message and by ending with a strong conclusion. Students may revisit a piece of their own writing and think about how they might reorganize their ideas to end with a direct message for their reader, such as how Linda Kranz concludes *Only One You* with "make it a better place."

LITERACY SNAPSHOTS IDEAS TO ADOPT OR ADAPT

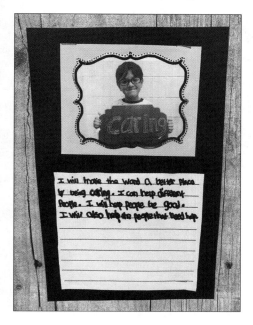

Building on the idea of one word to make the world a better place introduced in *Only One You*, invite students to share a specific word that illustrates how they will make a difference in their world.

Explore ways that your learners can impact your classroom as in this anchor chart created by second-grade students that connect their individual and collective goals for community.

CONTINUING CONVERSATIONS ADDITIONAL HEARTPRINT CONNECTIONS

One of a Kind, Like Me/Único Como Yo by Lauren Mayeno, illustrated by Robert Liu-Trujillo

Based on a true story, this bilingual English/Spanish text, explores the story of a boy who wants to be a princess for Halloween. This is a wonderful book to talk about acceptance and appreciation for individuality.

There's Only One You by Kathryn Heling and Deborah Hembrook, illustrated by Rosie Butcher

Add this to your collection of joyful picture books that celebrate individuality. In this inclusive text that follows a young girl through school, readers will encounter children of all kinds of personalities, character traits, physical aspects, and abilities. At the end of the day, the girl is picked up from school by her two moms. *There's Only One You* is another powerful text to highlight the beauty and diversity in our world.

The Many Colors of Harpreet Singh by Supriya Kelkar, illustrated by Alea Marley

Harpreet Singh is a boy who loves colors. He loves to match his outfits, especially his head covering, or *patka*, to reflect his moods. When he has to move away, everything seems to turn gray. Share this story of self-love and acceptance to spark discussions about dealing with change, belonging, and honoring individuality.

CONTINUING CONNECTIONS MORE LAYERS FOR LEARNING TOGETHER

One Little Word, a video from Ali Edwards, explores the power behind our words—even a single word. After viewing it with staff members, discuss its message and choose a word (any time of the year) that will guide you as a professional community to stay reflective and student centered.

We have to teach toward children who, individually and collaboratively,
make meaning and do meaningful things.

Peter H. Johnston, *Opening Minds: Using Language to Change Lives*

FROM THE MOMENT they first enter our buildings, we want students to know that we are all part of a community of learners who think and care for themselves and for others. Our students grow in the knowledge that who they are and what they do matter. Recent groundbreaking work is expanding the concept of agency, attaching mindsets and dynamic learning to relationships, feelings, and beliefs in ways that impact students' sense of self, their intellectual development, and their development as human beings (Johnston 2012). Agency—the internalized belief and drive that we can act to directly affect outcomes in our lives and our learning—involves habits of mind and heart. Shaped by these principles, this chapter is devoted to agency-driven connections that can influence a greater sense of self-direction, academic efficacy, and values that transfer to work in classroom communities and beyond school walls.

Stories can help ignite a passion for learning, spark curious minds and hearts, and get kids thinking about relevant real-world issues. With books and authors as our coteachers, stories also serve as "recruiters," getting students to care about our world. When we explore stories through a lens of critical care, we can layer in opportunities for agency and activism that can have profound implications for our teaching and learning. Ellin Keene (2012) maintains, "Sometimes when your heart aches, is filled with joy, or you feel strongly about something, it makes you want to take action. It makes you want to do something to make the world a better place" (25). Stories and three-dimensional characters help evoke thoughts, feelings, and questions that invite students to raise their voices and take action in our classrooms and in our global communities. These stories and our connected conversations around reading, writing, and thinking serve as a vision for what's possible.

Learners need to see big ideas in stories as having relevance to their own lives too. Agency, empathy, and activism are all bound together like the spine of a book. Through stories our students connect their growing understanding of issues and individuals to happenings in their lives and in their world. When readers are inspired by the journeys of the characters they are reading about, they can often find a sense of advocacy that leads them to act on the "life lessons" found on and off the pages. Students learn not just to walk in the shoes of others but also to allow those hearts to beat in rhythm with their own. So, we begin with stories and ideas that can stimulate discussions around the power of one's voice, social responsibility, and activism. Through the influence of these stories, we can affirm the power of their own voices and inspire them to use that voice to make a difference in their own lives and in the lives of others.

In this section of heartprint connections, you'll find examples of titles that will help students ache with caring. From our beginning conversations about the power of one's voice, we layer in conversations around other individuals as models who have acted on their desires and beliefs, overcome challenges, or aspired to achieve their dreams. We connect these stories to leverage process over product as our learners focus on reflective practice, decision making, and learning to make a difference. Using poetry, art, and story as transformative tools, we can support students in their personal learning journeys and expand their choices for ways of being. Together, we are always learning. We are shaped by the choices we make, and the heartprint books that follow will help students develop confidence and competence as their sense of agency evolves through the ongoing, shared experiences we have with story.

STUDENT VOICE with *RULES FOR SCHOOL*

HEARTPRINT BOOK: *Rules for School* by Alec Greven, illustrated by Kei Acedera

ABOUT THE BOOK: *Rules for School* was written by an eleven-year-old student addressing questions, concerns, and tips for school. This book includes "rules" followed by fun facts and a few outrageous explanations too. The author's humor and voice are appreciated by children of all ages.

LIFE LAYERS ♥ INVITATIONS TO SHARE CONNECTIONS, CARES, AND CONCERNS

Rules for School can serve as an entry point to conversations about kids taking ownership of their own learning in all aspects of school. Greven's book might provide more laughs than ahas, but it can also help initiate discussions about a collaborative culture of learning where all students have a voice and are active participants in their own learning.

Discussion Possibilities

- Invite students to reflect on which norms are part of their everyday routines and expectations. Consider how one's perspective might influence the rules they are most concerned about.
- Propose that your students reconsider or add to your list of classroom expectations that seem important from their perspectives.
- Provide time to address additional norms for more complex conversations. Share ways students can engage in more difficult conversations to ensure a healthy learning environment for all students.
- Be prepared to explore assumptions using "labels" from *Rules for School*. Greven shares his opinion and identifies traits he believes to be associated with various roles in the classroom. This aspect of the text can invite more intricate conversations around stereotypes and generalizations, equity, and inclusivity.

LITERACY CONNECTIONS 👥 POSSIBILITIES FOR NURTURING OUR READERS AND WRITERS

Based on the needs of your students and their instructional goals, consider the following possibilities for layering in reading and writing connections to complement your workshop, small-group, or individual conversations.

As a Reader	As a Writer
Making Connections Readers read to connect information in texts to their own lives. Guide students to notice when experiences match their own or seem different and use information provided in *Rules for School* to further develop and expand upon their ideas of school expectations.	**Developing Ideas** Writers write to explore their purpose or stance on a topic. Learners could discuss ideas and experiences they have strong opinions about, and, in a similar style as Greven, share their voice and experience. Students may want to write about their own rules, tips, lists, or procedures.
Analyzing Texts Structures Readers read and analyze text structures to determine how specific features of a text connect to one another and to the whole text. Invite students to consider how an author's intentions, emphasis, and choices and ideas are revealed. Have students reflect on how the parts connect to impact their understandings.	**Organizing Ideas** Writers reflect on text features and structures to analyze how an author presents information. Students could list noticings in *Rules for School* to use in their own writing, such as an introduction (to talk to the reader), a list of rules (in numbered order), and facts, tips, and statistics to add additional information.
Synthesizing Readers connect prior knowledge with new knowledge (facts, opinions, text evidence) and use that information to gain new understandings. Students can merge new ideas as they reflect on perspective, insight, and experience to understand the impact of rules and norms in various situations.	**Writing from Sources** Writers write from multiple sources to support opinions on a topic. Encourage your writers to search for books and resources to gather information on a subject of interest and consider collecting categories of information to guide their reader, as Alec Greven does in *Rules for School*.

LITERACY SNAPSHOTS IDEAS TO ADOPT OR ADAPT

Constructing lists together with students is a powerful way to get the community involved in creating and shaping shared expectations. Students create a list of dos and don'ts for productive conversations.

After sharing Alec Greven's *Rules for School*—or other similarly themed books, such as James Dean's *Pete the Cat's Groovy Guide to Life*, R. J. Palacio's *365 Days of Wonder*, and Kwame Alexander's *The Playbook*—invite students to collaborate on their own version of life's rules.

CONTINUING CONVERSATIONS ADDITIONAL HEARTPRINT CONNECTIONS

Library Lion by Michelle Knudsen, illustrated by Kevin Hawkes

Library Lion loves to visit the library. He enjoys his daily visits but not everyone else does. In this humorous story, readers get the chance to reflect on rules and how some rules are meant to be broken, especially when it comes to making friends and helping others. Added bonus: it's a celebration of reading and libraries!

Strictly No Elephants by Lisa Mantchev, illustrated by Taeeun Yoo

After a boy and his pet elephant are excluded from a club, they realize they can start their own club and make their own rules. Share this story to lead conversations about how our decisions and choices impact others and explore the ways rules should reflect inclusive, caring communities.

Plant a Kiss by Amy Krouse Rosenthal, illustrated by Peter H. Reynolds

In this sweet story, the main character plants a kiss and the community watches it grow. Although some suggest she keep it for herself, she decides to listen to her heart and spread kindness. Rosenthal's message, told through short, clever verses, and Reynolds's engaging artwork leave glittery marks on the page and in readers' hearts as they consider how their own rules might include ways to spread kindness.

CONTINUING CONNECTIONS MORE LAYERS FOR LEARNING TOGETHER

Share Todd Parr's Back-to-School Checklist as a model and mentor text for teachers or students to create their own version, including acts of kindness to make this school year the best it can be.

To arm students with guidelines to support more difficult conversations, you may want to take advantage of resources such as *Let's Talk! Discussing Race, Racism and Other Difficulties with Students*, from Teaching Tolerance (2016) which provides free resources for educators under its mission to inform and support practices for diversity, equity, and social justice education. In *Let's Talk!*, teachers can find an educator guide to rules for having difficult conversations and a bank of resources that include research, and student facing materials to extend this work further.

CELEBRATING CULTURE AND STORIES with *PLANTING STORIES*

HEARTPRINT BOOK: *Planting Stories: The Life of Librarian and Storyteller Pura Belpré* by Anika Aldamuy Denise, illustrated by Paola Escobar

ABOUT THE BOOK: This biography is an introduction and a tribute to the life of the influential librarian and author Pura Belpré, the first Latinx librarian in New York City who was also a champion for bilingual literature. She turned popular retellings of *cuentos folklóricos* into books. Each story was a seed planted and ready to grow, affirming culture and stories from across generations.

LIFE LAYERS ♡ INVITATIONS TO SHARE CONNECTIONS, CARES, AND CONCERNS

Books and stories can be opportunities to champion many voices. Pura Belpré worked with determination and persistence to ensure that books were available for children in languages other than English. Belpré's work echoes with many heartprint themes. Today, we continue to honor the influence of her work with an award established in her name by the American Library Association—the Pura Belpré Award, which is given to authors or illustrators whose books portray, affirm, or celebrate the Latinx cultural experience.

Discussion Possibilities

- Suggest students reflect on the ways that writing or sharing stories is like "planting seeds."
- Invite your students to think about whose stories might be missing in your library and whose stories they could they add.
- Recommend students consider additional ways literacy can change lives and ways individuals can act as role models for social change.
- Invite students to read, review, and book talk titles that are Pura Belpré award winners and additional books that celebrate the linguistic and cultural diversity of readers all across the world.
- Read and reflect on the power of storytelling and the "own voices" movement started by author Corrine Duyvis (#OwnVoices), which advocates for sharing stories about and by individual voices from marginalized groups and recognizing the domination of privileged voices in children's literature.

LITERACY CONNECTIONS 👥 POSSIBILITIES FOR NURTURING OUR READERS AND WRITERS

Based on the needs of your students and their instructional goals, consider the following possibilities for layering in reading and writing connections to complement your workshop, small-group, or individual conversations.

As a Reader	As a Writer
Thinking About the Text Readers use an author's notes to supplement their reading and provide additional information about a topic. *Planting Stories* includes suggested bibliography, articles, films, and more for further reading. Help readers access digital media to add to their knowledge about Pura Belpré.	**Exploring Language and Word Choice** Notice the way that Anika Aldamuy Denise included English and Spanish together to illustrate an idea. Your students may be inspired to draw from their own lives, using multiple language or more intentional word choices to give their reader a glimpse into their culture, tradition, or voice.
Inferring About Characters Readers read biographies to gather information and infer the importance of a subject's contributions to the world. Invite students to reflect on information that influenced their inferences and thoughts about Pura Belpré. Notice the impact of Pura Belpré who saw the lack of stories from her native land.	**Researching and Presenting Information** Writers collect information to write essays about inspiring individuals and their accomplishments. Students may want to research another individual using primary sources, interviews, and photos and then write to reflect on this research. Share back matter from *Planting Stories* for more examples.
Integrating Knowledge and Ideas Readers read to identify and discuss important, interesting, and surprising information found in a text, gathering evidence to support their ideas. Suggest readers discuss information they found interesting throughout the illustrations and the text. Guide students to develop ideas as they gather evidence across the pages. As they're ready, you might ask students to explore messages about representation, voices, and missing perspectives in children's literature.	**Analyzing Craft** Writers collect artifacts, quotes, illustrations, and information to include in informational pieces to make their writing more engaging to the reader. Reflect on these text features found in *Planting Stories* that may inspire your writers with new possibilities to add to their own writings or drawings.

LITERACY SNAPSHOTS IDEAS TO ADOPT OR ADAPT

As schools explore *makerspace*, as a constructivist approach to learning, real-world problem solving, and creativity, consider the ways you can connect those ideas to make space for reading and readers. These Little Free Libraries were constructed by high school students for the community as another way to provide access to books and reading all year long.

During the summer, Principal Joseph Tsaveras drives the book mobile around the neighborhood and invites students to select books to take home. The books include a variety of texts in multiple languages and many bilingual English/Spanish books to support their readers. In keeping with tradition of Pura Belpré, consider ways you can ensure access to books and stories all year long.

CONTINUING CONVERSATIONS ADDITIONAL HEARTPRINT CONNECTIONS

Schomburg: The Man Who Built a Library by Carole Boston Weatherford, illustrated by Eric Velasquez

This is the biography of Afro-Puerto Rican Arturo Schomburg, who illuminated African books, art, and contributions. Through paintings and poetry, readers learn the gift of his legacy and how his contributions to correct history through reflections on the achievements of Africans expanded research in black culture. This book can spark important conversations to reflect on and learn from history, heroes, and who is telling the story.

 Little Libraries, Big Heroes by Miranda Paul, illustrated by John Parra

Share the story of how Little Free Libraries came to be. Inspire others to spread book love with gift giving, by sharing books, and through ordinary people doing extraordinary things.

Library on Wheels: Mary Lemist Titcomb and America's First Bookmobile by Sharlee Glenn

This is the story of Mary Lemist Titcomb who is credited with inventing the bookmobile. Everyone should have access to books. Share this *Library on Wheels* to reflect on the importance of book access and to discuss possible ways to extend access to students and members of your learning community outside of school.

CONTINUING CONNECTIONS MORE LAYERS FOR LEARNING TOGETHER

Check out the American Library Association's landing page for the Pura Belpré Award, which expands on Belpré's biography and lists all award winners.

Explore additional ideas to help your community and others have access to books. Meet with high school students or other community members to reflect on ways to get involved in projects, such as starting a bookmobile, building Little Free Libraries (littlefreelibrary.org), or establishing story time and book buddy book clubs.

EXPLORATION AS LEARNING WITH *MY FOREST IS GREEN*

HEARTPRINT BOOK: *My Forest Is Green* by Darren Lebeuf, illustrated by Ashley Barron

ABOUT THE BOOK: Through rhythmic language and wordplay, a curious child explores an urban forest near his home and finds many ways to create and express himself. As a call for inquiry, creativity, and artistic exploration of nature, this heartprint book celebrates self-directed, personalized learning.

LIFE LAYERS ♥ INVITATIONS TO SHARE CONNECTIONS, CARES, AND CONCERNS

This book can encourage students to pursue their own interests and increase motivation to create something of their own as they learn about their world. *My Forest Is Green* can prompt conversations about personalized learning, genius hour, poetry, art, and nature. Share this book to discuss ways students can be active participants in their own learning while increasing motivation driven by their own interests, needs, and concerns.

Discussion Possibilities

- Consider the impact of the urban forest setting in this story. With this in mind, you might invite your students to step outside for a closer look and to record or sketch their observations and think about how their environment inspires them and promotes learning opportunities.
- Highlight the author's use of descriptive language and reflect on words that show size, shape, color, and textures. Ask your students to make observations about their classroom and their surroundings. Encourage them to use descriptive words that paint a picture of their emotions and feelings for these spaces.
- Remind students of the power of wondering and observing to aid discovery. Consider asking students to include a wonder of the day to inspire further conversations and connections. For additional ideas and inspiration, see wonderopolis.org.

LITERACY CONNECTIONS POSSIBILITIES FOR NURTURING OUR READERS AND WRITERS

Based on the needs of your students and their instructional goals, consider the following possibilities for layering in reading and writing connections to complement your workshop, small-group, or individual conversations.

As a Reader	As a Writer
Searching for and Using Information Readers notice the setting to determine how it impacts a character's perspective, the story, or the plot. Suggest students reflect on the narrator's different interpretations of a forest using background knowledge and text evidence (images and word choice) to understand the descriptions of this urban forest and share their observations.	**Writing Arguments** Writers expand on their opinions using reasoning and evidence to support their ideas. As your students read and reflect on the word choice in *My Forest Is Green*, consider ways they can include more descriptive words, examples, or illustrations to support their claims to their readers.
Exploring Vocabulary To enhance meaning, readers compare how specific words express mood, textures, and feelings. Suggest students reflect on the ways Darren Lebeuf uses descriptive words to indicate color, size, and shape in ways that add meaning to the message in the story.	**Expanding on Word Choice** Writers use precise words to create images for the reader and to convey ideas. Consider the ways that students may include specific vocabulary to describe a subject they are studying. As Lebeuf includes words that show color, shape, and texture, suggest your writers revisit a piece they are working on to add more precise words in a similar way.
Planning for Word Work Readers distinguish shades of meaning among words to show understanding. As students reflect on unknown words, invite them to notice connections, such as synonyms and antonyms, and to think about how these words enhance the meaning of the forest.	**Exploring Figurative Language** Writers notice use of figurative language to create stronger images. As an example, Lebeuf used playful personification to describe colors: "peekaboo purple, sneaky blue, carefree red and patient white." Invite your writers to reflect on ways their use of language and word choice can reveal more to their readers.

LITERACY SNAPSHOTS IDEAS TO ADOPT OR ADAPT

This outdoor garden serves as a space for learning and play where students are able to provide fresh vegetables for the lunch menu, including tomatoes, spinach, beets, and more. Connect authentic, real-world learning outside as a way to spark curiosity, collaboration, and creativity.

Consider exploring the Zentangle Method (a way of drawing using structured patterns called mosaics) to celebrate creativity, art, and mindfulness. Students added their silhouettes as the source for these Zentangle doodles, exploring colors, shape, and the design of their choosing.

CONTINUING CONVERSATIONS 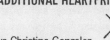 ADDITIONAL HEARTPRINT CONNECTIONS

 **Call Me Tree/Llámame árbol** by Maya Christina Gonzalez

Call Me Tree is a beautiful expression of our connections to nature and journeys of self-discovery. Written in English and Spanish, with the intentional absence of gender pronouns, the author shares how we are all like trees: unique, embracing our roots, and growing from within. This book can also lead to discussions of Gonzales's intentional use of gender-free pronouns and the messages behind that choice.

What If . . . by Samantha Berger, illustrated by Mike Curato

This picture book explores creativity, imagination, and inspirations made from one's heart. Read this story aloud to discuss the what-if possibilities that come from our own celebration of self-expression and creativity.

 Daniel Finds a Poem by Micha Archer

In this debut from Micha Archer, Daniel searches for the definition of poetry. He wanders through the park and asks each animal he sees, "What is poetry?" Through Daniel's search readers might explore the ways we all see things differently and how, through our per-sonal and connected experiences, we can learn more about our surroundings and find beauty in the world around us. Share Archer's story to connect the art of poetry as an important part of self-expression.

CONTINUING CONNECTIONS MORE LAYERS FOR LEARNING TOGETHER

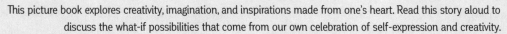 Consider hosting a meeting and inviting your colleagues to try the Zentangle Method to inspire creativity, art, and self-expression. Some find doodling in this way therapeutic, which could be a nice way to start or end a meeting.

PERSPECTIVES AND POSSIBILITIES WITH *JUST LIKE ME*

HEARTPRINT BOOK: *Just Like Me: Stories and Self-Portraits by Fourteen Artists* edited by Harriet Rohmer

ABOUT THE BOOK: This picture book examines self-portraits that highlight artists and personal stories about their lives. Each example showcases an inspirational artist with a self-portrait and statement, as well as photographs and stories about their journeys. Along the way, readers learn more about how these artists stayed true to themselves and believed in their ability to achieve great things.

LIFE LAYERS ♡ INVITATIONS TO SHARE CONNECTIONS, CARES, AND CONCERNS

Through art and stories children are invited to open their hearts, share more about themselves, and learn more about others, not only as inspiring writers and artists but also as humans.

Discussion Possibilities

- Suggest readers share new insights about the artists, their artwork, and their stories in *Just Like Me* to help them think about the choices and decisions individuals encounter as we grow.
- Invite your students to share which artists' personal stories most resonated with them, reflecting on the images and texts as they share their observations and interpretations.
- Highlight one selection and generate a list of observations the reading invokes, such as questions about the artists' family, background, or upbringing.
- Suggest readers revisit and compare two artists' self-portraits to find differences and similarities. Provide examples and facilitate a conversation about common elements that might have influenced those individuals in regards to their agency, self-determination, motivation, and success.

LITERACY CONNECTIONS 👥 POSSIBILITIES FOR NURTURING OUR READERS AND WRITERS

Based on the needs of your students and their instructional goals, consider the following possibilities for layering in reading and writing connections to complement your workshop, small-group, or individual conversations.

As a Reader	As a Writer
Analyzing Character and Texts Readers learn about a person's life through biographical essays. After reading *Just Like Me*, select one artist to discuss further, exploring how that individual's life was influenced by culture, family, or background experiences.	**Writing to Show Not Tell** Writers reveal something important about their subjects in biographies, sharing a specific event and its effect on the person's life journey. Invite your students to write autobiographically about a small moment that's shaped an outcome in their lives.
Thinking Beyond the Text Readers reflect on decisions authors and illustrators make to include symbols, graphics, and photographs to further develop an idea. Ask students to select one artist's self-portrait and reflect on the ways the art communicates the writer's ideas. As part of this study, consider the message behind Enrique Chagoya's statement that art is "an act of freedom and an act of trust"—and as a way to express his "concerns, dreams, and hopes for the society in which we live."	**Writing to Make a Claim** Writers study essays and images and, after careful research, choose a subject and state a claim. Invite your writers to select an inspiring individual for further study to write about. Students may choose to illustrate their findings through photo-essays, art, essays, or poetry, to share what they learn.
Making Connections Readers notice a variety of connections across and within texts to strengthen ideas. As they reflect on the artists' stories and paintings, suggest students consider how these connect to themselves, other texts, and their world.	**Developing Ideas** Writers get ideas about life lessons from stories and expand on those ideas after looking at mentor texts. Suggest students pair up to share important messages from *Just Like Me* and to discuss how the book's bigger ideas and lessons might influence their writing and their lives today.

LITERACY SNAPSHOTS IDEAS TO ADOPT OR ADAPT

To further explore the impact of cultural connections to artwork, students study and write about a variety of artists as part of a celebration of Hispanic Heritage in the Arts.

After reading *Just Like Me* students interviewed each other to share which artists inspired them and why. At Northern Parkway inspiring artists also got to learn from and with illustrator and author Peter Catalanotto.

CONTINUING CONVERSATIONS 📖 ADDITIONAL HEARTPRINT CONNECTIONS

Beautiful Shades of Brown: The Art of Laura Wheeler Waring by Nancy Churnin, illustrated by Felicia Marshall

This selection is an informational text about the art of Laura Wheeler Waring. Waring broke many barriers as an African American woman, artist, and contributor to the National Portrait Gallery. She was commissioned as an artist to expand recognition of important African Americans. Her portraits are exhibited in the Smithsonian's National Portrait Gallery. Beyond a celebration and representation of the beautiful shades of brown, her work will also inspire budding artists and activists.

Out of Wonder: Poems Celebrating Poets by Kwame Alexander, with Chris Colderley and Marjory Wentworth, illustrated by Ekua Holmes

Kwame Alexander (who received the 2015 Newbery Medal for his middle-grade novel *The Crossover*) created this powerful collection of poetry based on twenty-four poets who have made the contributors' "hearts sing and minds wonder." The format positions original poems next to a new poem inspired by that mentor text, which is a great way to show how studying the work of others can inspire our own. This book is a must-have to encourage writers to take risks and share their ideas with the world. Ekua Holmes received the 2018 Coretta Scott King Illustrator Award for her work on this book.

They Say Blue by Jillian Tameki

In this playful, poetic, and philosophical look at colors, author and illustrator Jillian Tameki explores perspective as the way we see and wonder about things. Tameki's watercolors appear to show movement and passage of time, as the reader sees through the eyes of a young child using observational skills, sensory language, and expanding perspectives of the known and unknown.

CONTINUING CONNECTIONS MORE LAYERS FOR LEARNING TOGETHER

In this video, Yuyi Morales talks about how her 2019 Pura Belpré Award–winning book, *Dreamers,* is more than her own immigration story, but is also a story for all of us to find ourselves and find hope, so we can tell own stories, too. Share this video for a behind the scenes look at *Dreamers* and a reflection on the power of setting a path and pursuing your dreams.

MAKING A DIFFERENCE WITH *COME WITH ME*

HEARTPRINT BOOK: *Come with Me* by Holly M. McGhee, illustrated by Pascal Lemaître

ABOUT THE BOOK: In the face of fear, a young girl and her family venture out determined to be brave, strong, and kind. This is a hopeful story set in trying times that connects to themes of community and humanity. It is also an important reminder about the influence of our words and actions because "your part in the world matters no matter how small."

LIFE LAYERS ♡ INVITATIONS TO SHARE CONNECTIONS, CARES, AND CONCERNS

This heartprint book was inspired by the events of September 11. Our world can be a scary place, but books can help provide the space and time for complex conversations during those difficult times. *Come with Me* offers opportunities for students to address fears and discuss reactions to real-world issues and events. This book can inspire conversations about making a difference, no matter how small, and reflections about individuals who have made a difference in our lives.

Discussion Possibilities

- Support students as they take the time to share those things that are on their minds, from little stressors to little celebrations. Read *Come with Me* to reflect on how small moments of kindness can impact humanity in a big way.
- Encourage students to consider how difficult situations can also create opportunities for bravery or acts of kindness.
- Revisit this book to discuss difficult current events that invariably come up across the school year. Be sensitive to the needs of your students and facilitate conversations that feel necessary in the moment.

LITERACY CONNECTIONS 👥 POSSIBILITIES FOR NURTURING OUR READERS AND WRITERS

Based on the needs of your students and their instructional goals, consider the following possibilities for layering in reading and writing connections to complement your workshop, small-group, or individual conversations.

As a Reader	As a Writer
Maintaining Fluency Readers read to express characters' feelings and moods in ways that reflect understanding about what's happening in the text. Explore examples in *Come with Me* where a character's emotions impact their fluency and comprehension.	**Writing Narratives** Writers use events that occur in their lives or to show significance or provide information. Suggest that your students consider writing about a personal event to express their feelings, share a message or convey a theme for their readers.
Inferring Readers make connections between a book's message and their lives to infer the author's implicit and explicit messages. For example, students can discuss what Holly McGhee means by the line, "Because as small as it may seem, your part matters to the world."	**Exploring Perspective and Point of View** Writers expand on ideas based on point of view to reveal sense of place and perspective. After reading *Come with Me*, notice how Holly McGhee and Pascal Lemaître use third person for the narrator and how that impacts various scenes in the text. Ask your students to explore writing from a different perspective in a text they are working on to consider how a different point of view might enhance their piece.
Synthesizing Information Readers interpret significant events, characters, themes, or lessons found within a text. As students explore *Come with Me*, discuss how its message can lead to action.	**Writing in Response to Reading** Writers write cards, letters, emails, and blogs to communicate with others about things that matter to them. Invite your students to write messages that support Holly McGhee's mission to get students to use their words in ways that positively impact others.

LITERACY SNAPSHOTS  IDEAS TO ADOPT OR ADAPT

Inspired by Holly McGhee's message, students share notes with staff members to communicate messages of appreciation, gratitude, and celebration of individuals who help in difficult times.

Come with Me connects positive identity and narratives about who we are and what we are capable of. Invite your students to use these card templates to write notes to themselves that inspire positive self-talk. Find them by searching *Come with Me* at allthewonders.com or have students make their own.

CONTINUING CONVERSATIONS 📖 ADDITIONAL HEARTPRINT CONNECTIONS

What Do You Do with a Problem? by Kobi Yamada, illustrated by Mae Besom

Now part of a trilogy, this text looks at a child struggling with worry and anxiety. The anxiety grows and manifests into something perceived to be real. Share this book to discuss how to deal with difficult situations and to explore ways we can be strategic when facing our problems.

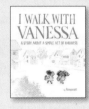

I Walk with Vanessa: A Story About a Simple Act of Kindness by Kerascoët

Based on a true story about an "upstander," this wordless picture book demonstrates that it just takes one small act to make a difference. This is another call-to-action book to stimulate rich discussions about making a difference in our classes, our communities, and our world.

The Little Hummingbird by Michael Nicoll Yahgulanaas

This picture book is based on a South American indigenous fable about a hummingbird who refuses to give up has many layers of life lessons. It is a great story to teach all ages that the one who is not afraid to act can make the biggest difference. It includes a message from the late Wangari Maathai, a Kenyan social, environmental, and political activist and the first black African woman to win a Nobel Prize.

CONTINUING CONNECTIONS MORE LAYERS FOR LEARNING TOGETHER

look up

To continue discussions about the themes from *The Little Hummingbird* and *Come with Me*, that even the smallest of us can make a difference, share this video from The Kid Should See This (TKSST). It features Nobel Peace Prize winner Wangari Maathai, who talks about how we all need to work toward doing the best we can.

SOCIAL RESPONSIBILITY WITH *LEND A HAND*

HEARTPRINT BOOK: *Lend a Hand: Poems About Giving* by John Frank, illustrated by London Ladd

ABOUT THE BOOK: The lessons of this collection of poems are that understanding, caring, and purposeful action can improve our lives and the lives of those around us. Each poem demonstrates how an individual can work to improve conditions, show compassion, and be an active and engaged member of society. Paired with moving illustrations, this collection of poetry shows ordinary people doing extraordinary things that can alter life paths and future outcomes.

LIFE LAYERS ♡ INVITATIONS TO SHARE CONNECTIONS, CARES, AND CONCERNS

Lend a Hand is a powerful addition to any classroom library that can inspire readers, writers, and thinkers. This collection of poems addresses many aspects of community, agency, respect, and empowerment. This book can also be used to prompt discussions about ways to connect with community members and help others.

Discussion Possibilities

- Help students to explore what it means to lend a hand.
- Consider the ways taking action for others can impact whole communities.
- Take some time for students to revisit poems from the book to share their thoughts about how the connected images complement the poems. Reflect on the ways those images add to, expand, or change their understanding.
- Invite students to reflect on how the illustrations might challenge or enable what author Chimamanda Ngozi Adiche describes as single stories. Single stories are incomplete and tell only one side, perpetuating misunderstandings and stereotypes. Students might reflect on the images and the text to discuss who is helping and who is being helped.

LITERACY CONNECTIONS 🗣 POSSIBILITIES FOR NURTURING OUR READERS AND WRITERS

Based on the needs of your students and their instructional goals, consider the following possibilities for layering in reading and writing connections to complement your workshop, small-group, or individual conversations.

As a Reader	As a Writer
Reading Fluency Readers strengthen their fluency as they read poetry using clues from the author, such as punctuation, stanzas, white space, and font choice, to reflect intonation, pausing, and phrasing. You might demonstrate a think-aloud using a poem from *Lend a Hand*, inviting students to consider the clues from John Frank's text as they search for examples that influence their fluency and comprehension.	**Drafting and Revising** Writers experiment with different forms and structures to affect meaning and visual display of their words. After exploring a variety of John Frank's poems, you might suggest that your students experiment with a piece of text or poem, playing with white space, line breaks, and placement of text.
Synthesizing Readers examine poems to analyze how lines, stanzas, and portions of the text connect to one another and impact meaning. Discuss the recurring themes and messages found across all of the poems. Students may also explore the ways a change in narrator and situation affects their interpretations of each poem.	**Revising Texts** Writers vary the arrangement of their words and lines to give their poems a certain rhythm and to affect meaning. Suggest students select one of their poems for revision and consider rewriting it to play with techniques such as white space, stanzas, and line breaks to see how the change impacts meaning.
Writing About Reading Readers read various poems by the same author to examine choices, similarities, and differences, using evidence to support their ideas. Students could compare two poems in *Lend a Hand*, to write about how they are alike and how they are different.	**Analyzing Craft** Writers can create or recreate poems inspired by others. Notice craft lessons found in Frank's poems or Ladd's illustrations that accompany the poems in *Lend a Hand*. Invite students to reflect on the author's and illustrator's words, phrases, images, and ideas that might inspire their own writing to make a difference.

LITERACY SNAPSHOTS IDEAS TO ADOPT OR ADAPT

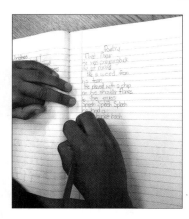

Borrowing from the ideas in *Lend a Hand,* demonstrate ways students can write their own poems. A fifth grader plays with white space to write a poem on a subject he cares a lot about, basketball. As students get comfortable, consider hosting a poetry slam. (See Kirah's poem in Chapter 3, performed at a fifth-grade poetry slam.).

Invite students to collect meaningful quotes and consider ways they can spread kindness like glitter. Readers may also display inspirational messages on the "glitter" boards (made simply from glitter paper in a photo frame) to brighten each other's day.

CONTINUING CONVERSATIONS ADDITIONAL HEARTPRINT CONNECTIONS

Most People by Michael Leannah, illustrated by Jennifer E. Morris

Readers are led through crowded streets of an urban area and get a glimpse of community members interacting. Written as a way to combat the scary messages kids see and hear about our world, this book looks at a world filled with kindness. Share *Most People* to explore messages about perspective, inclusivity, and doing good for oneself and for others.

Be Kind by Pat Zietlow Miller, illustrated by Jen Hill

After witnessing unkind acts, a child reflects on how one might respond to various situations using kind acts or words. *Be Kind* can stimulate important discussions about kindness. Share this text to reflect on the question, *What does it mean to be kind?*

The Can Man by Laura E. Williams, illustrated by Craig Orback

A boy wonders how he might save money to buy a skateboard, but he comes to understand the difference between needs and wants through his encounter with the Can Man who collects cans in his neighborhood to earn money to survive. This read-aloud can inspire social action and empathy for others, while inviting conversations about the dangers of stereotypes, labeling, and judging others.

CONTINUING CONNECTIONS MORE LAYERS FOR LEARNING TOGETHER

This heartprint video, "Unsung Hero," won Best Ad award in 2014. It was created as an advertisement for life insurance with the slogan "Believe in Good." Follow along to observe a day in the life of an ordinary man who does extraordinary things to bring good to strangers, friends, and neighbors. Share the video to facilitate discussions about the ripple effects of one person's actions.

To further explore the dangers of single stories, what this means, and how it can impact our teaching, consider reflecting on Chimamanda Ngozi Adichie's brilliant Ted Talk. You might also search for copies of her recent commencement speeches to add more layers to this conversation.

ART FOR TRANSFORMATION with *MAYBE SOMETHING BEAUTIFUL*

HEARTPRINT BOOK: *Maybe Something Beautiful: How Art Transformed a Neighborhood* by F. Isabel Campoy and Theresa Howell, illustrated by Rafael López

ABOUT THE BOOK: This book tells the true story of the Urban Art Trail in California where people came together to create art and revive a community. Volunteers from all backgrounds were invited to participate and share their talents.

LIFE LAYERS ♥ INVITATIONS TO SHARE CONNECTIONS, CARES, AND CONCERNS

Share *Maybe Something Beautiful* to inspire students to embrace art and creativity as a powerful tool for self-expression. Read this story to reflect on how a neighborhood became a work of art. The Urban Art Trail can motivate budding artists and writers and help students to make further connections between art and activism. Art can transform lives.

Discussion Possibilities

- Demonstrate to students how art and illustrations in any text enhance literacy. Select an image to reflect on further with your students. Invite readers to discuss how the illustrations and artwork add to this story. Share observations, responses, and reflections.
- Lead discussions on how the illustrations inspire emotional response or enhance word choice.
- Explain how illustrations can have different meaning for different people. Invite learners to share what individual images from the text mean them.

LITERACY CONNECTIONS 👥 POSSIBILITIES FOR NURTURING OUR READERS AND WRITERS

Based on the needs of your students and their instructional goals, consider the following possibilities for layering in reading and writing connections to complement your workshop, small-group, or individual conversations.

As a Reader	As a Writer
Analyzing Texts Readers examine illustrations and consider how they add to observations about a text. Reflect on the ways López's illustrations reveal information about the neighborhood, considering how the images impact interpretations about this neighborhood. For example, consider what biases the story might reinforce. Suggest your students look back to see how the images change through the course of the story (and in other stories) to determine what ways this might influence new thoughts, opinions, or observations.	**Strengthening Writing Ideas** Writers draw on their own historical and cultural connections to create personalized, meaningful texts. After exploring the story of the Urban Art Trail, students might be inspired to create their own drawing or writing to express pride in their community, neighborhood, family, or one another.
Thinking Beyond the Text Readers read images and texts, studying what they say explicitly and implicitly, to make inferences and draw conclusions. Discuss descriptive words and phrases, such as "Ms. López, the lady with the sparkling eyes." Or "The walls lit up like sunshine." In the same way art transforms, discuss how specific lines reveal new thinking about the characters in *Maybe Something Beautiful*.	**Establishing Perspective and Point of View** Writers include text about various characters to reveal relationships and to elaborate on events. Notice how the neighborhood became a "giant block party" with the contributions of various neighbors. Encourage your writers to consider adding conversations and/or inner thoughts from multiple viewpoints to elaborate on or to express in a moment they are writing about.
Thinking Within the Text Readers interpret words and images to analyze how positioning impacts meaning or tone. Consider the way the layout changes throughout *Maybe Something Beautiful*. Ask your students to consider the way lines such as "color, punch and pizzazz" might influence their thoughts and emotions.	**Analyzing Craft and Word Choice** Writers create images through their words and illustrations to convey their message. Notice the ways Campoy, Howell, and López used words and images to emphasize ideas. Suggest students share the possible ways they could adjust their own writing to emphasize an idea using images, color, size, shape, or organization.

LITERACY SNAPSHOTS IDEAS TO ADOPT OR ADAPT

Share images and more information from the Urban Art Trail at maybesomethingbeautiful.com to extend your conversations and inspire students to think about ways they might contribute art for their community.

Explore artists and activists. These first-grade students were inspired by their study of pop artist Romero Britto and created their own emojis on themes of love, happiness, and hope.

CONTINUING CONVERSATIONS ADDITIONAL HEARTPRINT CONNECTIONS

Hey, Wall: A Story of Art and Community by Susan Verde, illustrated by John Parra

In this book we learn about another community that is connected and strengthened by art. Susan Verde focuses on how walls can connect us rather than divide us. Share *Hey, Wall* to inspire children to take action as change agents in their own community.

Home Sweet Neighborhood: Transforming Cities One Block at a Time by Michelle Mulder

This informational text, told through photo-essays, reflects on the beauty of all neighborhoods. Readers can explore thriving community spaces and the connections that come from shaping our public spaces into more personal, communal sanctuaries. Explore more titles in the Orca Footprint series to encourage student to become activists and advocates for social responsibility and global citizenship.

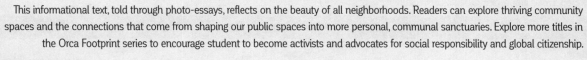

Martí's Song for Freedom / Martí y sus versos por la libertad by Emma Otheguy, illustrated by Beatriz Vidal

This bilingual biography (Spanish and English) explores the work of Cuban poet and political activist José Martí. Share this story and these poems to reinforce how we can use art, poetry, and music in transformational ways.

CONTINUING CONNECTIONS MORE LAYERS FOR LEARNING TOGETHER

Inspired by the work of pop artists such as Romero Britto and illustrator Rafael López, establish additional opportunities to connect poetry, art, and makerspaces. Invite your colleagues to be a part of the conversation and brainstorm possibilities. To get everyone on board, share the article "7 Ways to Use StickTogether Mosaic Posters in Your Library," by Liz Bowie (2018), or visit Romero Britto's website for more inspiration at britto.com.

AGENCY AND ACTIVISM with *DESTINY'S GIFT*

HEARTPRINT BOOK: *Destiny's Gift* by by Natasha Anastasia Tarpley, illustrated by Adjoa J. Burrowes

ABOUT THE BOOK: Destiny loves visiting her local independent bookstore and spending time with the owner, Mrs. Wade. They share a love for books, reading, writing, and the power of words. They care deeply for each other and have a special bond. When Mrs. Wade's store is in danger of closing, Destiny steps in to take action and to bring her neighborhood together.

LIFE LAYERS ♡ INVITATIONS TO SHARE CONNECTIONS, CARES, AND CONCERNS

Destiny's Gift has so many heartprint connections, beginning with Destiny's love for learning and her relationship with Mrs. Wade. Their friendship is an example of pure book love in action. Share this text to spark conversations about book bonds, as well as to reflect on our individual gifts and talents.

Discussion Possibilities

- Consider how Destiny loves words by reading and spends her Saturdays visiting Mrs. Wade's bookstore. Suggest students discuss the people who shape their thoughts for being active members or role models in their community.
- Launch an exploration of students' definition of role models. Help students notice Destiny's relationship with Mrs. Wade. Consider other possible role models, such as students' relatives, neighbors, teachers, and even fellow students.
- Invite students to share what they are passionate about modeled on Destiny and Mrs. Wade's passion for reading, writing, and the power of words.
- Have students reflect on the ways children can and do make a difference—as young Destiny demonstrates—in the lives of others in their community or at home.
- Reflect on the ways students could act in response to community issues and concerns, such as facilitating peaceful protests, fund-raising, block parties, and rallies.

LITERACY CONNECTIONS POSSIBILITIES FOR NURTURING OUR READERS AND WRITERS

Based on the needs of your students and their instructional goals, consider the following possibilities for layering in reading and writing connections to complement your workshop, small-group, or individual conversations.

As a Reader	As a Writer
Exploring Illustrations Readers pay close attention to the images to think more deeply about setting, character, and events. Invite your readers to go back and notice the ways the pictures add to the words in *Destiny's Gift.* There are lots of messages in the illustrations.	**Developing Ideas** Writers write about memories they want to celebrate and record those details. *Destiny's Gift* can provide inspiration for your writers to collect ideas to write about people, places, or books they love.
Exploring Vocabulary and Word Choice Readers look for words that have distinct meanings or powerful effects. Like Destiny and Mrs. Wade suggest, we can all be "word detectives." Recommend that students record new and/or beautiful words or phrases found in this book or in books they are reading on their own.	**Exploring Language and Word Choice** Writers look for and use specific words to add detail to their writing. Remind students they could use sketches or their own language to understand and collect unfamiliar words found in *Destiny's Gift* (or new words from their own reading) as a way to acquire and use new vocabulary.
Reading with a Critical Lens Readers evaluate power and perspective. Mrs. Wade's bookstore is in danger of closing. In response, ask your students to reconsider the various characters (landlord, neighbors, Destiny, Mrs. Wade) through the lens of questions—Who has the power in this story? Who has more? Who has less? Why may that be?	**Revising Texts and Titles** Writers reflect on titles and how they connect to the messages found in books. Consider Natasha Tarpley's choice: *Destiny's Gift.* Students can share opinions about this title and others, supporting their thoughts with rationales and examples, while considering ways they could revise titles in their own writing in a way that reflects their messages and big ideas.

LITERACY SNAPSHOTS  IDEAS TO ADOPT OR ADAPT

Help your students evaluate texts they read for larger issues like power, privilege, and fairness. A group of fifth graders brainstorm social concerns to think about critically as they read.

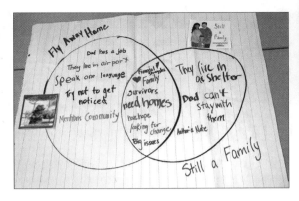

To highlight different author perspectives, students look at two similar stories that address homelessness with an eye toward how they differ in relation to larger social issues as well as their relationship to who is telling the story. Students are encouraged to look for alternative viewpoints, voices, and other sources of information.

CONTINUING CONVERSATIONS  ADDITIONAL HEARTPRINT CONNECTIONS

Turning Pages: My Life Story by Sonia Sotomayor, illustrated by Lulu Delacre

This is the autobiography of Supreme Court Justice Sonia Sotomayor. As a strong, powerful woman and the first Latinx Supreme Court judge, Sotomayor has inspired others to reach for their dreams. She shares the impact and power of books in her life. Sharing Sotomayor's story can help connect conversations back to role models we can find on and off the pages of a book.

Imagine by Juan Felipe Herrera, illustrated by Lauren Castillo

Juan Felipe Herrera, the son of migrant farmworkers, who grew up to be named the United States Poet Laureate, shares his life's story and his message: anything is possible if you imagine. *Imagine* is another powerful picture book that will spark conversations and action exploring literacy as a tool for change.

Still a Family: A Story About Homelessness by Brenda Reeves Sturgis, illustrated by Jo-Shin Lee

This book addresses homelessness from a different lens, where readers meet a loving family that, despite their circumstances, are viewed as active agents rather than helpless victims.

CONTINUING CONNECTIONS MORE LAYERS FOR LEARNING TOGETHER

Consider sharing Steven Zemelman's *From Inquiry to Action: Civic Engagement with Project-Based Learning in All Content Areas* (2016) to explore ideas to support students and teachers as responsible, active learners through project-based learning based in real-world situations.

LEARNING FROM ROLE MODELS WITH *SHAKING THINGS UP*

HEARTPRINT BOOK: *Shaking Things Up: 14 Young Women Who Changed the World* by Susan Hood, illustrated by Sophie Blackall et al.

ABOUT THE BOOK: This hybrid text blends art and information with additional sources and bonus quotes to showcase fourteen inspiring rebels, activists, trailblazers, and role models. This picture book has unique text structure with poetic verse, each illustrated by an equally inspiring and talented female illustrator. Additional resources—a bonus time line, famous lines, quotes, author's notes, and suggestions for further research—complement the paired text and poems.

LIFE LAYERS ♥ INVITATIONS TO SHARE CONNECTIONS, CARES, AND CONCERNS

In *Shaking Things Up*, Susan Hood captures the beauty of the words and deeds of inspirational female role models. Readers who recognize injustice will be encouraged to become active community members to stand up for themselves and for others. This informational picture book will inspire readers, writers, and researchers of all ages.

Discussion Possibilities

- Lead students in discussing the roles of women described in the book or others they admire.
- Encourage students to reflect on the following quote by activist Frances Moore Lappé in *Shaking Things Up*, "Every choice we make can be a celebration of the world we want." Facilitate their discussions about the type of world they want to live in and how their choices can contribute to this outcome.
- Ask students to think about other trailblazing individuals in history to include in this discussion.
- Consider extending this conversation to people from other informational texts or book characters who have made an impact in their lives.
- Recommend that learners discuss real-life individuals, such as family or community members, athletes, artists, and other people they admire.

LITERACY CONNECTIONS 👥 POSSIBILITIES FOR NURTURING OUR READERS AND WRITERS

Based on the needs of your students and their instructional goals, consider the following possibilities for layering in reading and writing connections to complement your workshop, small-group, or individual conversations.

As a Reader	As a Writer
Searching For and Using Information Readers scan texts to gather information from text features such as a drawing, a diagram, a caption, time lines to synthesize information, and ideas. Discuss how these features in *Shaking Things Up* add collectively to its overall message.	**Developing and Strengthening Writing Ideas** Writers use techniques such as interesting language, photos, and graphics to engage and entertain the reader as they share factual information. *Shaking Things Up* includes time lines, poetry, quotes, fun facts, and extensive back matter. Suggest students select an example from this mentor text to emulate in their own writing.
Inferring Readers draw conclusions about texts making inferences using titles, captions, and new words in context. Invite your students to pay close attention to the messages that the selected titles in *Shaking Things Up* might reveal. Notice how the titles such as "Books, Not Bullets" or "The Storyteller" add to inferences that support ideas about these "rebels with a cause."	**Writing Arguments** Writers form and express opinions using evidence to support or extend an argument. Use *Shaking Things Up* to help student writers think about the importance of justifying their own arguments by citing impactful quotes and information from sources.
Writing About Reading Readers use varying text structures to identify and share information. As readers reflect on information they read, they may consider writing about their reading using one of the structures provided, such as time line, ABC word list, or illustrations to share new learning from *Shaking Things Up*.	**Writing in Response to Reading** Writers may choose to research and write an essay or poem about others (from the text) who have used their talents to overcome challenges. Extend the connections by inviting your students to think about their own challenges, strengths, or talents and the path they wish to take in their lives inspired by these individuals.

LITERACY SNAPSHOTS IDEAS TO ADOPT OR ADAPT

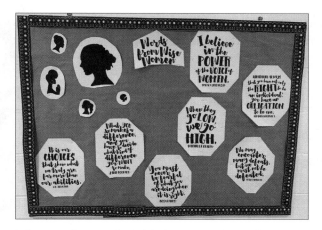

Invite your students to gather and display inspirational quotes from people in history and in our world. Students searched for and reflected on powerful quotes under the heading "Words from Wise Women" to extend their conversations and inspire further research.

Suggest your students select an inspiring individual or role model they want to read and learn about. Primary students share their research about important women in "Herstory."

CONTINUING CONVERSATIONS ADDITIONAL HEARTPRINT CONNECTIONS

Auntie Luce's Talking Paintings by Francie Latour, illustrated by Ken Daley

In this beautifully illustrated picture book, readers will find paintings that "talk back," telling stories about the history, culture, sounds, and language of Haiti. The book celebrates Haitian history and culture while sparking conversations about Luce Turnier, a ground-breaking artist who overcame obstacles for women of color and artists of all backgrounds.

Ada Byron Lovelace and the Thinking Machine by Laurie Wallmark, illustrated by April Chu

This fascinating woman, daughter of poet Lord Byron, had a passion for numbers, even though she was born into a world of poetry. Through her creativity and talents, she was one of the first computer programmers to recognize the poetry of science, examining the power of collaboration, curiosity, and creativity.

Sweet Dreams, Sarah by Vivian Kirkfield, illustrated by Chris Ewald

Sarah Goode made "herstory" as the first African American woman to receive a patent. The book's back matter includes a long line of ingenious women working to make life better for their communities. Share with your readers to generate conversations about women who acted on their beliefs, overcame challenges, and achieved their goals.

CONTINUING CONNECTIONS MORE LAYERS FOR LEARNING TOGETHER

To continue the conversation about women who have broken rules to overcome stereotypes and challenges, take a look at this collection of videos (from The Kid Should See This) that explore the lives and contributions of inspiring women in science, technology, engineering, and mathematics fields.

CARING FOR OUR WORLD with *GALÁPAGOS GIRL/GALAPAGUEÑA*

HEARTPRINT BOOK: *Galápagos Girl/Galapagueña* by Marsha Diane Arnold, illustrated by Angela Dominguez

ABOUT THE BOOK: This bilingual (English and Spanish) biography is about the early life that influenced young activist and conservationist Valentina Cruz. It was inspired by the author's visit to the Galápagos Islands and interview with Valentina Cruz. The book was illustrated by Pura Belpré Honor recipient Angela Dominguez. An added bonus for readers includes detailed author's notes, fun facts, and resources to extend the conversations and the learning.

LIFE LAYERS ♡ INVITATIONS TO SHARE CONNECTIONS, CARES, AND CONCERNS

In *Galápagos Girl/Galapagueña*, readers will learn the story of a young activist, Valentina, and her respect for nature, beginning with her volunteer work (at age twelve) at the Charles Darwin Research Center, which shaped her future. This book provides an important message about how kids can make a difference and how things happen when you have a "heart full of fire."

Discussion Possibilities

- Encourage readers to discuss the author's note and consider how the author's visit to the Galápagos and meeting Valentina Cruz inspired her to write this story.
- Lead students in discussing a person they would like to meet and/or interview who has done something they admire.
- Invite students to reflect on how Valentina's experience as a child and young activist impacted her life and her future.
- Ask students to share something they're passionate about, as demonstrated by Valentina, whose concern for the animals in the Galápagos Islands started in childhood.

LITERACY CONNECTIONS 👩🏻‍🦰👨🏾 POSSIBILITIES FOR NURTURING OUR READERS AND WRITERS

Based on the needs of your students and their instructional goals, consider the following possibilities for layering in reading and writing connections to complement your workshop, small-group, or individual conversations.

As a Reader	As a Writer
Making Connections Readers recognize that informational texts often reflect the customs, behaviors, and events of their locations. In *Galápagos Girl/Galapagueña*, students might discuss connections that help them infer how the setting impacts the information presented and how place impacts meaning even in informational texts.	**Writing in Response to Reading** Writers write in response to reading that connects events and details to expand on and strengthen ideas. Suggest students write about what it means to protect one's environment and what that might look like where they live.
Exploring Vocabulary and Word Choice Readers ask questions to deepen understanding of new vocabulary. As you reflect on unfamiliar words, provide opportunities for learners to stop and sketch or stop and jot notes in their own words to help expand vocabulary and understanding.	**Borrowing Craft Structures** Writers use a bibliography to cite sources from their research and to invite their readers to investigate further on their own. Students could revisit the back matter from *Galápagos Girl/Galapagueña* to spark their own research or as a model for including resources in their own informational writing.
Analyzing Ideas and Information Readers notice how writers blend narrative and informational text to give a real-world context for learning. Invite students to discuss the ways that Marsha Diane Arnold created scenes that add to their understanding and appreciation for the life of this young activist.	**Writing from Sources** Researchers take notes and record information from a variety of sources. Like Marsha Diane Arnold's use of interviews, fun facts searches, or in-person visits, students have options for making research fun and engaging. Invite your students to research a topic of their choice using interviews, websites, photos, magazines, and other student-selected sources.

LITERACY SNAPSHOTS IDEAS TO ADOPT OR ADAPT

Started nonprofit at 5.
Fed 20,000. So far.

SERVICE
PassItOn.com

Using content-area studies and inspiring stories of young activists like Valentina Cruz, help students investigate, write about, and celebrate other young activists. Students explored individuals like Mari Copeny—Little Miss Flint—who continues to fight for clean water in Flint, Michigan, and Joshua Williams, who started a food pantry at age five. Learn more about Joshua and others at passiton.com.

Inspired by Marsha Diane Arnold's work in *Galápagos Girl/Galapagueña*, students might choose a topic to write their own informational books and include additional resources for further learning through a variety of text features.

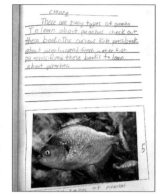

CONTINUING CONVERSATIONS 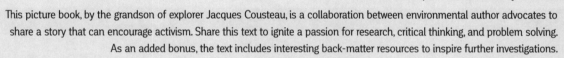 ADDITIONAL HEARTPRINT CONNECTIONS

A Is for Activist by Innosanto Nagara

Although this is an alphabet board book, it is a great entry point to reflect on the meaning of *agency* and *activism*. *A Is for Activist* can also be used as a mentor text to model the ABC format as a text structure to share research and learning.

Follow the Moon Home: A Tale of One Idea, Twenty Kids, and a Hundred Sea Turtles by Philippe Cousteau and Deborah Hopkinson, illustrated by Meilo So

This picture book, by the grandson of explorer Jacques Cousteau, is a collaboration between environmental author advocates to share a story that can encourage activism. Share this text to ignite a passion for research, critical thinking, and problem solving. As an added bonus, the text includes interesting back-matter resources to inspire further investigations.

Bravo! Poems About Amazing Hispanics by Margarita Engle, illustrated by Rafel López

This is a collection of biographical poems about inspirational Latinx individuals and their contributions to communities all around the world. Engle wrote these poems through her subjects' first-person perspectives. Your writers can try this technique as they work to connect research, poetry, and point of view.

CONTINUING CONNECTIONS MORE LAYERS FOR LEARNING TOGETHER

 Take a tour of the Galápagos Islands to help students build background knowledge and explore videos of many of the animals mentioned in Arnold's book.

 The website for Earth Echo, a nonprofit organization founded by Jacques Cousteau's grandchildren, will help students consider problems, gather information, and learn about the history of and ongoing work in environmental studies and sustainability.

THE POWER OF WORDS WITH *WORDS AND YOUR HEART*

HEARTPRINT BOOK: *Words and Your Heart* by Kate Jane Neal

ABOUT THE BOOK: In this heartprint book that's sure to leave its mark on hearts and minds, the narrator speaks directly to the reader about how the words that go into our ears, actually go straight to our hearts. *Words in Your Heart* offers a great message about the power of our words and a reminder to choose and use them with care.

LIFE LAYERS ♡ INVITATIONS TO SHARE CONNECTIONS, CARES, AND CONCERNS

This book explores the way in which words have the ability to harm or heal and how this connects to kindness, character, and nurturing communities. What we say and how we say it matters.

Discussion Possibilities

- Facilitate conversations that recognize the power of words.
- Invite students to reflect on those words that they view as positive or negative and discuss why.
- Suggest students reflect on words and images they might "collect" from stories and friends that encourage or inspire agency and action.
- Consider addressing situations where students missed an opportunity to use kind words.
- Help students reflect on the differences between negative and positive self-talk as well as the difference between specific feedback over empty praise.
- Be sensitive as students explore experiences with words that can be harmful.

LITERACY CONNECTIONS 👥 POSSIBILITIES FOR NURTURING OUR READERS AND WRITERS

Based on the needs of your students and their instructional goals, consider the following possibilities for layering in reading and writing connections to complement your workshop, small-group, or individual conversations.

As a Reader	As a Writer
Maintaining Fluency Readers pay attention to text formatting, examining how font choice, text size, and color influence interpretations of emotions and voice. Notice how the words in *Words and Your Heart* change in size, causing the reader to pause, speed up, whisper, or yell. Invite your students to look for similar clues during their independent reading.	**Exploring Words and Images** Writers use a variety of techniques (such as sound words and onomatopoeia) to create sensory details and to guide readers to interpret the text in a specific way. Invite your writers to explore additional ways they could add sensory details to their pieces to expand on an image or an idea.
Monitoring for Meaning Readers notice a writer's word choice and use of sensory details and images to impact visualization or convey feeling. Notice how the parenthetical messages in *Words and Your Heart* reveal feelings and express the author's intent. Kate Jane Neal expands on the idea of our hearts as "that little bit inside of you, that make you, you."	**Analyzing Craft** Writers make deliberate decisions about words to share their point of view or beliefs. Consider the craft choices made by Kate Jane Neal and invite your students to try out similar ideas, such as using parenthetical messages, for their readers.
Inferring Readers read to infer themes and to understand that there can be more than one interpretation. Examine the text to discuss how an author's message is revealed through images, emotions, and ideas.	**Writing Critiques** Writers express opinions about a text—analyzing illustrations, the author's craft, or the theme. Through writing, students can evaluate sections from *Words and Your Heart* by sharing their opinions and using examples as rationale.

LITERACY SNAPSHOTS IDEAS TO ADOPT OR ADAPT

To reinforce using our words to do "good," students can create compliment cards or posters to tear off and give to others.

Help students consider places around the school to post messages to nurture one another's hearts. These "You Matter" tear-offs were displayed in the bathroom.

CONTINUING CONVERSATIONS ADDITIONAL HEARTPRINT CONNECTIONS

Bookjoy, Wordjoy by Pat Mora, illustrated by Raúl Colón

This inspiring collection of poetry celebrates the power of words and all the joyful ways we can engage with words, books, and reading. Paired with beautiful illustrations by Raúl Colón that reflect the style of Mexican muralists, this book will leave your students wanting to sketch and write their own book of joyful words and ideas.

The Word Collector by Peter H. Reynolds

Another example of the impact and transformative power of our words, this heartprint author shares more life lessons about how we might use our words to do good. Consider pairing this book with *Destiny's Gift* by Natasha Anastasia Tarpley, another heartprint book that celebrates what it means to be a word collector.

Quiet Please, Owen McPhee! by Trudy Ludwig, illustrated by Patrice Barton

Trudy Ludwig's books are great for character studies and character education. In this book, the reader meets Owen, whose talking too much is somewhat problematic. This is a great read-aloud to discuss the power of listening and learning together. Read or revisit this title to connect to ways to reinforce successful routines in student-led conversations.

CONTINUING CONNECTIONS MORE LAYERS FOR LEARNING TOGETHER

As a staff, study Peter Johnston's *Choice Words: How Our Language Affects Children's Learning* (2004) to extend the conversation about how the words we use as teachers matter. This book will stir reflections about how the words we in use conferring conversations with students can either motivate them or hold them back.

FINDING INSPIRATION WITH *LIMITLESS*

HEARTPRINT BOOK: *Limitless: 24 Remarkable American Women of Vision, Grit, and Guts* by Leah Tinari

ABOUT THE BOOK: This is a unique collection of stories about groundbreaking women who have contributed to the arts, education, science, civil rights, fashion, technology, sports, and more. Artist Leah Tinari creates graffiti-style portraits in an appealing and inviting way to share research.

LIFE LAYERS ♥ INVITATIONS TO SHARE CONNECTIONS, CARES, AND CONCERNS

Read *Limitless* to spark conversations about the impact of perseverance and passion. Share it to introduce further investigations into what it means to be inspirational and the qualities of people that inspire us. In addition to her unique text layout and artwork, Tinari includes quotes, facts, and illustrations that will inspire endless possibilities for your researchers and artists.

Discussion Possibilities

- Ask students to think about which individuals and accomplishments they admired the most from the book and why.
- Revisit Tinari's style of art and illustrations. Together, analyze the choices she made and patterns she used throughout the text. Invite students to reflect on how the author's style choices affect their interpretations of her message.
- Raise the question about Tinari's selection of people, quotes, and information. Ask students to look for patterns that may illustrate why Tinari was inspired to write about these individuals.
- Suggest students consider who is represented and whose voices are missing from these selections. Discuss additions or changes they would make if they were to write something similar.

LITERACY CONNECTIONS POSSIBILITIES FOR NURTURING OUR READERS AND WRITERS

Based on the needs of your students and their instructional goals, consider the following possibilities for layering in reading and writing connections to complement your workshop, small-group, or individual conversations.

As a Reader	As a Writer
Analyzing Texts In *Limitless*, graffiti-style words add to the images. Readers might reflect on the purpose of this word art and how it enhances their understanding of the ideas presented.	**Analyzing Craft** Writers use a variety of techniques, such as graphics, quotes, and formatting, to communicate a message. Tinari incorporates stenciled quotes, facts, and information about these iconic and inspirational women. Invite students to play with some of Tinari's craft choices. Students might experiment with similar graffiti style, to demonstrate big ideas and information.
Analyzing Author's Purpose Readers notice how information, structures, and organization connect ideas within and across pages of a text. Using *Limitless*, invite your students to reflect on Leah Tinari's decisions. As students connect the texts, art, and ideas across the pages, invite them to look for patterns that might reveal more about the author's purpose.	**Developing Ideas** Researchers categorize information from a variety of sources to help their readers navigate through a text. Have students explore the way the layout and text structures thread the author's ideas together in *Limitless* and consider ways they can share information in a similar way.
Expanding Vocabulary and Word Choice As readers explore informational texts, they make note of new terms associated with the subject and add them to their vocabulary. Suggest your students practice using expert words as they speak or write about the subject or topic they are reading about.	**Exploring Word Choice** Writers deepen their vocabulary as they research and use specific terms to teach their readers more about a subject. Suggest students think about including content-specific expert words associated with a topic or person they are writing about.

LITERACY SNAPSHOTS IDEAS TO ADOPT OR ADAPT

Inspired by the art and ideas in *Limitless*, create displays that feature interpretations of artists, activists, and personal role models, such as this portrait with a quote from Maya Angelou.

As you continue to study inspiring individuals through reading, writing, and art, use Leah Tinari's work to inspire research displays. A fifth grader focused her study on Ruth Bader Ginsburg and then, using a similar structure, layout, and model of *Limitless*, shared her research.

CONTINUING CONVERSATIONS  ADDITIONAL HEARTPRINT CONNECTIONS

Heroes and She-roes: Poems of Amazing and Everyday Heroes by J. Patrick Lewis, illustrated by Jim Cooke

Your students will find lots of information in this collection of biographic poems that celebrate those "daring do-ers; heroes and she-roes." This book is a nice way to connect to your content areas or to spark further investigations of individuals and change makers in history. Readers will find inspiration for reading, writing, and living.

I Dissent: Ruth Bader Ginsburg Makes Her Mark by Debbie Levy, illustrated by Elizabeth Baddeley

Share this first picture book about the life of Supreme Court Justice Ruth Bader Ginsburg to continue explorations about "limitless" individuals in history.

Kate Warne: Pinkerton Detective by Marissa Moss, illustrated by April Chu

Like many of Marissa Moss's picture book biographies, this is another carefully researched story of a little-known groundbreaker. Kate Warne defied all expectations and became the first female detective in 1856! Share this picture book biography to discuss determined, fearless, inspiring individuals, and share the message that gender has no limits.

CONTINUING CONNECTIONS MORE LAYERS FOR LEARNING TOGETHER

Upstanders: How to Engage Middle School Hearts and Minds with Inquiry (Daniels and Ahmed 2015) is a professional development book that looks at ways we can connect academic instruction with a commitment to inquiry-based practices, justice, and action-oriented goals for students as individuals and as contributing members of society.

MAKING EVERY WORD COUNT with *SAY SOMETHING!*

HEARTPRINT BOOK: *Say Something!* by Peter H. Reynolds

ABOUT THE BOOK: In this engaging picture book, Peter H. Reynolds looks at the many ways one's voice matters. A great companion to his much-loved *The Word Collector*, Reynolds offers another simple but powerful message in *Say Something!*—each of us has the ability to use our voice to make a difference.

LIFE LAYERS ♡ INVITATIONS TO SHARE CONNECTIONS, CARES, AND CONCERNS

Share this inspiring book with readers of all ages to explore how we can "say something" through our words but also through our choices and our actions. Speaking directly to the reader, author and illustrator Peter H. Reynolds invites us to consider the many ways we can use our voice to speak out and make a difference.

Discussion Possibilities

- Suggest students take a closer look at the various ways Peter H. Reynolds shows children speaking out while exploring the meaning of the phrase "say something" based on their observations and experiences.
- Extend the conversation by curating a list of ways one can listen, be heard, or use their voice through creativity, words, and action.
- Students may choose to express their thoughts and words using the blank speech bubbles at the end of the book. Encourage your students to use this as a call to action or as recognition for the positive things happening in your community.
- Discuss how *Say Something!* might also prompt communities to think carefully about the harmful outcomes of discrimination and to recognize their individual and collective responsibility to speak up against prejudices and injustices.

LITERACY CONNECTIONS POSSIBILITIES FOR NURTURING OUR READERS AND WRITERS

Based on the needs of your students and their instructional goals, consider the following possibilities for layering in reading and writing connections to complement your workshop, small-group, or individual conversations.

As a Reader	As a Writer
Analyzing Ideas and Information Readers attend to the design elements, images, patterns, layout, and print an author and/or illustrator uses to communicate meaning. Reflect on the ways Peter H. Reynolds uses text boxes, thought, and speech bubbles to support his message about using one's voice in various ways.	**Analyzing Craft Lessons** Writers get ideas from other authors about options for sharing information in engaging ways. Encourage students to try a craft move from Peter H. Reynolds in their own writing, such as repetition of a line, use of dialogue, speech bubbles, or illustrations.
Inferring Central Message Readers notice the evidence a writer provides to support a message or lesson for the reader. Consider the central message from Peter H. Reynolds in *Say Something!* along with the techniques and clues he uses to get that message across.	**Writing for Change** Peter H. Reynolds serves as a mentor and a role model. He often has powerful messages in his books that inspire action. Lead an author study to help students think about the possible topics that they, like Reynolds, could write about to inspire change.
Critiquing Texts Readers talk critically about a text and what a writer does to connect to real-world issues or to make the topic interesting. Invite students to reflect on Peter H. Reynolds's message to his readers, and, if your students are ready, discuss his dedication to Emma González.	**Exploring Point of View** Writers make intentional decisions about point of view in a text. As an example, Reynolds used second person to talk directly to the reader to convince them to take the writer's point of view or take some action. Invite your writers to consider an issue and think how they might address their reader directly with facts or examples to support their reasoning.

LITERACY SNAPSHOTS IDEAS TO ADOPT OR ADAPT

Inspired by artists, poets, musicians, and athletes alike, primary students investigated role models for agency and advocacy. Here, a group studied football player Colin Kaepernick's role as an influential activist and change maker.

Teaching for joy and justice is part of everyday learning at Northern Parkway. Students are inspired through stories to explore social justice and *life* work.

CONTINUING CONVERSATIONS 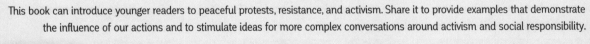 ADDITIONAL HEARTPRINT CONNECTIONS

One by Kathryn Otoshi

This picture book explores colors, numbers, and concepts but also stirs conversations about a complex message. Through the personification of colors and numbers, readers can explore the ways we can find strength in numbers and in our collective ability to support one another.

Peaceful Fights for Equal Rights by Rob Sanders, illustrated by Jared Andrew Schorr

This book can introduce younger readers to peaceful protests, resistance, and activism. Share it to provide examples that demonstrate the influence of our actions and to stimulate ideas for more complex conversations around activism and social responsibility.

Hello by Aiko Ikegami

This wordless picture book sends a powerful message about communicating and connecting with others. The illustrations portray an intergalactic child landing on Earth, only to find that most of the people are too busy or too involved on their devices to connect with him. When he meets a little girl, they form bonds of friendship through kindness. Share this with your readers to discuss the power that comes from spending time with others and making every word and moment count.

CONTINUING CONNECTIONS MORE LAYERS FOR LEARNING TOGETHER

 In this video, Peter H. Reynolds discusses his book *Say Something!* and shares more about his message that all of our beliefs, ideas, and dreams matter.

 To explore more books by Peter H. Reynolds and their connections to your heartprint work, check out one of my former blogs from the Nerdy Book Club.

HELPING OTHERS AS HELPING OURSELVES with *THE ONE DAY HOUSE*

HEARTPRINT BOOK: *The One Day House* by Julia Durango, illustrated by Bianca Diaz

ABOUT THE BOOK: *The One Day House* demonstrates what it means to be part of a caring community. Through the main character's conversations with neighbors and friends, readers will be inspired by the beauty and the power of working together to help others.

LIFE LAYERS ♥ INVITATIONS TO SHARE CONNECTIONS, CARES, AND CONCERNS

Being part of a caring community of learners, we need conversations that also incorporate the impact of our actions on others. Through stories like *The One Day House*, students connect the ideas of advocacy and agency to remember that they can and do have an impact in our world. Read this heartprint book aloud to address the interconnectedness of community, selflessness, agency, and activism.

Discussion Possibilities

- Help student reflect on and examine the ways they work together to demonstrate their support for one another and the members of their community.
- Ask readers to think about a list of possible problems in need of solutions. Invite students to think about directions they might take to change a real issue.
- Invite students to discuss the beautiful expressions in Durango's text. They might discuss what it means to be "all the sunshine one person needs" or to be "the song in someone's heart." Perhaps students can share similar phrases about individuals who have a similar impact in their lives.
- Suggest students think about how they might address real-world problems through project-based work, genius hour, and innovative student-centered projects.

LITERACY CONNECTIONS 👥 POSSIBILITIES FOR NURTURING OUR READERS AND WRITERS

Based on the needs of your students and their instructional goals, consider the following possibilities for layering in reading and writing connections to complement your workshop, small-group, or individual conversations.

As a Reader	As a Writer
Inferring Readers read and reflect on the significance of relationships between characters. Consider how Gigi and Wilson interact throughout *The One Day House*. Discuss how their interactions tell more about the author's message and big ideas. Suggest readers look back to reflect on additional images to add to their interpretation of the book.	**Argument Writing** Writers can research and raise awareness for issues and activism. Think about ways to extend and deepen investigations with authentic, relevant connections to real people who have impacted our world.
Analyzing Language Readers make note of an author's intentional use of language. Think about how Julia Durango uses repetition ("One day . . . ") and metaphors ("you are the song in my heart"). Readers can reflect on how those lines reveal more about the relationship between Gigi and Wilson.	**Organizing Craft Lessons** Writers use repeated words and/or images to illustrate an idea. Your students might notice how Julia Durango repeats the phrase, "One day . . ." as a balance of style and argument. Invite students to borrow the techniques as a source of inspiration for their own writing. Prompt writers to think about a repeated line or phrase that could reveal a bigger message to their readers.
Making Connections Read articles about current events to help raise students' awareness about community issues. For ideas, search the News ELA site (newsela.com) or use your community newsletter to spark conversations and actions.	**Writing to Research and Connect** Encourage writers to research some of the suggested groups found in the author's note, such as Habitat for Humanity and United Way. Suggest students consider a topic from the perspective of a change maker, think about ways to address a problem, and write about the ways they could get involved.

LITERACY SNAPSHOTS IDEAS TO ADOPT OR ADAPT

Share the author's note and back matter in *The One Day House*. Author Julia Durango suggests additional ideas for activism and volunteer work through a celebration of the "labors of love," inviting readers to get involved in various projects. Here, a group of students tend to a community garden.

Help students think about possibilities for connecting community and literacy. After reading *The One Day House.*, these students created tear-offs as a way to share book recommendations and spread a little book love in their community.

CONTINUING CONVERSATIONS 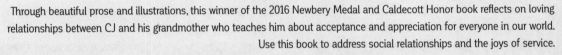 ADDITIONAL HEARTPRINT CONNECTIONS

Miles of Smiles by Karen Kaufman Orloff, illustrated by Luciano Lozano

In *The One Day House*, Wilson brings smiles to Gigi and it's "all the sunshine she needs." In *Miles of Smiles*, readers see the boomerang effect of smiles, laughter, and kindness. Share this picture book to discuss the impact of actions, however small, and reflect on the ways our smiles can affect our individual and collective learning environments.

Last Stop on Market Street by Matt de la Peña, illustrated by Christian Robinson

Through beautiful prose and illustrations, this winner of the 2016 Newbery Medal and Caldecott Honor book reflects on loving relationships between CJ and his grandmother who teaches him about acceptance and appreciation for everyone in our world. Use this book to address social relationships and the joys of service.

If You Plant a Seed by Kadir Nelson

Told through Kadir Nelson's beautiful words and paintings, this book illustrates how kind actions can grow into something beautiful. Readers can connect to the symbolic message of seeds of kindness growing into greater acts of compassion.

CONTINUING CONNECTIONS MORE LAYERS FOR LEARNING TOGETHER

Reflect on opportunities to volunteer in your own community or find other ways you can help others. In an effort to support community businesses, reading, and actively participating in one's neighborhood, you might plan a field trip to a local independent bookstore.

Spread smiles and share inspirational messages that illustrate a commitment to joyful learning environments through displays like the one found in this literacy lounge. What messages might your halls and walls reveal?

VISION AND COMPASSION with *BEAUTIFUL HANDS*

HEARTPRINT BOOK: *Beautiful Hands* by Kathryn Otoshi and Bret Baumgarten

ABOUT THE BOOK: All the symbols and illustrations in this book were made using the loving handprints and fingerprints of family members connected to the author and illustrator. Each page asks the reader to think about the many wonderful things our hands can do, such as reaching for dreams and planting ideas. The book was published as a memorial to the life of co-illustrator Bret Baumgarten.

LIFE LAYERS ♡ INVITATIONS TO SHARE CONNECTIONS, CARES, AND CONCERNS

Beautiful Hands can encourage readers to think about the tangible and intangible ways we can leave our mark on the world. Read to discuss the opportunities we have to nurture compassionate, curious, and caring community members. Otoshi reminds us, "When our actions are simultaneously used with good intentions, all these actions can add up to a much greater unforeseen vision."

Discussion Possibilities

- Inspire your readers to consider all the ways they can use their hands to support others.
- Encourage students to revisit *Beautiful Hands* and think about their responses to the open-ended questions found on each page throughout the book.
- Take a closer look to examine the illustrators' choices around colors, symbols, and shapes. Consider the ways they contribute to the meaning of the story.
- Share the author's note to learn more about the creators' decisions behind the art and explore how and why the handprints throughout the book contribute to the overall message in the text.
- Discuss Kathryn Otoshi's suggestion that students consider sharing their own individual and/or collective artwork created with their hands or fingerprints.

LITERACY CONNECTIONS 👧👦 POSSIBILITIES FOR NURTURING OUR READERS AND WRITERS

Based on the needs of your students and their instructional goals, consider the following possibilities for layering in reading and writing connections to complement your workshop, small-group, or individual conversations.

As a Reader	As a Writer
Searching for and Using Information Readers notice book and print features such as dedication pages, endnotes, and endpapers to add to their interpretation of a book. As a group, read and discuss the section "About the Story and Illustrations" and reflect on the impact of Bret Baumgarten's words and actions.	**Organizing and Presenting Ideas** Writers study an author's use of notes, dedications, and acknowledgments to support meaning and to inspire ways they might add to their own writing. Students may consider adding various features and back matter to a piece to include background for their readers through their own behind-the-story notes.
Monitoring for Deeper Meaning Readers recognize how an author's use of language impacts their interpretations. Notice how Kathryn Otoshi uses words that have multiple meanings to add to the images and ideas in this text. Consider how Otoshi uses symbolic language to plant or stretch ideas to deepen meaning.	**Exploring Word Choice** Writers make intentional decisions about word choice to create a strong image for their readers. As you discuss word choice in *Beautiful Hands*, invite your students to consider ways they could vary words and phrases to strengthen a piece of their writing.
Critiquing Texts Readers form opinions about texts they've read and give reasons to support their opinions. Students can contemplate which lines in the text or illustrations in *Beautiful Hands* they admired and why.	**Writing in Response to Reading** Writers draw or write to expand on an image or idea shared in something they've read. Students may be inspired to draw or write about what their hands can do or expand from other ideas presented in the text. Younger students may choose to create illustrations using their own handprints.

LITERACY SNAPSHOTS IDEAS TO ADOPT OR ADAPT

Consider creating your own symbol, word, or image to signify the ways you will work to leave your mark. Students proudly display bracelets they created with their one little word to illustrate the messages of their hearts.

Consider ways your students can create something to celebrate their connections and commitment to community. Kathryn Otoshi's work inspired these students to create images using their own handprints.

CONTINUING CONVERSATIONS  ADDITIONAL HEARTPRINT CONNECTIONS

Giant Steps to Change the World by Spike Lee and Tonya Lewis Lee, illustrated by Sean Qualls

In this motivational picture book about activism, readers learn about individuals who have taken big steps toward change. Each page introduces another step toward change and pairs it with a powerful quote from an inspiring individual from history. As your students read, help them reflect on the guiding question from the book, *What steps will you take to change the world?*

The Rooster Who Would Not Be Quiet! by Carmen Agra Deedy, illustrated by Eugene Yelchin

In this modern-day folktale about standing up to oppression, readers learn about the the power of one's voice. This book makes an important comparison about how like the roosters, children can use their voices to make a difference in our world and reminds us to speak up, to stand up, and to have the courage to "sing."

What Do You Do with a Chance? by Kobi Yamada, illustrated by Mae Besom

A child discovers that when you have courage, take chances, and try your best anything is possible. This picture book is part of the trilogy by Yamada that can spark additional conversations that nurture our students as individual readers, writers, and thinkers.

CONTINUING CONNECTIONS MORE LAYERS FOR LEARNING TOGETHER

Inspired by *Beautiful Hands* use handprint art to illustrate your school's missions, values, and/or beliefs. You might invite the school community to participate in creating a mural using everyone's hands to display and celebrate your vision for learning.

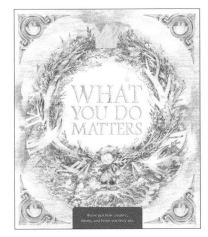

*It is the daily doses of authentic caring and mutual respect
that facilitate learning and empowerment.*
—Ernest Morrell et al., *Critical Media Pedagogy*

RESPONSIVE EDUCATORS use stories to engage their students wholeheartedly and to cultivate an inclusive community that respects individual differences through appreciating who its members are and who they can become. By sharing the pages of our favorite heartprint books, we can honor our students' identity, community, culture, traditions, and values and—through those stories—encourage habits of acceptance and respect.

Respect is about more than teaching students to treat others as they'd treat themselves. It's about opening our minds to the strengths in our differences and to celebrating the wonderful qualities that make each of us unique. True respect honors multiple perspectives and appreciates a variety of ways of being.

In this section of heartprint connections, we use stories to help learners appreciate others and nurture their social-emotional learning skills not only to support reading and writing communities but also to support learning as lifework. Through stories, we make connections about what matters to children, inviting them in and encouraging them to look for messages that speak to their hearts so they can grow beyond the book—to the story's impact on their lives and how they view the lives of others.

As our conversations evolve through our ongoing, shared reading experiences, students continue to think about how the books we explore can influence how they read, write, and live in the world. We invite our learners to use their personal connections to these stories to expand their understanding of themselves and others and to drive their curiosity to know more. Our read-alouds may set the stage for this, but it's the continuing community conversations that prepare their minds, hearts, and hands to do this important work.

Author Chimamanda Ngozi Adichie (2018) reminds us: "There's something wonderful and affirming about reading about your own reality and reading what is familiar to you. And that particular pleasure should never be denied anyone. But it is equally affirming to read about people who are *not* like you." So, in this chapter, you'll encourage learners to listen more, use inclusive language, explore hidden messages, talk back to texts, and honor the individuality of all the characters they encounter—regardless of age, gender, position, power, and culture—as they connect similar themes of respect across heartprint books. Through stories, we can encourage students to honor the lives of others and, in doing so, to find respect for themselves as readers, writers, *and* people.

RESPECTING OURSELVES AND OTHERS with *WE'RE ALL WONDERS*

HEARTPRINT BOOK: *We're All Wonders* by R. J. Palacio

ABOUT THE BOOK: The middle-grade success of Palacio's *We're All Wonders* inspired readers and the Choose Kind movement. Schools all across the country used her message and worked toward positive social change and respect for others. This picture book spin-off version gives a brief introduction to the story of Auggie, the extraordinary boy who wishes the world would see him as different not less than.

LIFE LAYERS ♥ INVITATIONS TO SHARE CONNECTIONS, CARES, AND CONCERNS

Palacio's stories speak to the universal messages of respecting our differences, finding our common connections, and addressing the universal need for belonging. Whether you use *We're All Wonders* to introduce or to complement the novel *Wonder* or as a stand-alone read-aloud, this book can be a catalyst to conversations that go beyond the clichéd suggestions pertaining to respect.

Discussion Possibilities

- Invite students to share their interpretations about what it means to show self-respect and respect for others.
- Encourage students to discuss the ways they show respect in your classroom and in your community. Consider ways they need to grow beyond kindness to go deeper in their respect for others.
- Facilitate student discussions about discrimination found in the novel, this picture book, or the popular film version, if they are ready. Suggest students consider characters in books as a starting point.
- Use scenarios in the book to explore connections around respect, appreciation, tolerance, and empathy.

LITERACY CONNECTIONS POSSIBILITIES FOR NURTURING OUR READERS AND WRITERS

Based on the needs of your students and their instructional goals, consider the following possibilities for layering in reading and writing connections to complement your workshop, small-group, or individual conversations.

As a Reader	As a Writer
Making Connections Readers think about the similarities and differences they see between events in a story and events in their own lives to make connections and understand the story more deeply. Suggest readers discuss connections to individual strengths and challenges and discuss the ways "we are all wonders."	**Developing Ideas** Writers write narratives with purpose and intention to develop big ideas about real or imagined experiences, using well-chosen images, words, and event sequences. Your writers could be inspired to write about an experience that was sparked by the message in *We're All Wonders*.
Inferring Readers examine the messages in texts that explore repeated images, words, and ideas to infer themes that can be reflected in their world and in their lives. For instance, Auggie says he can't change the way he looks, but maybe "people can change the way they see." Invite your readers to talk about what messages lines like this reveal.	**Showing Rather Than Telling** Writers use text clues with illustrations, words, phrases, actions, and/or dialogue to imply character attributes. R. J. Palacio describes Auggie by including others' actions and opinions others about him. Encourage your students to revise a piece of writing using the words and thoughts of others, to help the reader understand a character they are writing about.
Summarizing and Synthesizing Readers learn from vicarious experiences with characters in stories and develop ideas over the course of the text to build on a new understanding. After reading *We're All Wonders*, facilitate conversations about respect for people who are different than we are. Discuss how others are treated, and ask students to share new understandings in connection to Auggie and to society.	**Drafting and Revising** Writers use illustrations, symbols, and words to cumulatively disclose ideas and communicate messages connected across a text. Make time for your writers to reread, reflect, and rethink how they develop an idea across a page, in booklets, or in paragraphs. Writers might add more details or try an ending with a strong message, as does Palacio.

LITERACY SNAPSHOTS IDEAS TO ADOPT OR ADAPT

Celebrate YOU: Consider the messages your halls and walls send. Create wall spaces where you invite your students to display work they are most proud of along with messages about their *wonder*ful work, including goals and accomplishments. To make your display interactive, leave markers and sticky notes, with an invitation: "Comments, encouragement, and love are greatly appreciated: Please Write!"

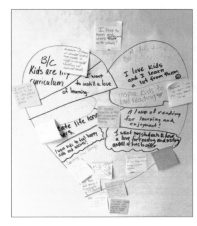

Respect for others includes respect for self. You might create a display where students can write, illustrate, or celebrate what they like about themselves and what makes them feel like wonders. Kindergarten students expanded on these ideas after reading Nancy Carlson's *I Like Me!*

CONTINUING CONVERSATIONS ADDITIONAL HEARTPRINT CONNECTIONS

I Like Myself! by Karen Beaumont, illustrated by David Catrow

I Like Myself! is a joyful read-aloud and a lighthearted affirmation of self. Told through both silly and serious rhyming text, it presents important messages about positive self-esteem, self-acceptance, and self-respect.

Quit Calling Me a Monster by Jory John, illustrated by Bob Shea

Jory John's text paired with Bob Shea's illustrations make for a great read-aloud and even greater discussion about respect for others. Share this playful but thought-provoking text to encourage readers to discuss the damaging effects of name-calling and stereotypes and, more important, the need to affirm our unique qualities and recognize individuals for who they are inside and out.

Life by Cynthia Rylant, illustrated by Brendan Wenzel

This book looks at life's joys and challenges and is paired with messages of respect and appreciation for our natural world. Page after page, readers are given a glimpse into all there is to love about life through the various lens of animals. In addition to discussions about respect for beauty in the world around us, share this book with students as a springboard to spark connections about what they appreciate about life.

CONTINUING CONNECTIONS MORE LAYERS FOR LEARNING TOGETHER

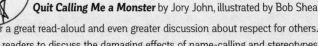

We can connect themes from *We're All Wonders* to remind us to consider professional development through a model of strengths as opposed to deficits. The Not This, But That series (organized like the Eat This, Not That books) is a short, practical resource that reminds us to look at learning, routines, and behaviors through positive, research-based, and student-centered practices. Titles in the series include *No More Culturally Irrelevant Teaching* (Souto-Manning et al. 2018), *No More Taking Away Recess: And Other Problematic Discipline Practices* (Cassetta and Sawyer 2013), and *No More Low Expectations for English Learners* (Nora and Echevarría 2016). This series is a great way to reflect on instructional practices that may need a little healthy improvement.

EMPATHY AND EXPERIENCES with *THEY ALL SAW A CAT*

HEARTPRINT BOOK: *They All Saw a Cat* by Brendan Wenzel

ABOUT THE BOOK: In this 2017 Caldecott Honor Book, the reader is invited to view a cat from multiple viewpoints. Brendan Wenzel's brilliant picture book explores complex concepts around point of view, including how experiences, perspectives, and biases can shape what we see.

LIFE LAYERS ♥ INVITATIONS TO SHARE CONNECTIONS, CARES, AND CONCERNS

Through artful text and images, readers can explore multiple perspectives and interpret changing points of view. Explore this book as a model to help facilitate complex conversations about the influence of privilege and power, and invite students to connect these messages to those found in other books, in media images, and in life. *They All Saw a Cat* is a simple picture book with multiple layers you will want to revisit again and again.

Discussion Possibilities

- Ask students to share opinions about the various animals in the story, not just the cat.
- Begin with connections to animals. Ask your students to share their opinions and ideas about animals. As you go deeper, you might encourage more complex conversations about how individual viewpoints inform our opinions.
- Lead students in discussing how each animal's perception of the cat changes and in reflecting on what messages are revealed through these changes.
- Invite students to share their observations and perceptions about the text and images from the book.
- Suggest students reflect on the ways previous knowledge, biases, or experiences can influence one's opinions and beliefs.

LITERACY CONNECTIONS POSSIBILITIES FOR NURTURING OUR READERS AND WRITERS

Based on the needs of your students and their instructional goals, consider the following possibilities for layering in reading and writing connections to complement your workshop, small-group, or individual conversations.

As a Reader	As a Writer
Analyzing Text and Point of View Readers analyze the voice an author chooses in a text to gain perspective. After reading *They All Saw a Cat*, invite your students to discuss their observations based on the various perspectives and viewpoints. Ask them to share their interpretations based on the different points of view.	**Writing Narratives to Develop Real or Imagined Ideas** Writers choose images or ideas to express meaning. Think about the ways that Brendan Wenzel used illustrations to demonstrate point of view. Students might choose a place in their writing where they can elaborate ideas through the eyes of a character, adding details through the lens of someone else's perspective.
Reading with a Critical Lens Readers revise their thinking as they read. Have readers select various pages to see which character is observing the cat and how that view connects to conversations about perspective and power (for the mouse, child, fox). As readers change their lens, it shifts their thinking. Facilitate discussions to consider how reading through the lens of power, position, identity, culture, or bias can influence how we read and interpret texts.	**Revising to Strengthen Our Ideas** Writers use various techniques to show how a character is feeling. Brendan Wenzel relied solely on images. Invite your students to revise a piece by using illustrations to reveal more about a character's feelings.
Inferring and Synthesizing Readers reflect on images to draw conclusions and develop ideas further. Suggest readers share the ways images, objects, and colors shape their inferences in *They All Saw a Cat*.	**Exploring Voice and Point of View** Writers can play with alternate viewpoints in their own writing. Invite students to take a new perspective and write through that lens. Encourage them to think about ways to be more precise with words, feelings, and actions that demonstrate how multiple characters are feeling in a scene.

LITERACY SNAPSHOTS IDEAS TO ADOPT OR ADAPT

To make thinking visible and to encourage kids to value different perspectives, students can sketch how they revise their thinking. Here, a fourth grader illustrates her inferences while looking at the same information from two points of view.

To help readers can gain a deeper appreciation for others, show them how to read a selection through the lens of a particular character. Create an anchor chart to guide your readers toward concepts to think about and ideas to develop.

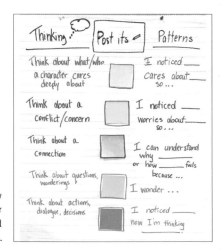

CONTINUING CONVERSATIONS ADDITIONAL HEARTPRINT CONNECTIONS

Duck! Rabbit! by Amy Krouse Rosenthal, illustrated by Tom Lichtenheld

Like *They All Saw a Cat, Duck! Rabbit!* is another must share to inspire discussions about multiple perspectives. (See Chapter 2.)

When the Cousins Came by Katie Yamasaki

A welcome spin to the lessons found in traditional city mouse and country mouse tales, Leo, a young Japanese American girl who lives in a rural area, is excited to host her "city" cousins, Rosie and Takeo, for a summer visit. Through small moments and memories, the cousins learn from and with one another as they celebrate their differences. Read *When the Cousins Came* to help students ponder family and friendships and appreciate cherished time with both.

Another by Christian Robinson

Expand perspectives and blow minds with this wordless narrative from Caldecott and Coretta Scott King Book Award honoree author and illustrator Christian Robinson, which begs to be read as an interactive book. Through unique artwork and use of white space, readers are taken on a journey they will want to return to again and again. Robinson brilliantly highlights our similarities and differences in two parallel worlds—a celebration of all children.

CONTINUING CONNECTIONS MORE LAYERS FOR LEARNING TOGETHER

For a sneak peek of *They All Saw a Cat* and to illustrate the messages discussed in the book, share this animated clip and book trailer created by Chronicle Books.

In this interview, Christian Robinson talks about illustration as a form of communication. He talks about his process and thoughts behind his experience in publishing and his mission to show all kids they matter in books.

THE IMPACT OF OUR WORDS WITH *TROUBLE TALK*

HEARTPRINT BOOK: *Trouble Talk* by Trudy Ludwig, illustrated by Mikela Prevost

ABOUT THE BOOK: Trudy Ludwig addresses the consequences of "trouble talk," such as gossip, sharing secrets, and talking about others. Maya's friend Bailey talks to everyone, but she is often insensitive and makes rude, inappropriate comments about other people's business to gain attention. This realistic fiction addresses the too often true-to-life problems among so-called friends that is, unfortunately, a common occurrence in many grade levels and schools. A powerful book and important vehicle for conversations and reminders about the importance of being respectful members of a community.

LIFE LAYERS ♥ INVITATIONS TO SHARE CONNECTIONS, CARES, AND CONCERNS

Share *Trouble Talk* to take a closer look at honesty, friendships, and respecting other people's feelings. Ludwig's books are an invaluable way to stir conversations about authentic social situations, such as when friends use harmful talk, spread rumors, and share others' secrets. This is an instructive book for addressing similar issues in social media interactions and the need to use our words respectfully.

Discussion Possibilities

- Ask students to discuss their various interpretations of the meaning of "trouble talk." Consider the sensitive nature of this conversation and the difficult examples it might bring up.
- Be prepared to help students recognize ways to respond to trouble talk with empathy, respect, and understanding.
- Discuss the harmful effects of talking about other people and prompt further discussion about the damage that can be done by spreading rumors or gossip of any kind.
- Encourage students to address respectful listening, true friendship, and not telling someone else's story that isn't yours to tell.
- Prompt children to reflect on the ways one can stand up or speak up when they hear hurtful comments from others.
- Discuss the importance of thinking before we speak.

LITERACY CONNECTIONS 👥 POSSIBILITIES FOR NURTURING OUR READERS AND WRITERS

Based on the needs of your students and their instructional goals, consider the following possibilities for layering in reading and writing connections to complement your workshop, small-group, or individual conversations.

As a Reader	As a Writer
Understanding Plot and Story Elements Readers use academic language to talk about story elements (such as conflict, resolution, character change) and use that language to develop their ideas further. Prompt students to discuss the multiple layers of conflicts and consider how stories often have more than one problem or conflict.	**Writing in Response to Reading** Using *Trouble Talk* as an example, model for students how to share written responses about narratives based on connections to the *narrator, conflict, turning point,* or *conclusion.*
Inferring Readers reflect on clues that show what a character is thinking to reveal more about that character's perspective in a problem or an event. Readers are privy to Maya's concerns as they "see" the thoughts she "wouldn't say out loud," such as "Bailey is all mouth and no ears." Ask your readers to consider the ways these clues impact their thoughts about Maya's character.	**Writing Craft Lessons** Writers use descriptive dialogue tags (such as *laughed, blurted, boasted*) to add voice and convey emotions. Invite your students to revisit *Trouble Talk* and/or other texts in search of dialogue tags, making note of the emotional messages those tags might reveal to their reader and considering ways to do the same in their own writing.
Making Connections After exploring the story and learning about Maya's experience with Bailey, take some time to reflect on your students' possible connections to the problem or the characters and how they might be able to use what they have learned from this book, such as respecting friends and others, in their own lives.	**Writing Real or Imagined Experiences** Writers develop their characters through the inner thoughts, actions, dialogue, and responses to events. Suggest your writers think about how they could further develop a character by including what the character does, thinks, or says in response to a situation.

LITERACY SNAPSHOTS IDEAS TO ADOPT OR ADAPT

Invite your readers to revisit a book and search for lines that might reveal or strengthen an idea with more specific text evidence. Partners went back to find examples of multiple places that showed Maya's inability to stand up for her friends, discussing quotes and lines that showed missed opportunities for Maya to do the right thing.

Encourage students to think about and build on the lessons they've learned in books. After exploring Ludwig's book, these students are reflecting on the ways they could turn trouble talk into healthy talk.

CONTINUING CONVERSATIONS 📖 ADDITIONAL HEARTPRINT CONNECTIONS

The Honest-to-Goodness Truth by Patricia McKissack, illustrated by Giselle Potter

After getting in trouble for lying, Libby decides to "always" tell the truth. Libby's new truths get her into a bit of trouble, and she learns that being completely honest isn't always the right thing to do. Share this with readers to examine consideration and respect for others' feelings.

Better Than You by Trudy Ludwig, illustrated by Adam Gustavson

This book can provide another lens to discuss different kinds of harmful talk and challenges associated with bragging and boasting. Jake's constant bragging is problematic, as he often makes his friends feel bad about themselves by constantly comparing what he can do better. This book is a powerful way to illustrate the difference between *doing* our best and *being* the best—a message children will need to apply in and beyond school.

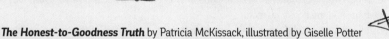

Nerdy Birdy Tweets by Aaron Reynolds, illustrated by Matt Davies

In this cautionary tale, readers meet Nerdy Birdy who has become obsessed with a new video game and his online "Tweetster" friends. Sound familiar? This humorous story provides a playful way to guide conversations on nurturing our friendships and with kindness and respect for others.

CONTINUING CONNECTIONS MORE LAYERS FOR LEARNING TOGETHER

To help your staff or students remember to stay respectful with their social media use and proper online etiquette, share and discuss the T.H.I.N.K. acronym (Roberts and Wright 2018, 57) that encourages users of social media of any kind—emails included—to stop before posting or commenting and *think* about the following questions:

T   Is it True?

H   Is it Helpful?

I   Is it Inspiring?

N   Is it Necessary?

K   Is it Kind?

FINDING STRENGTH IN DIVERSITY with *WHY AM I ME?*

HEARTPRINT BOOK: *Why Am I Me?* by Paige Britt, illustrated by Sean Qualls and Selina Alko

ABOUT THE BOOK: In this collaborative picture book by Paige Britt and husband and wife illustrators Selina Alko and Sean Qualls, readers meet two children pondering questions about identity. The narrators simultaneously wonder philosophical questions: "Why am I me and not you? Who would I be?" The text is presented as an exchange between children with poetic text and beautiful illustrations that showcase a variety of people in an urban setting.

LIFE LAYERS ♡ INVITATIONS TO SHARE CONNECTIONS, CARES, AND CONCERNS

This book is a celebration of humanity as well as a reflection of diversity, discovery, and compassion for others. The poetic text—"Imagine a world where there is no you or me, only we"—and correlating images will stimulate curiosity and conversations about our individual and collective learning and appreciation for self and others.

Discussion Possibilities

- Lead a conversation with your students about how they might answer the question, "Why am I me?" Discuss how we learn from one another as we seek understanding through the questions we ask and the books we read.
- Ask students to reflect and share their thoughts about the illustrations and ideas from their interpretations of the messages they find in this book.
- Guide students as they share the narrators' wonderings and discuss their thoughts about some of the same questions—What might it mean if they perceived themselves to be different (e.g., taller, faster, lighter, darker, older, bolder . . .)?
- Prompt students to share additional words they would use to describe who they are and who they might be.

LITERACY CONNECTIONS 👥 POSSIBILITIES FOR NURTURING OUR READERS AND WRITERS

Based on the needs of your students and their instructional goals, consider the following possibilities for layering in reading and writing connections to complement your workshop, small-group, or individual conversations.

As a Reader	As a Writer
Analyzing Texts and Messages Readers pay close attention to the images and art in a text to deepen their understanding about the author's and illustrator's messages. Illustrators Sean Qualls and Selina Alko both describe their art as "vehicles for social justice." Suggest your readers look back to explore how the images might connect to their message and develop that idea further.	**Drafting and Publishing** Writers create illustrations to enhance a piece of writing and influence its interpretations. Notice how Selina Alko and Sean Qualls share the message of connectedness and community using various images and media to produce a collage effect. Explore the techniques and tools your writers could use to enhance a piece of their writing through different forms of media (such as graphics and illustrations) to support the message in a piece of their own writing.
Writing About Reading To practice using writing to enhance their comprehension of books, readers can contemplate the question, *Why am I me?* and process their reflections through writing, citing the text, and personal experiences to support their observations, opinions, and thoughts.	**Writing in Response to Reading** Students can respond to major themes found in the texts they read through writing. For example after reading *Why Am I Me?*, students might extend their thoughts by writing about their connections to the illustrators' work as artists for social justice.
Asking Questions *Why Am I Me?* is a journey of self-reflection and consideration of others. It allows readers, writers, and thinkers to examine big ideas and philosophical questions. Invite your students to keep track of questions as they read and discuss how those questions help them engage deeper with the text.	**Developing Ideas** The collective work of Paige Britt, Selina Alko, and Sean Qualls shows the power of collaborating and connecting various perspectives in one piece. Suggest your writers team up with a partner or another group to collaborate on a piece, focusing on "we," not "me." Suggest students explore different roles of author, illustrator, editor, compositor, and designer.

LITERACY SNAPSHOTS IDEAS TO ADOPT OR ADAPT

Primary students share who they are and where they are from in their native language and in English. Invite your students to share their messages and celebrate how we find strength in our individuality and diversity.

In an effort to celebrate their connections and highlight the school's character goals, students teamed up with the art teacher to plan for and create this mural to highlight what they value—respect, care, and responsibility.

CONTINUING CONVERSATIONS ADDITIONAL HEARTPRINT CONNECTIONS

Carl and the Meaning of Life by Deborah Freedom

Carl is an earthworm who enjoys tunneling through the soil. One day, he is asked what he is doing and why. Confused by the questions, Carl goes off in search of his purpose. He leaves the soil neglected and, in doing so, discovers his purpose in life.

 Matthew A.B.C. by Peter Catalanotto

Imagine a class where every student was named Matthew! Mrs. Tuttle has no problem with this because she values each Matthew for his unique attributes. With an added layer of alliterative wordplay and complementary illustrations that extend the message, readers will laugh and learn, while celebrating what makes each one of us who we are.

The Home Builders by Varsha Bajaj, illustrated by Simona Mulazzani

Readers get a glimpse into a variety of animals that, though decidedly different, all have rituals to provide and care for their young. *The Home Builders* is a nice way to use our natural world to illustrate respect for differences and an appreciation for commonalities.

CONTINUING CONNECTIONS MORE LAYERS FOR LEARNING TOGETHER

 To spark conversations about public and professional practices, your staff may want to revisit Shelley Harwayne's timeless book *Going Public: Priorities and Practices at the Manhattan New School* (1999), which explores ways literacy leaders at the Manhattan New School embody respect for their community of learners.

ACKNOWLEDGING OUR RIGHTS WITH *I HAVE THE RIGHT TO BE A CHILD*

HEARTPRINT BOOK: *I Have the Right to Be a Child* by Alain Serres, illustrated by Aurélia Fronty

ABOUT THE BOOK: Alain Serres reframes the universal rights embodied in the document created by the United Nations' Convention on the Rights of the Child with simple text and images that illustrate human rights "for every child, for every right."

LIFE LAYERS ♡ INVITATIONS TO SHARE CONNECTIONS, CARES, AND CONCERNS

Read this book aloud to focus conversations on the idea that—beyond basic rights of food, water, and shelter—every child needs to feel valued, safe, and protected. Knowing and talking about these rights is an important step toward implementation, which can lead to greater respect and understanding for all.

Discussion Possibilities

- Facilitate a conversation about which rights students feel are the most important to them and discuss why.
- Ask students to discuss the term *right* and what makes something a universal right.
- Ask students to reflect on the various rights as they're interpreted by Alain Serres's words and Aurélia Fronty's illustrations, and share their noticings and wonderings.
- Share what readers might have been surprised to learn or how their thoughts have grown or changed by the text and images.
- Invite student to consider how people from different backgrounds, cultures, traditions, ages, and religions might view various rights differently.
- Reflect on differences between rights, privileges, and needs.
- Explore concepts of humanity, compassion, and respect for the rights of every child, in every community.
- Share and ask your students to reflect on which rights are most evident in your classroom and in your community.

LITERACY CONNECTIONS 👥 POSSIBILITIES FOR NURTURING OUR READERS AND WRITERS

Based on the needs of your students and their instructional goals, consider the following possibilities for layering in reading and writing connections to complement your workshop, small-group, or individual conversations.

As a Reader	As a Writer
Synthesizing Readers deepen understanding of a text by connecting what they may already know with new knowledge to gain more information. After reading and discussing *I Have a Right to Be a Child*, ask your students to discuss how their thinking may have changed about rights, equality, and equity for all.	**Researching to Grow an Idea** Writers research a topic of interest asking questions and collecting information as they search selected sources or interviews to gain information on a subject. Model ways students can stop and jot to pause and reflect on new ideas and understandings.
Inferring Readers use images and symbols in a text to expand on their thinking. Suggest students reread to examine how the connections of the pictures and text in *I Have the Right to Be a Child* influence their inferences and why the illustrator chose to include particular graphics. Students could share specific images and examples to support their thinking.	**Writing Arguments** Writers use multiple forms of information to write essays and arguments. Suggest students consider arguing for or against a particular issue or position pertaining to rights, and use research information to support those opinions.
Making Connections Readers read across texts to connect ideas and support their thinking. Ask your readers to look for additional texts that might send messages about a variety of human rights.	**Writing to Develop an Idea** Writers can collect information and examples from additional mentor texts such as images, advertisements, or media that strengthen an idea about a topic. Students could explore ways to include information from research as examples to illustrate their thinking about a right presented in the book in a new way.

LITERACY SNAPSHOTS IDEAS TO ADOPT OR ADAPT

Our teaching needs to respond to the needs of our learners' hearts and minds. Gun violence in schools and in the world is real. In this school, students exercised their rights, participated in their own walkout, had T-shirts made to reflect their mission, and made posters to share their concerns as part of a schoolwide protest against gun violence.

Here, students created posters to reflect rights, and continued to discuss those rights and the rights of others as part of their lifework.

CONTINUING CONVERSATIONS ADDITIONAL HEARTPRINT CONNECTIONS

Everyone . . . by Christopher Silas Neal

Share this much lighter book to explore universal feelings. Through empathy and understanding, we can use *Everyone . . .* to respect and layer connections between the feelings and the rights of everyone.

Every Human Has Rights: A Photographic Declaration for Kids by National Geographic Society

Take another look at the 1948 United Nations Declaration of Human Rights in this collection that pairs an array of photographs and poems to illustrate the rights of every human and stir conversations about respect for individuals in our class and in our global community.

We Are All Born Free: The Universal Declaration of Human Rights in Pictures by Amnesty International

Continue the exploration of rights through this collection of illustrations provided by various artists and illustrators that deepen understanding and connect messages that validate the rights of every human being.

CONTINUING CONNECTIONS MORE LAYERS FOR LEARNING TOGETHER look up!

 Amnesty International created this animated video as an introduction to the articles in the United Nations Declaration of Human Rights. After sharing it with your students, consider expanding on its message through follow-up student-led conversations and a variety of creative written or artistic responses.

 HONORING CELEBRATIONS with *EVERY MONTH IS A NEW YEAR*

HEARTPRINT BOOK: *Every Month Is a New Year* by Marilyn Singer, illustrated by Susan L. Roth

ABOUT THE BOOK: This collection of poetry highlights the many wonderful festivities inspired by the phases of the moon and days that represent a new calendar year all across the world. The book has an interesting layout with symbols of calendar-style grids and informative back matter that shares additional research about the time and traditions of cultural observances of seasons and their associated rituals.

LIFE LAYERS ♥ INVITATIONS TO SHARE CONNECTIONS, CARES, AND CONCERNS

Read Marilyn Singer's poetry collection to explore an array of beautifully diverse, cultural, and religious traditions that occur year-round. In addition to encouraging a respect for these festivities, this book can stir deeper investigations of the personal significance of celebrations around the world.

Discussion Possibilities

- Invite your students to explore the beauty of multicultural celebrations in our world. Ask students to share more about what they learned and what surprised them.
- Provide time for each child to share the variety of celebrations and traditions in their own families.
- Suggest students consider the less visible ways culture can impact our understanding and interactions with others in our world as they explore the concepts of culture, celebrations, and holidays.
- Address the problematic approach to observing certain festivities through the lens of a single story and, instead, invite unique and multiple perspectives for considering various celebrations.
- Be sensitive to those children who, as part of their culture and traditions, may not observe certain holidays.

LITERACY CONNECTIONS POSSIBILITIES FOR NURTURING OUR READERS AND WRITERS

Based on the needs of your students and their instructional goals, consider the following possibilities for layering in reading and writing connections to complement your workshop, small-group, or individual conversations.

As a Reader	As a Writer
Making Connections	**Writing to Present Knowledge**
Readers use personal knowledge as an entry point to make connections to ideas and to learn more. Students connect their own identity to other cultures by considering ways they are similar and ways they are different to grow understanding and respect.	Writers of informational text use information from their own knowledge and from multiple sources to express what they know about a topic. Students can explore the author's note to reflect on the way Marilyn Singer shared information with her readers and consider including their own author's note with introductions, pronunciation guides, glossaries, or back matter to better inform their readers.
Exploring Word Choice and Vocabulary	**Exploring Craft Lessons**
Readers notice and reflect on author's use of words and phrases to illustrate images and ideas. Guide readers to revisit a selection or selections from the poems to deepen their understanding of poetic language or vocabulary that reflects new understanding about another language, culture, or tradition.	Writers of poetry read and rewrite to experiment with layouts on the page, white space, and word choice. Invite your writers to use Marilyn Singer's poems as mentor texts and try out a few of her ideas, such as a reverse poem (starting at the end and working backward) or a free verse poem.
Analyzing the Text	**Writing to Integrate Ideas**
Readers identify and analyze a writer's or illustrator's use of images and features that impact feeling or add meaning to a poem. Guide students to search for patterns and ideas as they read. Students could reflect on the reasons that Susan Roth included a map, used calendar grids, or incorporated mixed media collage and think about the universal messages these might reveal.	Writers collect entries and ideas across a topic of interest. After exploring the many ways Marilyn Singer and Susan L. Roth explored celebrations, encourage your writers to consider creating or curating their own collection of poems, or entries in their own notebooks around a topic they are passionate about.

LITERACY SNAPSHOTS IDEAS TO ADOPT OR ADAPT

Several times in the school year at P.S. 66, families are invited to celebrate writing, reading, and learning. Look for opportunities to connect literacy celebrations to honor your students as well as their families and cultures.

To celebrate the "gift of reading," invite students and their family in for a book swap. To ensure that everyone goes home with a book, consider having a collection of extra titles on hand.

CONTINUING CONVERSATIONS ADDITIONAL HEARTPRINT CONNECTIONS

Going Down Home with Daddy by Kelly Starling Lyons, illustrated by Daniel Minter

This charming heartprint book is a beautiful expression of traditions and history celebrated among multiple generations that illustrates bonds and love of family. Lil Alan and his family are going "down home" for a reunion. As part of the celebration each year, members pay tribute to the family's history. Lil Alan is worried that he won't have the right gift to share. The artwork is captivating and complements the beautiful language that will inspire readers, writers, and storytellers of all ages.

 This Is How We Do It: One Day in the Life of Seven Kids from Around the World by Matt Lamothe

This informational book gives readers a glimpse into the lives of seven children from the time they wake, until they go to sleep. Share this book to add to the conversations about how we all have traditions that make us different but many that remind us that we're all the same.

Under the Same Sun by Sharon Robinson, illustrated by A. G. Ford

For another beautifully illustrated book that explores family and traditions, share *Under the Same Sun*. In this story, written by the daughter of Jackie Robinson, Grandmother Bibi and Aunt Sharon visit relatives in Tanzania for Bibi's eighty-fifth birthday celebration. In addition to celebrating international and cross-cultural connections among these families, Robinson shares parts of their visit to a slave-trading post in recognition of the resilience of her African American ancestors.

CONTINUING CONNECTIONS MORE LAYERS FOR LEARNING TOGETHER

Think about reimagining your family literacy night with a theme that positions literacy to honor the variety of cultures and traditions in your school community. For instance, students can share storytelling, interviews, book displays, and poetry that highlight backgrounds and customs from home. Invite families to celebrate their own stories and traditions through literacy.

CARING FOR OURSELVES WITH *BENJI, THE BAD DAY, AND ME*

Heartprint Book: *Benji, the Bad Day, and Me* by Sally J. Pla, illustrated by Ken Min

About the Book: After having a very bad day, Sammy feels upset about his own needs being overlooked, thinking everyone attends to his brother, Benji, too often. This is a moving story about sibling relationships that also addresses respect for the wide range of our neurological differences and the spectrum of our emotions on any given day.

LIFE LAYERS ♥ INVITATIONS TO SHARE CONNECTIONS, CARES, AND CONCERNS

Benji, the Bad Day, and Me is an emotive and a relatable fictional story that touches on real sibling issues while encouraging respect for our various strengths, interests, and needs. This is a powerful heartprint book that will leave its mark.

Discussion Possibilities

- Invite your readers to discuss what it means to have a bad day. Students could look back to reflect on Sammy's day or share their own experiences with a bad day.
- Ask students to consider who they feel more connected to, Benji or Sammy, and talk about why.
- Ask students to share their experience with being an older sibling, younger sibling, or an only child. (Sammy, the narrator of *Benji, the Bad Day, and Me*, is Benji's older brother.) Guide children in a discussion to explore their opinions on the advantages and disadvantages within those roles. Be sensitive to family situations, and support as needed.
- Lead discussions for students who may want to share how they coped with frustration toward a friend, a sibling, or other family member.
- Encourage your students to discuss what needs and issues they (self or classmate) might be more sensitive to and treat more respectfully.
- Have students discuss how they can support a friend who is having a bad day.

LITERACY CONNECTIONS 👥 POSSIBILITIES FOR NURTURING OUR READERS AND WRITERS

Based on the needs of your students and their instructional goals, consider the following possibilities for layering in reading and writing connections to complement your workshop, small-group, or individual conversations.

As a Reader	As a Writer
Inferring Readers make inferences about characters and messages in a story based on the clues the title may disclose. Ask students to think about the title, *Benji, the Bad Day, and Me*, and how it connects to events and the characters.	**Writing About Our Experiences** Writers write narratives to express feelings, moods, and experiences. After reading about these siblings and Sammy's bad day, invite students to write or share a story about a time they experienced a strong feeling in the same way.
Exploring Point of View Readers reflect on point of view to see how the narrator's perspective influences the story. Invite your students to discuss Sally J. Pla's reasons for choosing to tell the story through Sammy's perspective and how the story might change if the point of view of the narrator changes.	**Showing Rather Than Telling** Writers use exact actions and examples to illustrate character traits and feelings. Notice the examples that illustrated Sammy's bad day: getting yelled at during recess, missing out on lunch, and the bus driver missing Sammy's spot. Your writers may want to go back to try this craft move in a piece they are working on.
Synthesizing Readers learn about characters through relationships and notice how those relationships change from the beginning of the story to the end. Consider the way Benji and Mom make Sammy feel at the end. Students could discuss how and why their thinking changed throughout the story based on the characters' interactions.	**Exploring Point of View** Writers use point of view and perspective to tell a story through a specific lens. Benji's story might skew differently from his mother's point of view. Writers can experiment in revisions by shifting a story's perspective to see how it might change the message. Suggest students return to a previously written narrative piece and try out different characters' viewpoints.

LITERACY SNAPSHOTS IDEAS TO ADOPT OR ADAPT

To further illustrate respect for individual differences, students can create posters that celebrate the strengths and talents of all children. After reading about neurodiversity issues, students chose to focus on autism awareness: "We are all children that just want to be loved."

As you continue to explore emotions and feelings, invite students to share the wide range of emotions they experience across any given day through writing or drawing. Here, a primary writer shares about a time he was feeling MAD!

CONTINUING CONVERSATIONS ADDITIONAL HEARTPRINT CONNECTIONS

Benny Doesn't Like to Be Hugged by Zetta Elliott, illustrated by Purple Wong

Told through rhyming text, this story is about appreciating and respecting our differences. Benny likes things in a very specific way and can be really fussy at times. The unnamed narrator is a true friend who supports him and his needs, professing the universal truth that "true friends accept you for who you are."

 Enough Is Enough! by Barney Saltzberg

Many children can relate to enough-is-enough moments. Whether it is from a sibling, a friend, or a situation, sometimes we feel we have too much to handle and we need a little space. Share this simple text to invite complex conversations about recognizing our own needs and being mindful of the needs of others.

Miss Maple's Seeds by Eliza Wheeler

Miss Maple knows that no two seeds are alike and she nurtures seeds of all kinds. In the summer, she gives special attention to seeds that haven't taken root yet. Read about Miss Maple to celebrate the seasons while spreading a whole lot of love in this metaphor for life to reinforce that we are all different and full of potential.

CONTINUING CONNECTIONS MORE LAYERS FOR LEARNING TOGETHER

To expand your libraries to deepen your understanding of respect and dignity for all, A Novel Mind database—created by three writers, including the author of *Benji, the Bad Day, and Me*—features a collection of titles that highlight mental health and neurodiversity. This resource can help focus your critical lens as you preview and consider titles to add to the book collections you share with children.

BELIEFS AND PRACTICES with *LAILAH'S LUNCH BOX*

HEARTPRINT BOOK: *Lailah's Lunchbox: A Ramadan Story* by Reem Faruqi, illustrated by Lea Lyon

ABOUT THE BOOK: As a new girl in a new school and a new country, Lailah is worried about fitting in and missing her friends. She is excited about Ramadan because she is finally old enough to abstain from eating during this religious holiday; yet, she's also worried about what other people will think if she doesn't bring her lunch to school. Based on the author's own experiences immigrating to the United States as a child, readers learn about the common feelings, worries, and experiences that can connect us all.

LIFE LAYERS ♥ INVITATIONS TO SHARE CONNECTIONS, CARES, AND CONCERNS

During Ramadan and other religious observances, individuals follow certain routines, such as fasting or prayer. For Lailah and author Reem Faruqi, religion is an important part of those beliefs. Share this story to help students gain an appreciation for Ramadan and to discuss respecting those family beliefs. Share this book to encourage all students to have the courage to celebrate their beliefs and to respect others' beliefs.

Discussion Possibilities

- ■ Discuss the significance of Ramadan and the Muslim holy month. Invite your students to add to the discussion with their knowledge, experience, and understanding of that celebration and others. Suggest students discuss familiar holidays and traditions.
- ■ Encourage students to share their families' rituals and practices as they consider Lailah's determination to participate in the fasting ritual.
- ■ Suggest students make a list of questions, wonderings, and ideas they wish to explore.
- ■ Ask students to discuss the feelings stirred by learning about Lailah's moving away from Abu Dhabi and her experience with old and new friends.
- ■ Request that students think about safe places or people they can turn to when they feel upset or alone. For Lailah—and the author—the library was a sanctuary.

LITERACY CONNECTIONS 👥 POSSIBILITIES FOR NURTURING OUR READERS AND WRITERS

Based on the needs of your students and their instructional goals, consider the following possibilities for layering in reading and writing connections to complement your workshop, small-group, or individual conversations.

As a Reader	As a Writer
Asking Questions Readers ask questions before, during, and after reading to monitor their reading and to clarify confusions. Suggest readers discuss questions about Lailah and consider how the messages implied in the pictures and words direct them to possible answers.	**Exploring Text Features** Writers include text features to give readers more information and to enhance their understanding. The author added a glossary of terms to further explain words associated with Ramadan. Suggest your students consider including their own expert word list or guide in their informational or narrative writing.
Thinking About the Text Readers discuss interesting book and print features that provide additional information. Students could think about how Reem Faruqi included a glossary of terms and an author's note to illustrate how her own experiences shaped this story.	**Writing with Flashbacks** Writers sometimes tell stories in a nonlinear way and may use flashbacks to illustrate a particular moment in time to strengthen an idea. Consider the way Reem Faruqi and Lea Lyon include images and examples of when Lailah was back with her friends, Hend and Ishrat. Suggest your writers think about revising a piece to include a flashback to a memorable experience or moment in an effort to further develop an idea in the present.
Analyzing the Impact of Setting Readers read and analyze setting to consider how it may influence the story. Lailah shares a map to show where she came from. Suggest students look at how pictures and words are significant to the setting.	**Writing in Response to Reading** Writers write to share their feelings after reading a piece. After reading the author's notes, students might write about their impressions of the story behind the story, inspired by the author's and illustrator's connections to *Lailah's Lunchbox*. Model how to write book trailers, blog posts, or correspondences to the creators.

LITERACY SNAPSHOTS IDEAS TO ADOPT OR ADAPT

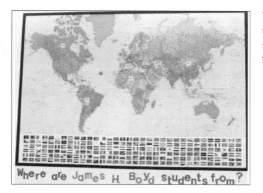

To support welcoming inclusivity and celebrations of where your community members are from, use a large a map to highlight your global connections. This map is prominently placed in a school's cafeteria and also includes an interactive component for students to highlight places they have been or want to learn more about.

As a response to inclusive conversations about respecting traditions and backgrounds, a group of students created a chart to showcase and celebrate the variety of languages spoken in their school community.

CONTINUING CONVERSATIONS 📖 ADDITIONAL HEARTPRINT CONNECTIONS

A Heart Just Like My Mother's by Lela Nargi, illustrated by Valeria Cís

Anna wishes she was more like her mother. She hears stories about when her mother was little and thinks they are nothing alike. But when Anna uses her *tzedakah*, the Hebrew word for a charitable contribution, for an act of kindness, she realizes they are more alike than she thinks. Share this story as celebration of cultural traditions with layers of family, charity, and kindness.

Señorita Mariposa by Ben Gundersheimer, illustrated by Marco Almada Rivero

In this Spanish and English text inspired by the author's travels, readers see phrases in both languages that share the journey of the monarch butterflies from Canada to Mexico. Lyrical language and messages—"It's hard to say goodbye / Es difícil adiós . . ."—add a poetic layer to an already engaging book.

In a Village by the Sea by Muon Van, illustrated by April Chu

In this wonderfully illustrated picture book set in a Vietnamese village, a fisherman at sea is longing for home. As they turn the pages, readers will notice that the images depicting the comforts of home and family continue to get larger as the fisherman gets closer to his beloved home. This heartprint book will connect to feelings of finding comfort in the places we each call home as well as respect and appreciation for the differences in everyone's home.

CONTINUING CONNECTIONS MORE LAYERS FOR LEARNING TOGETHER

Check out this idea for Welcoming Libraries (from a nonprofit organization in Portland, Maine) that center on picture books featuring new arrival and new American families to spark community conversations about immigration and commonalities all families share. Consider ways you might create your own Welcoming Library in a prominent space in your building, online, or in your literacy lounge.

INCLUDING OTHERS WITH *THE INVISIBLE BOY*

HEARTPRINT BOOK: *The Invisible Boy* by Trudy Ludwig, illustrated by Patrice Barton

ABOUT THE BOOK: This heartprint book explores a boy who is timid yet talented in so many ways. Brian expresses himself through his artwork instead of verbally. No one ever seems to notice or include Brian, the Invisible Boy, until a new student arrives and makes him feel welcome.

LIFE LAYERS ♥ INVITATIONS TO SHARE CONNECTIONS, CARES, AND CONCERNS

Friend groups can be challenging. Trying to fit in and avoid standing out all add up to feeling disconnected. With unique artwork that demonstrates Brian's invisibility in soft grays and changes to full color when he starts to feel valued, this book may inspire students to widen their circle of inclusion and will allow for greater conversation about taking action for others.

Discussion Possibilities

- Suggest students discuss and compare what it means literally and figuratively to be invisible.
- Explain the difference between inner and outer traits to lead a conversation around aspects of our identities that are visible and invisible.
- Think about individuals in our community, society, or the world and what contributes to their visibility or invisibility.
- Suggest students explore what it means to exclude others and discuss ways to be more caring and inclusive.

LITERACY CONNECTIONS POSSIBILITIES FOR NURTURING OUR READERS AND WRITERS

Based on the needs of your students and their instructional goals, consider the following possibilities for layering in reading and writing connections to complement your workshop, small-group, or individual conversations.

As a Reader	As a Writer
Making Connections In *The Invisible Boy*, Brian feels invisible because he is excluded. Invite your readers to discuss times they felt invisible or perhaps made someone else feel invisible. Think back to examples in the text when Brian was excluded and felt invisible to prompt further conversations and connections.	**Writing About Real-World Issues** Writers can reflect facts and statistics from research through stories. Consider how Trudy Ludwig incorporates research about school issues associated with invisibility and equality. Invite your writers to discover stories that reflect real-world issues from their own lives.
Synthesizing Readers read to analyze the development of theme over the course of the text. Suggest students look for examples, such as events, that support themes of exclusion, invisibility, and inclusion. Students might want to discuss how these big ideas are connected to issues in their life, school, or community.	**Writing Real or Imagined Narratives** Suggest students write a story from the perspective of someone feeling invisible or from the perspective of the bully, the bystander, or the upstander.
Analyzing Texts and Illustrations Take a look back with students to explore the illustrator's artful and intentional use of color throughout the story. Invite your readers to discuss how these illustrations influence their interpretations and how the story and visual presentation connect to extend the message. Encourage readers to find and share examples to support their ideas.	**Writing Opinions** Writers read and share their opinions about texts, topics, and themes using text evidence to support their point of view. After reading *The Invisible Boy*, students might write an opinion piece to share their thoughts on an issue that is important to them.

LITERACY SNAPSHOTS IDEAS TO ADOPT OR ADAPT

In this elementary school, the entire student body read and discussed *The Invisible Boy* through a one-book, one-school experience and created a mural to reinforce welcoming inclusivity and respect for all.

Extend recess interactions by establishing lots of opportunities for playing and connecting with classmates with makerspaces, board game areas, and a buddy bench, where children can invite friends old and new to play.

CONTINUING CONVERSATIONS 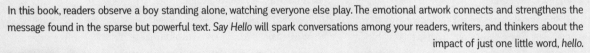 ADDITIONAL HEARTPRINT CONNECTIONS

The Buddy Bench by Patty Brozo and illustrated by Mike Deas

After a huge snowstorm, when most of the children stay inside for recess, one child heads out alone to the playground and finds a spot on the buddy bench, which signals that he is looking for a friend. This sweet story told through rhyming is a perfect introduction to the concept of the buddy bench and can extend conversation about welcoming, valuing, and making space for new friends.

Say Hello by Jack Foreman and Michael Foreman

In this book, readers observe a boy standing alone, watching everyone else play. The emotional artwork connects and strengthens the message found in the sparse but powerful text. *Say Hello* will spark conversations among your readers, writers, and thinkers about the impact of just one little word, *hello*.

Each Kindness by Jacqueline Woodson, illustrated by E. B. Lewis

Jacqueline Woodson's message about inclusiveness and change has been evident in every one of her heartprint books. In *Each Kindness*, a new girl moves into a school and is judged by what she wears and how she looks. She tries unsuccessfully to connect with her classmates but eventually moves again. After she's gone, lessons are learned about how every action and inaction has consequences.

CONTINUING CONNECTIONS MORE LAYERS FOR LEARNING TOGETHER

 Host a faculty meeting to learn about Teaching Tolerance's Mix It Up at Lunch Day, a way to make the lunchtime experience more inviting for others. Brainstorm ways you can mix it up during recess, library, music, gym, or art.

SELF-EXPRESSION with *JACOB'S ROOM TO CHOOSE*

HEARTPRINT BOOK: *Jacob's Room to Choose* by Sarah Hoffman and Ian Hoffman, illustrated by Chris Case

ABOUT THE BOOK: In this companion to *Jacob's New Dress*, an important book about appreciating individual gender expressions, the conversation continues when Jacob and Sophie feel uneasy about which bathroom to use. Their teacher rallies the class to teach lessons of acceptance and respect for others. The class decides to change the bathroom rules, so no one is made to feel uncomfortable.

LIFE LAYERS ♡ INVITATIONS TO SHARE CONNECTIONS, CARES, AND CONCERNS

This book can spark conversations including gender expressions as part of a spectrum of identities. Share this book to help widen perspectives and to nurture inclusive, caring communities where differences and similarities are respected and celebrated.

Discussion Possibilities

- Lead students in a discussion of various forms of expression, such as how we dress, what we eat, what music we listen to, and which stories we like to read.
- Talk about the important message that all children should feel respected and comfortable in our communities.
- Revisit the dangers of harmful stereotypes, labeling, and single stories.
- Reflect on the ways the students came together to value and support Jacob and Sophie.
- Ask students to share new wonderings and possible ideas for spreading the important message about appreciating everyone's right to express themselves.
- Invite discussion of gender roles found explicitly and implicitly in other texts.

LITERACY CONNECTIONS POSSIBILITIES FOR NURTURING OUR READERS AND WRITERS

Based on the needs of your students and their instructional goals, consider the following possibilities for layering in reading and writing connections to complement your workshop, small-group, or individual conversations.

As a Reader	As a Writer
Inferring and Analyzing for Character Readers analyze characters in a story to compare and contrast how their experiences are similar or different. Suggest that your students think about the main character's challenges, how other characters responded, and how those characters' appreciation or understanding changed.	**Writing and Developing Ideas** After reading *Jacob's Room to Choose*, explore how writers introduce and develop characters from the first page to hook the reader. Provide time for your writers to consider starting a new piece with a similar hook that introduces characters, a problem, or starts in the middle of the action.
Analyzing Plot Readers reflect on problems in a story and notice how characters respond to that problem. Ask students to consider the ways the class comes together to find a resolution in *Jacob's Room to Choose*.	**Writing Arguments** Writers write an argument to express perspectives and opinions about a topic or an important issue. Suggest students explore a topic of concern to write a narrative or essay about, using research and information to highlight and support their opinions about that topic.
Determining Author's Purpose Readers read and reflect on author's purpose. Consider what message Sarah and Ian Hoffman want their readers to think about and learn through Jacob's story. Invite your readers to explore the authors' note from the Hoffmans about their firsthand experience raising a gender-nonconforming son.	**Critiquing the Texts** Writers share their thoughts and opinions about texts and topics they care about. Invite your writers to think about *Jacob's Room to Choose* and share a written response or drawing with specific examples to express their thoughts and feelings about this story.

LITERACY SNAPSHOTS IDEAS TO ADOPT OR ADAPT

Be mindful of the unintended messages character portrayals may send. Here, students consider the male character in *I Hate Picture Books*, who expressed a dislike for reading, which led to a discussion about misconceptions about "boy" books versus "girl" books. As your students read, invite them to dig deeper to expand their appreciation for unique preferences not driven by gender.

Invite your students to revisit various texts to discern implied messages on gender roles. These third-grade students work together to examine the portrayal of characters in books in their classroom library with a critical lens.

CONTINUING CONVERSATIONS 📖 ADDITIONAL HEARTPRINT CONNECTIONS

When Aidan Became a Brother by Kyle Lukoff, illustrated by Kaylani Juanita

Aidan was born as a girl but always knew he was a boy and, with his parents' help, became who he was meant to be. Now, in anticipation of his new role as a big brother, Aidan can't wait to welcome a new baby and is ready to help with the transition for his growing family. Share this book to introduce messages of acceptance and affirmation for being who you want to be.

Willow's Whispers by Lana Button, illustrated by Tania Howells

In this series about a quiet but resourceful girl named Willow, readers learn that she has a hard time speaking up. She is often misunderstood, because her voice is barely above a whisper. Read this book to discuss ways to find your voice and to help others to find theirs. In addition to layers about communication, share this book to address various personality types, such as introverts and extroverts, while celebrating the strengths found within each characteristic.

Sparkle Boy by Lesléa Newman, illustrated by Maria Mola

Meet Casey, who loves lots of items, including blocks, puzzles, and glittery, sparkly things. Casey is happy to wear glittery, sparkly articles of clothing and does so with pride. Casey doesn't care what other people think. This book can encourage honest conversations around sibling issues, acceptance, self-expression, and respect.

CONTINUING CONNECTIONS MORE LAYERS FOR LEARNING TOGETHER

To connect your ongoing discussions about individual preferences, styles, and choices to how we all have inclinations that influence our reading lives, consider studying Donalyn Miller's *The Book Whisperer: Awakening the Inner Reader in Every Child* (2009) or Teri Lesesne's *Naked Reading: Uncovering What Tweens Need to Become Lifelong Readers* (2006).

Teaching for Change created a tool to support conversations and to guide work in critical exploration of texts for harmful, undermining stereotypes in books. You can find resources for selecting anti-bias books and more at the website.

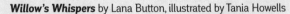

APPRECIATING FAMILY with *WHEN I FOUND GRANDMA*

HEARTPRINT BOOK: *When I Found Grandma* by Saumiya Balasubramaniam, illustrated by Qin Leng

ABOUT THE BOOK: Maya longs for her grandmother who lives thousands of miles away. One day she is thrilled to find that Grandma has arrived for a visit, but Maya quickly begins to have trouble navigating their generational and cross-cultural environments. As she learns to respect their differences, Maya's relationship with her grandmother grows into a beautiful symbol of compromise, acceptance, and loving understanding.

LIFE LAYERS ♡ INVITATIONS TO SHARE CONNECTIONS, CARES, AND CONCERNS

Share this endearing story about the evolving relationship between a young girl and her grandmother to explore respect for elders and traditions and to revisit conversations about love for family and appreciating people who help to shape our beliefs and identities.

Discussion Possibilities

- Encourage students to share their feelings about family members they may live near or be separated from, drawing from Maya's experience of missing her grandmother and wishing she would visit.
- Be prepared and make room for supportive conversations as children discuss the benefits and challenges of families. Be sensitive to children who may have experienced recent loss or separation.
- Invite students to think about the way Maya treats her grandmother upon arrival. Encourage students to consider Maya's lack of respect for her elders and how her attitude changes over the course of the story.
- Revisit the text that discusses the festival of colors known as Holi that announces the arrival of spring and passing of winter. Suggest students connect to other holidays, celebrations, and festivities within their own families and communities.

LITERACY CONNECTIONS 👥 POSSIBILITIES FOR NURTURING OUR READERS AND WRITERS

Based on the needs of your students and their instructional goals, consider the following possibilities for layering in reading and writing connections to complement your workshop, small-group, or individual conversations.

As a Reader	As a Writer
Making Connections	**Showing Rather Than Telling**
Readers reflect and connect to characters' experiences. As you read Maya's story, invite students to share thoughts and feelings that come to mind and how connecting to those help them understand the message behind *When I Found Grandma*.	Writers use a variety of techniques to illustrate what a character is thinking and feeling. When Maya tasted Grandma's special treats, she said, "I tasted her treats. I liked cupcakes better." Invite your writers to consider ways dialogue in their own writing can reveal a character's inner thoughts and feelings.
Exploring Point of View	**Exploring Point of View**
Readers determine who is telling the story and how the narrator influences their interpretations. Throughout the text, we see Maya's first-person (*I*) point of view. Invite your readers to consider Grandma's point of view and how it might differ.	In *When I Found Grandma*, the author tells the story in her own voice. Discuss this as model for how to enhance writing through the voice telling the story. Students might experiment with point of view by adding more than one perspective about a family experience.
Thinking About the Text	**Analyzing Craft Lessons**
Readers notice the way an author chooses to craft an ending and consider what message that might reveal. Look back at the last page and invite your readers to discuss why the author chose to end with the visit of another student's grandma. Discuss the significance of that event and the author's message.	Writers make intentional decisions about their endings. In *When I Found Grandma*, we might describe the ending as a "circular" structure where the events start and end in a similar way. Invite your writers to try using a circular ending in a piece of their own writing.

LITERACY SNAPSHOTS IDEAS TO ADOPT OR ADAPT

My Family Portrait
By: _____

After reading stories that reflect families, encourage students to draw or write about what makes their family unique. Consider poems, portraits, or personal narratives. These second-grade students drew portraits to tell about their families.

After reading about Maya's experience and exploring other family stories, these third-grade students wrote essays about their families and what they appreciate about them.

My Family
By: Francisco

my famivy is like a school. I live wirt my mom and day, brother and grama. my granma is fun but slow. My mom works 3 Jobs to give me a home and food. my dad is a good man because my dad he gives me toy and can make me toy car. my das nams is Rogger He gets mad at me because when I come down th a stairs he get scared and mad. My broke is nice and annoying to me I go rollerskating with my brother. I can do a har of a back flip. I really really love my family.

CONTINUING CONVERSATIONS 📖 ADDITIONAL HEARTPRINT CONNECTIONS

Going Home, Coming Home / Về Nhàm, Thăm Quê Hư'o'ng by Truong Tran, illustrated by Ann Phong

In this bilingual English and Vietnamese text, readers follow a young girl's journey to visit her grandmother in Vietnam, a place her parents still consider home. Readers learn about appreciating cultural differences, immigration, and having more than one place to call home.

Drawn Together by Minh Lê, illustrated by Dan Santat

This beautifully illustrated heartprint book explores another grandchild and grandparent relationship. A young boy visits his grandfather, and they struggle to communicate because they lack a common language. But their joint appreciation for art and storytelling strengthens their relationship and solidifies their bond. With very few words, the art and message in this book will leave you "speechless."

Far Apart, Close in Heart: Being a Family When a Loved One Is Incarcerated by Becky Birtha, illustrated by Maja Kastelic

This book looks at the emotional realities and experiences of a diverse array of children who have experienced separation from an incarcerated loved one. With each example, readers see a variety of individuals with equally unique reactions to the experience.

CONTINUING CONNECTIONS MORE LAYERS FOR LEARNING TOGETHER

 Explore the collection of essays edited by Django Paris and H. Samy Alim titled *Culturally Sustaining Pedagogies: Teaching and Learning for Justice in a Changing World* (2017) to stimulate conversations about ways to celebrate families and access the knowledge and resources they have to offer.

ENCOURAGING AND SUPPORTING OTHERS WITH *YOU HOLD ME UP*

HEARTPRINT BOOK: *You Hold Me Up* by Monique Gray Smith, illustrated by Danielle Daniel

ABOUT THE BOOK: Written as a list of actions we can do to show respect and compassion for our community members, *You Hold Me Up* affirms the ways we can all love, respect, and support one another. The illustrations depict Indigenous families, and the author's note addresses the power that comes from reconciliation, unity, and mutual respect.

LIFE LAYERS ♡ INVITATIONS TO SHARE CONNECTIONS, CARES, AND CONCERNS

Indigenous author Monique Gray Smith wrote *You Hold Me Up* as a form of healing, explaining that this is "a book about love, building relationships and fostering empathy." Share this book to spark conversations about compassion and respect for others.

Discussion Possibilities

- Lead a conversation to discuss what it means to "hold someone up" and how this connects to the themes of the book.
- Suggest your students discuss ideas for supporting members of their classroom and their community as described in *You Hold Me Up*.
- Take the time to share the author's note from Monique Gray Smith. Encourage students to discuss her reasons for dedicating the book to children and families of Indigenous backgrounds.
- Explore the author's note to connect the message of forgiveness and reconciliation to historical contexts.

LITERACY CONNECTIONS 👥 POSSIBILITIES FOR NURTURING OUR READERS AND WRITERS

Based on the needs of your students and their instructional goals, consider the following possibilities for layering in reading and writing connections to complement your workshop, small-group, or individual conversations.

As a Reader	As a Writer
Thinking About Print and Book Features As readers reflect on the messages of empathy, respect, and compassion for community in *You Hold Me Up*, encourage them to extend their learning by sharing their new understandings after reading the author's note from Monique Gray Smith.	**Writing Narratives** Writers share events that occur in their lives as inspirational stories. Suggest your students write about a time when someone "held them up." Consider using repeated phrases or examples, like those used in *You Hold Me Up*, to illustrate important details of the moment.
Making Connections Readers reflect on information they've read and pursue follow-up research to add to their understanding of a text. Invite your readers to explore additional information about the wellness of Indigenous families and communities.	**Writing Arguments** Writers express their opinions using evidence to support their ideas. Consider ways your writers could share their point of view on an important subject and take a stance like Monique Gray Smith does in *You Hold Me Up*. Prompt students to consider specific perspectives they might write from and why.
Inferring Writers use illustrations to support interpretations of texts to further develop their ideas about a message from the author. As your students read *You Hold Me Up*, invite them to go back and consider how the images reflect the writer's message.	**Writing Conclusions** Writers use conclusions to leave the reader with an important idea or to empower the reader to take action. Notice how Monique Gray Smith used her conclusion to reinforce her message. Ask your students to revisit a piece to revise the ending in ways that leave their readers with a powerful message or desire to take action.

LITERACY SNAPSHOTS IDEAS TO ADOPT OR ADAPT

In response to *You Hold Me Up*'s call to be informed citizens and advocates for respect for all people, students discussed matters that were important to them. Inspired by Maya Angelou's words, they reflected on the harmful effects of the words we use on the mental and emotional well-being of others.

To highlight ways we can lift one another up, students can reflect on individual words of support and encouragement. Here, a third grader illustrates her pledge to spread happiness.

CONTINUING CONVERSATIONS ADDITIONAL HEARTPRINT CONNECTIONS

A World Full of Kindness by editors and illustrators of Pajama Press

Share *A World Full of Kindness* to inspire meaningful discussions that help readers reflect on how kind their actions truly are. Several scenarios are presented in this text that allow readers to consider the choices they would make in various situations and why. The series of child-friendly questions can encourage more compassionate behaviors in your classroom and reinforce the messages of respect for everyone.

Mango, Abuela, and Me by Meg Medina, illustrated by Angela Dominguez

An award-winning author and illustrator bring to life a tale that shows how love transcends language. In this beautiful story, a young child's too-faraway grandmother comes to live with the family in the city, leaving behind mango trees and sunshine. But the two have trouble unlocking the words that connect them both. Their language barrier highlights similar experiences of many multigenerational families and immigrants, who, through their support for one another, find ways to communicate love in many languages.

Early Sunday Morning by Denene Millner, illustrated by Vanessa Brantley-Newton

In this heartwarming story, we follow June as she prepares to sing her first solo in her church choir. Overcome with fear, June is given advice from her loving family that helps her conquer her fears and find her voice. Readers will be treated to a celebration of family, faith, music, and traditions.

CONTINUING CONNECTIONS MORE LAYERS FOR LEARNING TOGETHER

 Share this video of Monique Gray Smith as she reads from *You Hold Me Up* and expands on its messages. Viewers will be inspired as they learn more about Smith's experiences and how they informed her work in book.

EMBRACING DIFFERENCES with *MIXED*

HEARTPRINT BOOK: *Mixed: A Colorful Story* by Arree Chung

ABOUT THE BOOK: In this town of three colors, everyone lives in harmony, until, one day reds, then yellows, and blues argue over who is "the best." Chaos ensues and the town is torn apart, separated into color-specific areas. Over time, some colors start to "notice" one another and appreciate their unique qualities. Eventually, they "mix" and so the story goes, with a message of hope and acceptance for all.

LIFE LAYERS ♡ INVITATIONS TO SHARE CONNECTIONS, CARES, AND CONCERNS

With the primary colors, red, yellow, and blue, masterfully personified, this thought-provoking picture book illuminates an important message. Share this with students of all ages to address inclusivity, equity, tolerance, and respect for all.

Discussion Possibilities

- Reflect on the big ideas found in *Mixed* and invite readers to share thoughts and wonderings that this text evokes. Students may want to share about how it feels to be excluded or how they dealt with a disagreement in a positive way.
- Support students as needed to explore the intricate conversations that may arise around complex subjects, including stereotypes, prejudice, labeling, and all forms of discrimination.
- Help students connect these conversations to the concept of respecting the differences of other people as well as negotiating issues without conflict. Revisit the varying levels of conflict and resolution within the texts and tie them to real-world applications.
- Remind students to listen respectfully as they share the text's deeper messages.

LITERACY CONNECTIONS 👥 POSSIBILITIES FOR NURTURING OUR READERS AND WRITERS

Based on the needs of your students and their instructional goals, consider the following possibilities for layering in reading and writing connections to complement your workshop, small-group, or individual conversations.

As a Reader	As a Writer
Thinking Beyond the Text Readers reflect on an illustrator's use of colors and symbols to support inferences. Ask students to consider the effectiveness of Arree Chung's use of colors to explore social justice and equality. Remind students to support their ideas with evidence from the text.	**Showing Rather than Telling** In *Mixed*, characters' emotions are emphasized through facial expressions. Notice how expressive the colors are and help learners accomplish similar effects through writing. For instance, students might brainstorm different ways of describing facial reactions with words.
Analyzing Plot Readers pay attention to how the sequence of events in a story connect cumulatively as a problem and its solution evolve across a story. Invite students to notice how the events in *Mixed* build on and affect one another, from the original conflict to its eventual solution.	**Establishing Voice** Writers establish voice through behaviors and attitudes of their characters using devices such as formal and informal speech, descriptive dialogue tags, and second-person point of view. Talk about the various ways Arree Chung demonstrated his characters' voice in *Mixed* that your students might use in their own writing.
Thinking Beyond the Text Readers reflect on the ways an ending can strengthen a message. Ask students to consider how the images and lessons connect at the end of *Mixed*. Guide a discussion about how your students' thinking may have been changed or been influenced by reflecting on the final message in *Mixed*.	**Writing Opinions** As writers read and reflect on messages in a text, they write to share their opinions and reactions to what they are reading about. Encourage students to discuss their opinions as they read *Mixed* and include their reactions to the book, lifting lines from the text to support their thinking.

LITERACY SNAPSHOTS IDEAS TO ADOPT OR ADAPT

After exploring several messages about respect and appreciation for diversity of everyone, students were asked to create a self-portrait to reflect on their bea-YOU-tiful selves. Consider an array of options for students to create self-portraits, including words, poetry, images, artifacts, and multimedia.

In this hallway display, students were encouraged to think about and celebrate what makes them remarkable. Children posted sticky notes that highlighted the qualities about themselves that make them proud.

CONTINUING CONVERSATIONS ADDITIONAL HEARTPRINT CONNECTIONS

The Colors of Us by Karen Katz

The Colors of Us affirms the incredible array of skin colors that make up our communities. Seen through the eyes of seven-year-old Leana—and with an artist's appreciation for colors—the language and illustrations in this book create beautiful imagery to help readers of all ages appreciate our unique qualities.

Remarkably You by Pat Zietlow Miller, illustrated by Patrice Barton

An affirming rhyming text that will invite conversations about all of our remarkable ways of being. *Remarkably You* threads together themes of *community*, *agency*, *respect*, and *empowerment* as part of a larger message that reminds readers to "be completely, uniquely, remarkably YOU."

Can I Touch Your Hair? Poems of Races, Mistakes, and Friendship by Irene Latham and Charles Waters, illustrated by Sean Qualls and Selina Alko

This unique collection of poetry explores perspectives of two fifth-grade classmates learning to understand their different experiences. The authors, Irene Latham and Charles Waters, collaborated to share messages about race, mistakes, and friendships that can provide a springboard for additional life lessons and conversations.

CONTINUING CONNECTIONS MORE LAYERS FOR LEARNING TOGETHER   *look up*

Share photographer Angelica Dass's interesting TED Talk about the beauty and infinite array of colors found in our human skin. In this informative presentation, she focuses a scientific lens to question assumptions and to elaborate on the complexities of skin color in our world.

HONORING TALENTS AND CREATIVITY with *EMILY'S ART*

HEARTPRINT BOOK: *Emily's Art* by Peter Catalanotto

ABOUT THE BOOK: Emily loves to draw. Excited to enter an art contest, she becomes upset when her cherished portrait of her dog, Thor, is mistaken for a rabbit. In addition to Emily's frustrations with her art being "misunderstood," Emily is hurt by the judge's decision in the contest and feels that she is no longer worthy of painting or sharing her art.

LIFE LAYERS ♡ INVITATIONS TO SHARE CONNECTIONS, CARES, AND CONCERNS

As an aspiring artist Emily loves to paint from her heart. With the upcoming school art contest, Emily will get to showcase her talents, but is disappointed when the judge, "Ms. Fair," doesn't see what she sees. Share this book to encourage conversations about art, interpretations, and life lessons.

Discussion Possibilities

- Raise the question, "What makes art?" Reflect on the many possibilities that define art, and discuss examples of art in music, words, and images.
- Consider what makes someone an artist and lead a conversation about appreciating the artistic and creative talents in all of us.
- Talk about what it means to be "the best" and who is given the power to decide such things.
- Think about Emily's experience of her work being judged. Suggest students reflect on how that might make them feel or share their reactions to similar experiences.
- Discuss the difference between opinions and brainstorm ways we can listen and respond to others' opinions—even if they aren't our own.
- Invite students to share about artists they may know and admire and the specific qualities they appreciate in their work. Connect the conversation to artists and illustrators from books your students know and love.

LITERACY CONNECTIONS 👥 POSSIBILITIES FOR NURTURING OUR READERS AND WRITERS

Based on the needs of your students and their instructional goals, consider the following possibilities for layering in reading and writing connections to complement your workshop, small-group, or individual conversations.

As a Reader	As a Writer
Reading to Share Opinions Readers respond to texts with opinions and offer rationale to support those opinions. After reading *Emily's Art*, suggest students discuss whether "Ms. Fair" was actually being fair and offer text evidence to support their perspective.	**Exploring Word Choice and Craft Moves** Writers make intentional decisions about names, traits, and actions to develop well-rounded characters. Students might revisit the way the author does this in *Emily's Art*, and try some of the craft moves in a piece they are writing to demonstrate a character's personality (such as actions, thoughts, dialogue, and names like "Ms. Fair").
Thinking Beyond the Text Readers look for patterns to develop ideas about a character in the text. Help students explore the patterns that Peter Catalanotto used to reveal Emily's feelings. Consider that colors change in the illustrations to show shifting emotions in the story.	**Using Illustrations to Elaborate** Writers use various techniques to demonstrate actions, movement, or feelings. Notice how Peter Catalanotto painted the mom showing movement by adding four of the same images in different positions. In addition, he used large ears to show Thor "hears everything." You might invite your writers to revisit the illustrations and consider trying some of the same techniques from *Emily's Art* in their writing.
Writing About Reading After reading *Emily's Art*, and exploring the value of different opinions, use the book to model responding to reading with personal opinions. Connect this to writing book reviews and encourage your students to write reviews for books in your classroom library based on a variety of agreed-upon criteria.	**Exploring Figurative Language** Writers use figurative language to create images and to demonstrate how a character is feeling. Consider the line "Emily's heart twisted." Invite your writers to explore ways they could use similar language (similes, metaphors, or personification) to strengthen an image or an idea in their writing.

LITERACY SNAPSHOTS IDEAS TO ADOPT OR ADAPT

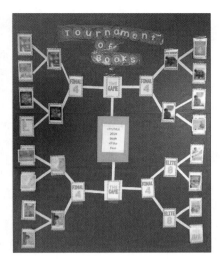

In appreciation of all books, invite readers to participate in literacy celebrations, such as Picture Book Madness or Battle of the Books (both based on best-of brackets).

To connect student talents with learning, suggest your students plan and conduct a literacy presentation of their choosing. Here, students participate in an appreciation for words and performance during a schoolwide poetry slam. They even had cued up walk-on songs ready to go.

CONTINUING CONVERSATIONS 📖 ADDITIONAL HEARTPRINT CONNECTIONS

A Day So Gray by Marie Lamba, illustrated by Alea Marley

A child shares her observations on a dull, gray day—until things are transformed. When she looks closely, she finds beauty and sees things in a new way. This is another book to help readers think about the importance of the lens through which we view the world.

Yesterday I Had the Blues by Jeron Ashford Frame, illustrated by R. Gregory Christie

This book highlights how people have different moods at different times and encourages respect for various opinions and perspectives. Full of beautiful metaphors, *Yesterday I Had the Blues* can also serve as a mentor text for readers to reflect on and for writers to borrow.

Music from the Sky by Denise Gillard, illustrated by Stephen Taylor

A young girl and her grandfather look for the perfect branch to carve a flute. Along the way she learns the power of finding and making your own beautiful music. Share this text to connect conversations about music, family, and, finding beauty in our hearts and our histories.

CONTINUING CONNECTIONS MORE LAYERS FOR LEARNING TOGETHER

 Work with a team of students and teachers to plan an event to celebrate individual student talents. Invite learners to showcase their talents by being a part of poetry slams, art exhibits, musical recitals, and dance performances.

RESPECTING INDIVIDUALITY with *LOVELY*

HEARTPRINT BOOK: *Lovely* by Jess Hong

ABOUT THE BOOK: Through an array of images and words, readers consider multiple interpretations of the word *lovely*. Though this heartprint book is light on text, it will give students lots to think about.

LIFE LAYERS ♥ INVITATIONS TO SHARE CONNECTIONS, CARES, AND CONCERNS

Words can take shape based on beliefs, biases, and values. With this simple text, readers can reflect on what it means to be "lovely" while its images help them expand their ideas of diversity and inclusivity. *Lovely* promotes two powerful messages: respect differences and everyone is beautiful in their own way.

Discussion Possibilities

- ■ Review the theme of *Lovely* with students, and consider its central question: What does it means to be lovely?
- ■ Have students reflect on ways the texts and images expand the meaning of the word *lovely*, discussing new ways and new words they might use to describe it.
- ■ Invite students to share how words take on new meaning with every picture as your students read and reflect on what it means to be lovely.
- ■ Encourage students to consider other indistinct words could be open to interpretation and redefinition (such as *perfect, smart,* and *best*).

LITERACY CONNECTIONS POSSIBILITIES FOR NURTURING OUR READERS AND WRITERS

Based on the needs of your students and their instructional goals, consider the following possibilities for layering in reading and writing connections to complement your workshop, small-group, or individual conversations.

As a Reader	As a Writer
Critical Reading Readers analyze pictures and words to develop ideas and interpretations about what they have read. As your students reflect on the messages in *Lovely*, discuss the ideas they might agree or disagree with and encourage readers to reflect on how the author and illustrator might challenge their ideas.	**Argument Writing** Writers can make a claim or state an opinion and use evidence to support that claim—using phrases such as "In my opinion," "I believe," and "one reason"—to connect and develop their ideas. In *Lovely*, every page describes what "lovely" is. Prompt students to choose a particular word and write about what it means to them.
Analyzing and Critiquing Texts After reading *Lovely*, consider what the illustrations say or leave unsaid. Invite students to go back to a page or selection to expand on their ideas and noticings.	**Examining Structures and Craft** Writers connect ideas across pages using labels, words, and examples to clarify or strengthen an idea. Revisit several selections in *Lovely* to see how the pages alternate with connected ideas. Jess Hong uses descriptive words that are opposites, color words, or specific adjectives to show a variety of meanings. Suggest your readers plan for and use a similar organizational pattern in their writing.
Exploring Vocabulary Readers connect to their personal and cultural background knowledge to inform meanings of new words. Ask students to reflect on words they encounter in *Lovely* and how their experiences may impact what they mean.	**Examining Word Choice** Writers consider personal and social connections to word meanings. Talk about the words Jess Hong uses to describe *lovely* and suggest students play with words by creating a book all about one word (e.g., *kind, respectful, proud*) that explores its various interpretations and shades of meaning.

LITERACY SNAPSHOTS IDEAS TO ADOPT OR ADAPT

After exploring the ideas in *Lovely*, students created their own interpretations of its theme about respect and appreciation for all kinds of lovely.

Using a student-generated word web, invite your students to brainstorm various meanings around a concept word like *lovely*. Here, a group considers the word *brave* and its various personal and social interpretations.

CONTINUING CONVERSATIONS ADDITIONAL HEARTPRINT CONNECTIONS

A Is for Awesome by Dallas Clayton

Share this alliterative alphabet book with rhyming phrases to help readers celebrate awesome qualities and explore all the various ways someone can be awesome. This is an *awesome* text to bring in additional wordplay or a to model the ABC text structure, which can be easily adapted for a variety of instructional purposes.

My Heart Fills with Happiness written by Monique Gray Smith, illustrated by Julie Flett

My Heart Fills with Happiness is a board book that makes for a great read-aloud to celebrate memories and moments that bring us joy. This uplifting book will inspire readers and writers of all ages to find the little joys in life.

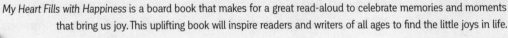

Courage by Bernard Waber

Share this concept book to reinforce and expand interpretations about courage based on different perspectives and points of view. You might also layer in conversations about what it means to have courage.

CONTINUING CONNECTIONS MORE LAYERS FOR LEARNING TOGETHER

Learn more about Todd Parr and his messages of respect and acceptance by visiting his website. Take a look at some of his free shareable graphics that could inspire continued reflections in your learning community.

*We do not need magic to change the world, we carry all the power we need
inside ourselves already: we have the power to imagine better.*
—J.K. Rowling, Commencement Address at Harvard

EMPOWERMENT is about understanding that each of us has the potential to make a difference in our world and affect the path our lives take. When our learners feel empowered, they begin to access that promise within themselves. Though this revelation may feel spellbinding, no trip to Hogwarts is required. Instead, through read-alouds, we can invite students on a journey across the pages of heartprint books, creating conditions and building conversations that inspire them to recognize their full inner potential.

Carefully chosen literature can set the stage for this type of heart magic. Empowerment incorporates qualities from its fellow CARE elements—*community, agency,* and *respect*—to round out our discussion of effective practices that build trust through collaborative community experiences and remind learners to honor themselves and others as they take steps to make their world a better place. As we focus on empowerment through the lens of the Heartprint Framework, we'll continue to think beyond the pages of the book to examine perspectives and motivations, while capitalizing on ways to help children find their own "powers."

During his Newbery acceptance speech, Kwame Alexander (2015) argued that books are "doors to a life of sustainability and success, to our lives, and each of us has a responsibility to walk through them." With that in mind, the titles you'll encounter in this chapter celebrate a wide variety of voices, choices, characters, and communities, while inviting our learners to do the same. These heartprint selections continue to serve as coteachers to help us challenge our ideas, accept new realities, and push ourselves to grow page by page, story by story.

Empowerment is about a vision for a better world—one that begins by calling all learners to be part of a more compassionate, caring classroom community. In the following heartprint connections, you'll find a wide range of titles that promote equity, empathy, and inclusivity while championing mindsets where each individual recognizes their abilities and strives to become their best self. Together, we can learn how to make these practices a reality as we celebrate books that encourage all learners to approach life with an outlook of magical wonder, potential, and hope.

GROWING IN CONFIDENCE with *THE KING OF KINDERGARTEN*

HEARTPRINT BOOK: *The King of Kindergarten* by Derrick Barnes, illustrated by Vanessa Brantley-Newton

ABOUT THE BOOK: In this joyful read-aloud, a boy is full of pride and enthusiasm as he gets ready to begin kindergarten. With the support of his family, and in anticipation of the royal treatment, he is confident that he will be the "king of kindergarten" this year. Follow him as he sets off with authority to meet his royal subjects and enter the kingdom of kindergarten. Readers might recognize the work of award-winning author Derrick Barnes, who has gifted readers with a new crown!

LIFE LAYERS ♥ INVITATIONS TO SHARE CONNECTIONS, CARES, AND CONCERNS

A great read-aloud to celebrate new beginnings with a reassuring sense of confidence and delight, *The King of Kindergarten* can focus conversations on the importance of self-esteem and how learners can embrace new challenges with excitement and anticipation.

Discussion Possibilities

- Brainstorm a list of new experiences (riding a bike, first day of school, first sleepover) and invite learners to discuss their feelings about them.
- Discuss the empowering mindset the narrator chose for this new school situation and how his attitude affected his day.
- Ask your students to share what they hope to accomplish this year and discuss actions they might take and attitudes they can adopt to help them reach those goals.
- Talk about how *The King of Kindergarten* is the hero of his own story and how we all have the ability to take charge of our own lives and learning.

LITERACY CONNECTIONS POSSIBILITIES FOR NURTURING OUR READERS AND WRITERS

Based on the needs of your students and their instructional goals, consider the following possibilities for layering in reading and writing connections to complement your workshop, small-group, or individual conversations.

As a Reader	As a Writer
Analyzing Book and Print Features Discuss the quote from Benjamin Mays in the dedication: "A child must learn early to believe that he is somebody worthwhile and that he can do many praiseworthy things." Invite your readers to revisit the quote before and after reading to develop their ideas further.	**Analyzing Craft** Writers use a variety of techniques to provide the reader with clear examples and interesting descriptions, such as Barnes's threaded metaphor about the royal experiences at school. Suggest your students consider ways they could write using a recurring metaphor in a piece of their own.
Exploring Language and Vocabulary Readers expand on new word meanings through context. Invite your readers to discuss the royal references (such as riding the big yellow carriage to the grand fortress, finding his royal seat) to clarify the meaning and consider what additional messages those word choices reveal.	**Exploring Language and Word Choice** Writers use well-chosen details to develop a focus for their reader. Derrick Barnes used figurative language through repeated references to royalty to influence feelings about the start of kindergarten. Invite your students to look for places where they can use more precise language in their own writing to help create a stronger image or focus.
Maintaining Fluency Readers read with intention—pausing, speeding up, or emphasizing words based on their comprehension and clues in the text that influence their fluency. Students may revisit various lines to experiment with reading certain phrases more fluently from *The King of Kindergarten,* such as "brushing Ye Royal Chiclets," or "greeting everyone with a brilliant, beaming, majestic smile."	**Revising Texts** Writers read and reread their work alone or with partners to find places they can write more effectively. As writers notice Derrick Barnes's use of pictures and words in *The King of Kindergarten,* encourage them to think about ways they can revise to add a fun font, images, or words to make their writing magnificent!

LITERACY SNAPSHOTS IDEAS TO ADOPT OR ADAPT

Confidence is king! Students who view themselves with confidence are empowered and take the role of lead learners in their own lives. As this slogan states, "We are all leaders." Invite your students to explore and create their own slogans with empowering messages.

Inspired by the optimistic mindset of *The King of Kindergarten*, these students reflected on previously held beliefs that they now viewed more positively.

CONTINUING CONVERSATIONS 📖 ADDITIONAL HEARTPRINT CONNECTIONS

Lena's Shoes Are Nervous: A First-Day-of-School Dilemma by Keith Calabrese and Juana Medina

In this first day of school dilemma, with a different twist, Lena is ready to start kindergarten. She is excited, but the problem is, "her shoes are nervous." She gains confidence as the day goes on and as she "talks" with her clothing to make it feel more confident and ready for her to attend her first day of school. Keith Calabrese's humor paired with Juana Medina's charming illustrations create a reading experience that's sure to leave its mark.

Butterflies on the First Day of School by Annie Silvestro, illustrated by Dream Chen

This sweet story brings the expression "butterflies in your stomach" to life. A little girl starting school is overcome with *that* feeling in her belly. Each time she tries to speak, butterflies that only she can see fly out. As the story goes on, she gains confidence for herself and, feeling empowered, is able to help a new friend who she finds alone under a tree, holding her own belly.

I Used to Be Afraid by Laura Vaccaro Seeger

In an artistic blend of story and puzzle, Seeger's narrator reflects on thoughts and fears she *used* to have. With each page, die-cuts support the text to offer a fresh new look that show readers how she revised her thinking to overcome a particular fear. *I Used to Be Afraid* will remind readers that they are in control of how they choose to view things.

CONTINUING CONNECTIONS MORE LAYERS FOR LEARNING TOGETHER

To kick off a new school year, share *Kids First from Day One: A Teacher's Guide to Today's Classroom* by Christine Hertz and Kristine Mraz (2018). The book focuses on routines and expectations for a year filled with heartwork, where all learners view themselves with a positive, empowering lens.

FINDING COURAGE with *JABARI JUMPS*

HEARTPRINT BOOK: *Jabari Jumps* by Gaia Cornwall

ABOUT THE BOOK: Jabari has been taking swimming lessons and preparing for a big day. As he plans for his big leap off the diving board, the readers see his many forms of procrastination, as well as the loving support of his patient and encouraging dad.

LIFE LAYERS ♥ INVITATIONS TO SHARE CONNECTIONS, CARES, AND CONCERNS

Beyond the ties to what it takes to be brave in this book, students finds lots of connections to stories from their own lives about taking chances and trying something new. Read *Jabari Jumps* to discuss how some things take more courage than others. The expressive illustrations will add to your discussions on perspective and mindsets.

Discussion Possibilities

- Stories can help us talk about important feelings we all have. Invite students to share their thinking about a time when they were brave or a time when they were scared but found the courage to face their fears.
- Ask students to share feelings that are on their mind or encourage discussions on experiences tied to powerful emotions. As a class, discuss how students might validate one another's feelings—especially when they're feeling sad or scared.
- Suggest students discuss what it's like to try or learn something new and to consider when the experience is positive or scary.
- In *Jabari Jumps*, Jabari is supported by his loving dad. Encourage students to consider who they turn to when they need help finding a little extra courage to take a big leap.

LITERACY CONNECTIONS 🗣 POSSIBILITIES FOR NURTURING OUR READERS AND WRITERS

Based on the needs of your students and their instructional goals, consider the following possibilities for layering in reading and writing connections to complement your workshop, small-group, or individual conversations.

As a Reader	As a Writer
Inferring Readers make inferences based on text evidence, such as events and actions, that support their understanding of characters' problems and feelings. For example, students can infer what it means when Jabari's dad squeezes Jabari's hand.	**Revealing Perspective with Illustrations** Writers deliberately choose how to illustrate perspective to express ideas more clearly. Look back at the techniques Gaia Cornwall uses (e.g., size, shape, and objects from various angles) to discuss possibilities that your writers might want to try to convey perspective in their own work and think about how this might be done in words as well as in illustrations.
Monitoring for Fluency Readers use inferences based on clues from the text to read with fluency and expressions, noticing when to put stress on words based on punctuation, text formatting, and word choice. Curate a list of examples from *Jabari Jumps*. Invite your writers to find examples from their own texts that might cause them to read with more expression in similar ways.	**Showing Rather Than Telling** Writers use techniques such as thought bubbles, dialogue, and actions to demonstrate what a character is thinking or feeling. Notice the way that Gaia Cornwall includes actions about how Jabari was *scared* but never used the word. With your students, chart out lines that reveal how Jabari is feeling. As students name those techniques, encourage them to try this craft more in their own writing.
Inferring from Illustrations Readers think about how illustrations connect to a story to describe people, places, and things to express ideas clearly. After reading *Jabari Jumps*, invite students to share their thoughts about images that add to their interpretation of Jabari's bravery during his "big leap."	**Elaborating Text Through Illustration** Writers use boldfaced words, fonts, sound words, and phrases to show feelings and convey emotions. Gaia Cornwall includes large type in a wavey font to show Jabari *splash* in the pool. Suggest students consider using or illustrating sound words to show an action or feeling in a piece they are working on.

LITERACY SNAPSHOTS IDEAS TO ADOPT OR ADAPT

Inspired by the ideas in *Jabari Jumps* and Gaia Cornwall's craft lessons, students explored techniques such as speech bubbles, illustrations to show movement, and symbols to indicate setting. These kindergarteners show a time when they felt brave like Jabari.

After discussing fears and anxieties, sixth-grade students posted a list of empowering declarations on the classroom door. Consider posting empowering text your students collect from texts they read.

CONTINUING CONVERSATIONS 📖 ADDITIONAL HEARTPRINT CONNECTIONS

There Might Be Lobsters by Carolyn Crimi, illustrated by Laurel Molk

Set during a day on the beach, readers meet a little girl and her dog, Sukie. Sukie is afraid of everything, especially the beach with bouncy balls, waves, and water. As her owner, Eleanor, encourages Sukie to overcome those fears, readers will be touched by the event that causes Sukie to finally go in the water. Share *There Might Be Lobsters* with students to discuss ways we can empower others.

The Happiest Tree: A Yoga Story by Uma Krishnaswami, illustrated by Ruth Jeyaveeran

Meena uses yoga training to gain confidence as she prepares to learn something new. With an author's note that includes tips for breathing exercises and more, *The Happiest Tree* explores various emotions and ways we can take control of our mind and body when we're overcome by challenging feelings.

Small Things by Mel Tregonning

This wordless, visual narrative reads like a graphic novel. The story depicts a boy struggling with childhood pressures and all of the complex emotions and intense feelings associated with those fears. Since the fears are personified in this more complex exploration about anxieties, this powerful picture book may be better suited for mature readers.

CONTINUING CONNECTIONS MORE LAYERS FOR LEARNING TOGETHER

Be on the lookout for ways to connect your conversations about courage to content areas and other parts of your day. To extend the exploration about what it means to be brave and to try something new, share this wonder of the day from wonderopolis.org. It could be employed to stir further discussions about fortitude when you undertake something unfamiliar.

MINDSETS AND MOTIVATIONS with *EXCELLENT ED*

HEARTPRINT BOOK: *Excellent Ed* by Stacy McAnulty, illustrated by Julia Sarcone-Roach

ABOUT THE BOOK: The extraordinary Ellis family and each of its members, Elaine, Emily, and Elmer, are all excellent at something, except Ed. Their dog, Ed, narrates the story and doesn't think he is exceptionally good at anything. Through joyful alliteration and wordplay, get to know more about the Ellis family while learning exceptional lessons about self-esteem and unconditional love.

LIFE LAYERS ♥ INVITATIONS TO SHARE CONNECTIONS, CARES, AND CONCERNS

Read aloud this playful picture book to help students relate to empowering concepts such as learning from our challenges, nurturing our strengths, setting goals, and exploring positive mindsets. *Excellent Ed* also spotlights affirming families, love, and finding what makes each one of us special.

Discussion Possibilities

- Ask students to reflect on what it might mean to be "excellent." Consider ways to help learners expand their understanding of excellence—from a fixed mindset to a more dynamic perspective that addresses growth and effort.
- Discuss your learners' reading and writing goals and the types of outlooks that will best prepare them to reach those goals.
- Ask your readers to reflect on the talents they admire in their friends, family, or people in your school community and how we can affirm the talents and efforts of others.

LITERACY CONNECTIONS 👥 POSSIBILITIES FOR NURTURING OUR READERS AND WRITERS

Based on the needs of your students and their instructional goals, consider the following possibilities for layering in reading and writing connections to complement your workshop, small-group, or individual conversations.

As a Reader	As a Writer
Inferring Readers search for clues in pictures, patterns, and phrases and notice how the writer or illustrator uses them to understand a text. Your students could look back to explore how the alliterative phrases connect to the illustrations in *Excellent Ed* to show the Ellis family and their interests and passions.	**Exploring Figurative Language** Writers use figurative language and make intentional decisions about word choice that impact sound, fluency, and message. After reading about the "Excellent Ellis" family members, invite your writers to try playing with repeated words or sounds to add rhythm to a piece of their own writing.
Exploring Sentence Fluency and Grammar Readers pay attention to conjunctions that signal relationships and connect ideas, such as *because, and, or, but*. Notice how Ed continues to compare himself to each Ellis child and gives examples with connected reasons to show he is not as excellent at the same things they are.	**Writing with Elaboration** Writers use specific examples to explain an idea further to the reader. Notice the way the talents of the Ellis family are explained ("Edith was an excellent ballerina . . .") and the examples to support the claim ("she could twirl on her toes"), Ask your students to find places in their writing to add descriptive examples to give the reader a stronger image.
Exploring Plot Readers pay attention to the important elements of a story, including the introduction, problem, and ending. After Stacy McAnulty introduces the Ellis family and describes the problem with Ed, help students reflect on how the actions of the characters help lead to a resolution.	**Writing Personal Narratives** Narrative writers consider story elements that include characters, setting, problem, and solution. After reading about the excellent Ellis family, suggest your student write about their own family, with specific attention to how these elements could add detail to their personal narratives.

LITERACY SNAPSHOTS IDEAS TO ADOPT OR ADAPT

After sharing their goals and ideas for what they want to learn and become better at, kindergarten students drew and wrote about what they will work hard at to be when they grow up.

As students reflect on the importance of mindset, invite your students to write essays or poems to illustrate what the word means to them. This fifth grader shares her feelings about the concepts of excellence and perfection.

Be Happy, Not Perfect
by Skye Dubose

There is no such thing as "perfect"
Where did the word come from?
The perfect student, the perfect parents,
The perfect future, the perfect life

We are all human, living in a human world
Most are nice, sincere, loving, and even strict
But perfect causes such unhappiness

Perfect is unreal, untouchable
Accept good, well done, and wonderful
Do your best, be your best
There is no such thing as perfect
Be happy, not perfect

CONTINUING CONVERSATIONS 📖 ADDITIONAL HEARTPRINT CONNECTIONS

The Book of Mistakes by Corinna Luyken

Ink smudges become new inspirations in this beautifully illustrated book of mistakes. Explore messages of experimentation and the importance of a mindset that recognizes that all mistakes can lead to something greater. You just have to be willing to look.

The Good Egg by John Jory, illustrated by Pete Oswald

In this companion to *Bad Seed*, readers will fall in love with the narrator who is a very good egg. But sometimes, "being good can be rotten," and he eventually finds the pressure to be perfect so unbearable, "he almost cracks." *The Good Egg* is filled with playful, "punny" humor, charming illustrations, and an empowering message about self-care.

It's Tough to Lose Your Balloon by Jarrett J. Krosoczka

Lost balloons. Sandy sandwiches. Some things are never fun, but if we think about problems in a different way, maybe we can find the bright side. Told through simple paired texts, and with examples to demonstrate the "but" for every situation, this book advocates for an optimistic, empowering view of our world.

CONTINUING CONNECTIONS MORE LAYERS FOR LEARNING TOGETHER

As you continue to explore mindsets and outlooks and how your teaching practices can help students approach goals and learning with a flexible frame of mind, consider this video of Carol Dweck, the author of *Mindset: The New Psychology of Success* (2016). Dweck demonstrates that we are never done learning.

SELF-ACCEPTANCE with *I AM ENOUGH*

HEARTPRINT BOOK: *I Am Enough* by Grace Byers, illustrated by Keturah A. Bobo

ABOUT THE BOOK: This book is a poetic expression about self-acceptance with patterns of rhyming text, similes, and illustrations that reinforce the message of loving oneself.

LIFE LAYERS ♥ INVITATIONS TO SHARE CONNECTIONS, CARES, AND CONCERNS

Although this text is about girls, it invites many opportunities beyond gender to read and discuss the empowering message of honoring our own strengths and advocating for our own potential. Grace Byers's message can support all children on their journey to self-acceptance.

Discussion Possibilities

- Initiate discussions on themes students find in *I Am Enough* and explore these ideas by sharing examples about being comfortable, confident, and pleased with exactly who you are.
- Challenge students to reflect on times they didn't feel like they were enough and—just as important—times when they felt confident and sure.
- Explore the opportunities to celebrate each of our unique qualities with affirmations for all children to love exactly who they are.
- Invite students to share those qualities they love about themselves and others.

LITERACY CONNECTIONS 💬 POSSIBILITIES FOR NURTURING OUR READERS AND WRITERS

Based on the needs of your students and their instructional goals, consider the following possibilities for layering in reading and writing connections to complement your workshop, small-group, or individual conversations.

As a Reader	As a Writer
Inferring Readers notice language that might say one thing and mean something more. Notice how the author uses similes to create clearer images in *I Am Enough*. Invite your readers to discuss examples of figurative language that strengthen an inference or help them to further understand an idea from the text.	**Exploring Figurative Language** Writers make comparisons using figurative language to create stronger images for readers. Notice how Grace Byers uses similes to demonstrate that we are all more than enough. After highlighting some of the similes from the text, suggest students try using *like* or *as* to enhance descriptions in their own writing.
Writing About Reading Select an image or page from the text and show students how they can use writing to extend their interpretation of the author's message. For instance, responding "I am enough," they might demonstrate writing to contemplate their personal connections to the theme of self-acceptance.	**Revising Titles and Texts** Writers purposefully choose titles that connect to the messages found in the text. Consider Grace Byers's decision to title this book after the phrase "I am enough." Ask students to discuss this craft move and consider ways they could revise titles from their own writing to more clearly illustrate their message for their readers.
Thinking About Themes Readers read to determine how themes in a text can be interpreted in more than one way. Prompt your readers to discuss alternative interpretations from *I Am Enough* that might reveal additional messages beyond self-acceptance using evidence from the text to support their ideas.	**Exploring Conclusions** Writers choose to end their texts to leave the reader with a specific feeling, thought, or resolution. Notice the circular ending Byers uses to reflect the book's title in the last line. To practice crafting conclusions, help students brainstorm alternative endings that could also echo the central message of *I Am Enough*.

LITERACY SNAPSHOTS IDEAS TO ADOPT OR ADAPT

To help students connect literacy to their lives, consider crafting a noticings chart like the one seen in this second-grade class that highlights connections your students make as readers, writers, and humans across a heartprint text.

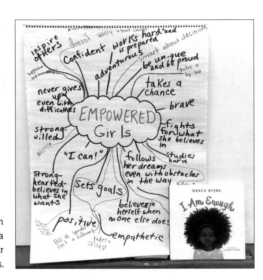

After reading and discussing themes from *I Am Enough*, these students created a concept web to share and extend their thinking about empowering girls.

CONTINUING CONVERSATIONS 📖 ADDITIONAL HEARTPRINT CONNECTIONS

Crown: An Ode to the Fresh Cut by Derrick Barnes, illustrated by Gordon C. James

Crown, a wonderful collaboration between author Derrick Barnes and illustrator Gordon C. James earned multiple awards, including both a Newbery and a Caldecott Honor. In poetic, rhythmic verse, this empowering book celebrates pride and self-esteem while reinforcing the message that confidence is king.

Be Who You Are by Todd Parr

Todd Parr begins this book with a message to readers about not being afraid to be who you are and connects that concept to thoughts of love, acceptance, and pride. With its empowering pictures and simple text, *Be Who You Are* highlights themes you'll want to return to again and again.

The North Star by Peter H. Reynolds

Peter H. Reynolds's allegory about how to seek our own path in learning and life encourages readers to explore and consider the many ways individuals can pursue learning and creative thinking. This story about following one's heart, being true to oneself, and self-determination will invite conversations around dreams, goals, and personal navigation.

CONTINUING CONNECTIONS MORE LAYERS FOR LEARNING TOGETHER

Empowerment isn't just about students! We support our learners by investing in ourselves and in growing our instructional skills. In the hustle and bustle of the school year, it can be difficult to find quality options for professional development, but many teachers are finding a new type of learning network in Twitter. If you aren't already connected, take a look at this free Teaching Channel resource about using this social media platform to inform your practices and how you can get started.

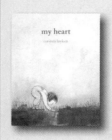

NURTURING FEELINGS WITH *MY HEART*

HEARTPRINT BOOK: *My Heart* by Corinna Luyken

ABOUT THE BOOK: This poetic text with equally beautiful illustrations examines words and images associated with one's heart. Using metaphors for the heart such as a compass, a puddle, a fence to keep the world out, or even a window, opened or closed, the narrator illustrates that a heart can be many things and that, ultimately, we get to decide.

LIFE LAYERS ♥ INVITATIONS TO SHARE CONNECTIONS, CARES, AND CONCERNS

Corinna Luyken's emotive artwork and thought-provoking metaphors will create opportunities for reading, writing, and thinking about feelings. Share *My Heart* to empower learners to see that they all have the ability to listen to their heart and decide their feelings.

Discussion Possibilities

- Ask students to consider and describe what their heart is like.
- Highlight Corinna Luyken's text and images. As your students make observations about the metaphors in this book, remind them to discuss and connect the images to examples from their own lives. For example, could they elaborate on a metaphor about a time when their heart was like a puddle or an open window.
- Suggest students think about the many messages in this text. As they consider the connected themes, invite them to discuss how they can decide to take care of their hearts too.

LITERACY CONNECTIONS 👥 POSSIBILITIES FOR NURTURING OUR READERS AND WRITERS

Based on the needs of your students and their instructional goals, consider the following possibilities for layering in reading and writing connections to complement your workshop, small-group, or individual conversations.

As a Reader	As a Writer
Making Inferences Readers read closely to analyze what a text explicitly says and make logical inferences about its implicit messages. Student might reread to identify implied messages about the heart from *My Heart*, supporting their inferences with specific examples of words or images.	**Drafting Ideas** Writers emulate craft ideas from authors they admire. After reading *My Heart*, suggest students list possible ways to describe a single object (like a heart), perhaps borrowing Corinna Luyken's pattern: "My _____ is _____."
Analyzing Illustrations Readers pay attention to color and shading in illustrations to reflect tone and evoke an emotional response. Work with students to identify changes in the images across the pages of *My Heart* that lead the reader to further interpretations.	**Developing Ideas** Writers reference texts and connected images as effective models to tell a story, express a feeling, or share an idea. After reading all the images and ideas associated with *My Heart*, encourage your writers to select one idea to develop.
Analyzing Style and Language Readers reflect on types of poetic verse (such as rhyme, repetition, free verse, and imagery) and consider how this impacts the rhythm and reading of a text. Ask students to share their observations about the language in this poem turned into a picture book. Readers might also reflect on the ways the writer uses imagery to balance light and darkness.	**Analyzing Craft and Figurative Language** Writers use language to impact meaning and affect the reader's interpretation. Author and illustrator Corinna Luyken uses metaphors to compare the heart to various objects that resonate with the reader. With your writers, explore ways to employ a recurring metaphor to enhance a piece of writing.

LITERACY SNAPSHOTS IDEAS TO ADOPT OR ADAPT

Love is when you hear your family cheering you on.

Love is when you're scared and someone helps you out of the dark.

Love is when you score your first goal and your friends are all there to watch you.

Love is when someone inspires you to do your best.

Love is when you are sad and your family makes you smile.

Love is when you win an award and your friends are in the crowd clapping for you.

   Love is so many things.
   Love is possibilities.

Explore ways students can find mentor texts and borrow ideas from other writers. Inspired by *My Heart*, this student wrote a personal piece about the meaning of love.

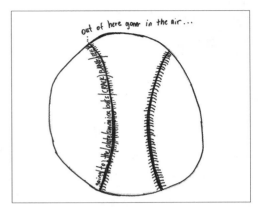

out of here gone in the air...

To merge passions and literacy, students might experiment with different styles to write about topics they love. This student decided to write a concrete poem inspired by his enthusiasm for baseball.

CONTINUING CONVERSATIONS ADDITIONAL HEARTPRINT CONNECTIONS

In My Heart: A Book of Feelings by Jo Witek, illustrated by Christine Roussey

In My Heart's unique artwork often includes die-cut peek-a-boo pages to extend her messages. This story addresses the continuum of our feelings. A little girl expresses those feelings using similes and metaphors to describe her wide range of emotions.

Sometimes I'm Bombaloo by Rachel Vail, illustrated by Yumi Heo

Rachel Vail created a story that portrays a very honest look at what happens when our emotions get the best of us. (My three grown sonshines still know what it means when I say, "I am sorry for being bombaloo.") Share this story to highlight how it feels to forgive and to be forgiven and the good things that can come when we're able to acknowledge those "bombaloo" feelings.

The Rabbit Listened by Cori Doerrfeld

Something terrible has happened to Taylor, and all of his stuffed animal friends have an opinion about how he should react. Share this emotional read-aloud to explore feeling upset, overwhelmed, or extremely sad. Cori Doerrfeld's book reminds readers that we can share difficult feelings when we're ready—and often find strength just from having someone to listen.

CONTINUING CONNECTIONS MORE LAYERS FOR LEARNING TOGETHER

To remind students of their ability to control their own feelings, behaviors, and attitudes, reflect together on the Collaborative for Academic, Social and Emotional Learning's social and emotional capacities (such as self-awareness, relationship skills, and responsible decision making) and brainstorm how your learning community might incorporate those layers further into your student-led conversations (CASEL 2013).

RECOGNIZING INTELLIGENCES with *HOW WE ARE SMART*

HEARTPRINT BOOK: *How We Are Smart* by W. Nikola-Lisa, illustrated by Sean Qualls

ABOUT THE BOOK: This hybrid collection of short texts, poems, and biographical sketches combines art, poetry, and information inspired by work around multiple intelligences. Readers will get a glimpse into the lives of exceptional individuals from various backgrounds: musicians, artists, athletes, politicians.

LIFE LAYERS ♥ INVITATIONS TO SHARE CONNECTIONS, CARES, AND CONCERNS

W. Nikola-Lisa's text can prompt students to rethink the meaning of *smart* as they investigate theories of intelligence and reconsider its definition to include motivation and mindsets. Share *How We Are Smart* to empower your readers as they pursue their passions with an emphasis on potential and possibility.

Discussion Possibilities

- Ask students to discuss their thoughts about the statement "Intelligence is not about how smart you are, but how you are smart" and the various ways they can showcase their brainpower.
- Suggest students discuss patterns, similarities, and differences among the intelligences highlighted by the author and think about what it means to be differently intelligent.
- Ask your students to share inspiration, new learning, and questions after reading *How We Are Smart* and how the book changed or affirmed the way they view their own talents.
- Prepare for students' questions about whose voices are represented in *How We Are Smart* as they consider the author's choice of individuals, information, and illustrations.

LITERACY CONNECTIONS 🎧 POSSIBILITIES FOR NURTURING OUR READERS AND WRITERS

Based on the needs of your students and their instructional goals, consider the following possibilities for layering in reading and writing connections to complement your workshop, small-group, or individual conversations.

As a Reader	As a Writer
Analyzing Texts Readers read informational texts, paying attention to important and interesting information that supports the author's message. Ask students to reflect on the purpose of the art in *How We Are Smart* and discuss how it supports their understanding of the intelligences addressed in this text.	**Analyzing Craft** Writers use a variety of techniques, such as graphics, quotes, and illustrations, to engage the reader and share information. Invite your writers to consider how they might try craft lessons found in *How We Are Smart*. Students could add poems or biographies to their accounts of a person's life or time lines to their research writing.
Expanding Vocabulary As readers explore informational texts, they make note of new words or terms associated with the topic. In *How We Are Smart*, W. Nikola-Lisa uses a variety of terms to describe intelligences. Suggest your learners keep track of expert words and vocabulary they learn as they read about a new subject.	**Developing Ideas** Writers write to explore a purpose or a stance on a topic. W. Nikola-Lisa chose to highlight individuals with very different backgrounds who were similar in the ways they've inspired others. Students may want to write about one of these individuals or an idea from *How We Are Smart* to share diverse perspectives or inform their readers about a topic that matters to them.
Inferring Readers use information from the texts to infer the importance of a subject's accomplishments. Guide students to use the information provided in a selected biopoem to think about how or why the author selected these individuals to showcase as multiple intelligences.	**Writing in Response to Reading** Writers write in response to reading, choosing a lens to guide their thinking as they search for information. After reading about an individual in *How We Are Smart*, ask students to gather information and evidence to support a theory about that person's accomplishments. Your students might want to write with a focus on their subject's talent or challenges.

LITERACY SNAPSHOTS IDEAS TO ADOPT OR ADAPT

To focus on honoring and growing talents, students investigated individuals whose accomplishments inspired their own. Notice this kindergartener's interpretation of Frida Kahlo.

After sharing *How We Are Smart* and participating in student-led conversations about our mindsets to grow and learn, this kindergarten display was created for students to showcase the passions that drive their goals.

CONTINUING CONVERSATIONS 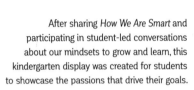 ADDITIONAL HEARTPRINT CONNECTIONS

Flight School by Lita Judge

Little penguin has the "soul of an eagle" and is determined to fly, so he enrolls in flight school and indeed receives lots of lessons. Penguin learns about the joy that comes from pursuing your passions with perseverance and a little help from your friends.

Everyone Can Learn to Ride a Bicycle by Chris Raschka

All students and teachers can relate to first-time experiences such as learning how to ride a bike. Raschka's text and joyful illustrations can serve as a reminder of the emotional ups and downs that come with new and challenging experiences.

Game Changers: The Story of Venus and Serena Williams by Lesa Cline-Ransome, illustrated by James E. Ransome

This picture book biography about the incredible record-breaking sisters, tells more about their bond and the story of their achievements. The Ransomes focus on the early years of the Williams sisters, two little girls with big dreams. Read this book to celebrate the impact of these strong role models on and off the court, and inspire your students to work hard and follow their dreams.

CONTINUING CONNECTIONS MORE LAYERS FOR LEARNING TOGETHER

Explore Peter Johnston's powerful book *Opening Minds: Using Language to Change Lives* (2012) to reflect on language and learning that nurtures agency, positive self-theories, intellectual curiosity, and the social imagination of our growing readers, writers, and thinkers.

BEING EXTRAORDINARY with *I WILL BE FIERCE!*

HEARTPRINT BOOK: *I Will Be Fierce!* by Bea Birdsong, illustrated by Nidhi Chanani

ABOUT THE BOOK: In this empowering story, readers meet a young girl who faces every day ready to explore new worlds. Readers travel with her on an epic adventure from home to school and back again, where she dares to "break away from the ordinary."

LIFE LAYERS ♥ INVITATIONS TO SHARE CONNECTIONS, CARES, AND CONCERNS

I Will Be Fierce! can help lead conversations about finding the extraordinary in everyday moments. Share this joyful and empowering read-aloud to encourage children to be the heroes in their own stories.

Discussion Possibilities

- ▪ Invite your learners to discuss feelings they associate with the word *fierce* and facilitate conversations about having a fierce mindset.
- ▪ Explore with students the different meanings for the word *fierce*, reflecting on why the author may have chosen it to illustrate confidence.
- ▪ Brainstorm ideas for how we can apply fierceness to meeting our life goals and taking charge of our own learning.
- ▪ Invite children to discuss adventures in their lives and how these experiences connect to confidence, resolve, and resiliency.

LITERACY CONNECTIONS POSSIBILITIES FOR NURTURING OUR READERS AND WRITERS

Based on the needs of your students and their instructional goals, consider the following possibilities for layering in reading and writing connections to complement your workshop, small-group, or individual conversations.

As a Reader	As a Writer
Making Connections Readers use personal knowledge to make connections to ideas in texts and to enhance understanding of themes. Students can connect to *I Will Be Fierce!* by comparing it to their own experiences and how it might inspire them to find the extraordinary in everyday moments.	**Developing Ideas** Writers observe places, people, and experiences to share more about those ideas. Ask your students to consider writing a narrative, inspired by *I Will Be Fierce!*, about a time when they felt empowered.
Inferring from Word Choice Readers think about how the author's use of language impacts their mental images and understanding of a text. Consider the epic word choice used to describe people and places, such as the librarian as the "guardian of wisdom." With students, look back to reflect on Bea Birdsong's word choice and how it adds to their understandings of the characters throughout the book.	**Exploring Figurative Language** Writers use a variety of techniques to create unique descriptions and convey messages to the reader. Invite your students to discuss the many situations that show how fierce the main character can be. Students can discuss the unique descriptions and word choice, and they might try to incorporate a recurring word or metaphor in a narrative of their own.
Exploring Fluency and Voice Readers read phrases, words, and dialogue with appropriate expression (noticing font formatting, word choice, punctuation, and meaning). Students can reread *I Will Be Fierce!* to consider how these elements affect their fluency and voice.	**Analyzing Texts** Reflect on the possible ways students could write about a topic of their own choice using a particular point of view or repetition of a phrase to help emphasize an idea. Notice how Bea Birdsong writes using first-person statements connected to affirmations—"I will . . ." and repeats that pattern to illustrate the main characters' confidence and capabilities.

LITERACY SNAPSHOTS IDEAS TO ADOPT OR ADAPT

Set up time for students to discuss some of the empowering messages found in books and in their lives. This second grader posted a message and reminder to "Be a Good Sport!!" and always have fun.

Inspired by *I Will Be Fierce!*, students discussed craft choices made by Bea Birdsong and made connections to other mentor texts on bravery. Students then reflected on the craft moves they found inspiring.

CONTINUING CONVERSATIONS 📖 ADDITIONAL HEARTPRINT CONNECTIONS

Mary Had a Little Glam by Tammi Sauer, illustrated by Vanessa Bradley-Newton

Modeled after the nursery rhyme "Mary Had a Little Lamb," this picture book version has a twist. Mary loves to accessorize! She spreads glam wherever she goes, but overdoes it and learns a little lesson of her own, as her attempt to fancy everyone up becomes problematic. This sweet story encourages everyone to be comfortable with who they are.

Sumo Joe by Mia Wenjen, illustrated by Nat Iwata

Sumo Joe loves wrestling, but he also really loves his little sister. When Joe's sister, Akido, challenges him to a match, Joe has to decide whether girls should be allowed into the ring. An empowering story about siblings, gender roles, and pursuing your passion, this rhyming story illustrates real elements of martial arts and includes back matter with Japanese vocabulary from the book.

The Big Bed by Bunmi Laditan, illustrated by Tom Knight

The Big Bed has heart and humor that will have you rolling on the floor laughing. Readers meet a young girl who plots to get her dad out of the big bed, so she can sleep with her mommy all by herself. Her proposals are interesting, and her negotiating tactics include a formal presentation to dad. This book definitely makes its mark for writing with voice, but it's also one to discuss as a powerful model for presenting and supporting ideas with evidence.

CONTINUING CONNECTIONS MORE LAYERS FOR LEARNING TOGETHER

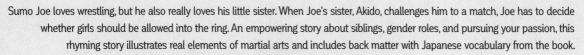

Though author Caroline Paul focuses on raising girls, explore this TED Talk to stir conversations about bravery and empowering all children. When we caution children rather than allowing them to take risks, how do they become brave? In this video, Paul discusses the significance of "risky play" that teaches resilience and confidence and more life lessons about bravery.

EMPOWERING RELATIONSHIPS with *HAIR LOVE*

HEARTPRINT BOOK: *Hair Love* by Matthew Cherry, illustrated by Vashti Harrison

ABOUT THE BOOK: Zuri is proud of her amazing hair. She can wear it like a princess, in two puffs, or like a superhero—and it can even do magic tricks! One day she enlists her dad (who has his own amazing locs) to help her get ready for a special day.

LIFE LAYERS INVITATIONS TO SHARE CONNECTIONS, CARES, AND CONCERNS

Based on Cherry's animated film and documentary, this picture book is a pure joy read-aloud with breathtaking illustrations. More than an ode to loving one's natural hair, this empowering picture book also celebrates a strong, loving relationship between a dad and his daughter.

Discussion Possibilities

- Discuss the powerful relationship and connections Zuri has with her dad, and invite students to reflect on how individuals provide love and support in their lives. Students may want to share thoughts about the people in their lives that care for them and those that they care for.
- Invite students to share their opinions about Zuri's sense of self and her relationships and consider how she takes care of herself and her family.
- Help learners think about the connections among the concepts of confidence, self-esteem, love, and family.

LITERACY CONNECTIONS 👥 POSSIBILITIES FOR NURTURING OUR READERS AND WRITERS

Based on the needs of your students and their instructional goals, consider the following possibilities for layering in reading and writing connections to complement your workshop, small-group, or individual conversations.

As a Reader	As a Writer
Making Connections Readers make connections to personal experiences throughout texts to enhance their understanding. Invite your students to reflect and make connections about the family members in their own lives who support and empower them as Zuri's dad does.	**Developing Ideas** When writers write about experiences, they intentionally decide to include specific details to help readers understand their ideas. Prompt your students to go back to look for small moments throughout the images and text in *Hair Love* that convey love of Zuri, her dad, and her mom, and consider ways they can replicate these feelings using words and images to reinforce themes in their own personal narratives.
Synthesizing Readers read to find the theme and big ideas the author wants to convey, asking themselves as they read, what a character or an event might be teaching them about life or the world. With students, discuss the variety of lessons they learn as you share *Hair Love*.	**Strengthening Ideas** Writers craft engaging beginnings such as establishing a situation, introducing a character, or providing precise descriptions to give the reader a clear picture of a real or an imagined experience. Matthew Cherry and Vashti Harrison begin *Hair Love* by introducing Zuri with rhythmic language and beautiful illustrations about hair. Encourage students to try similar techniques as they revisit a piece to try out a new, engaging beginning.
Evaluating Illustrations Readers notice how illustrations can add to or reflect the theme of a text. Invite students to go back to revisit Vashti Harrison's illustrations to share their thoughts about images that best contribute to their interpretations about the story. Ask readers what meaning they place on the images of Zuri making cards and the welcome sign in the final illustration of *Hair Love*.	**Exploring Characters** Writers include minor characters whose actions and dialogue add detail to the story. Discuss the role Zuri's dad plays in *Hair Love* and consider ways students can write background characters into their own stories to help their readers better understand the main character and plot.

LITERACY SNAPSHOTS IDEAS TO ADOPT OR ADAPT

Students can explore themes and life lessons found in their books using six-word memoirs, a unique storytelling form that synthesizes information (Gallagher 2011).

Invite students to share their interpretations of messages from books by sketching about quotes or lines that illustrate the big ideas. This model demonstrates using personal connections to infer the theME (messages to ME) from Lynda Mullaly Hunt's *Fish in a Tree*.

CONTINUING CONVERSATIONS ADDITIONAL HEARTPRINT CONNECTIONS

Mommy's Khimar by Jamilah Thompkins-Bigelow, illustrations by Ebony Glenn

Mommy's Khimar is another celebration of a relationship between a parent and child. With its expressive text and joyful images, *Mommy's Khimar* can serve as a mentor text for writing personal narrative, poetry, or essays about those objects that connect us to memories with people we love.

Real Sisters Pretend by Megan Dowd Lambert, illustrated by Nicole Tadgell

This loving story is told through the conversation (speech bubbles) between two sisters as they discuss being family, adopted sisters with different birth parents. A beautiful illustration of sibling relationships that also highlights a loving family with two moms, this empowering book will spark connections about love that exists and extends beyond families to relationships of all kinds.

A Hand to Hold by Zetta Elliott, illustrated by Purple Wong

A little girl loves the comfort she finds in holding her daddy's hands. She doesn't want to let go even for the start of school. In a *Hand to Hold*, Zetta Elliot shares an important lesson: "You have to keep your hands open if you want to grab something new." This heartprint book will stir conversations about finding our inner strengths and knowing who we can lean on.

CONTINUING CONNECTIONS MORE LAYERS FOR LEARNING TOGETHER

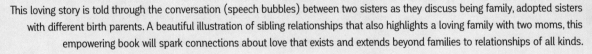

Books are most empowering when readers are inspired to imagine themselves as heroes through personal connections to the story. This is why it's so important for the books we share to mirror our students' lives and experiences. Take a moment to reflect on titles from your classroom libraries, book-of-the month choices, and recent read-alouds, paying special attention to inclusivity. As you evaluate your selections, ask yourself: *What messages does this book send? Whose voices are valued? Whose experiences are missing? How can this book speak to and empower our community of learners?*

LITERACY AS POWER WITH *MY PEN*

HEARTPRINT BOOK: *My Pen* by Christopher Myers

ABOUT THE BOOK: Written by the son of children's book author Walter Dean Myers, Christopher Myers shares a message narrated by an unnamed young artist who reflects on all of the power and possibilities that exist in a pen. The narrator talks directly to the reader with a powerful message about all the ways we can create and celebrate communication of ideas.

LIFE LAYERS ♥ INVITATIONS TO SHARE CONNECTIONS, CARES, AND CONCERNS

Through poetic verse and illustrations, words and images in *My Pen* celebrate all that is possible through writing, drawing, and using one's voice. Read this book to spark conversations about the marks of men and women whose words have impacted our world and empower all students to discover, create, and share their words.

Discussion Possibilities

- Invite students to discuss the phrases and images that resonated with them from *My Pen* and brainstorm how they can use their words and talents to inspire others or to facilitate change.
- Suggest your learners discuss the strong connection between reading, writing, and art in this text, specifically considering Myers's use of black-and-white sketches to evoke images of a sketchbook or notebook.
- Ask students to discuss the possibilities and inspiration they could find from Christopher Myers's ideas and share the ways they can or already do use their notebooks.

LITERACY CONNECTIONS 👥 POSSIBILITIES FOR NURTURING OUR READERS AND WRITERS

Based on the needs of your students and their instructional goals, consider the following possibilities for layering in reading and writing connections to complement your workshop, small-group, or individual conversations.

As a Reader	As a Writer
Writing About Reading Readers write about reading to reflect and identify key ideas. After reading *My Pen*, demonstrate how students can respond to texts they are reading through words or sketches.	**Developing Ideas** Writers borrow ideas and inspiration from texts. Students could reflect on Christopher Myers's statement about "the million worlds" that live inside their pens that can inspire a variety of possible topics to write about.
Analyzing Texts Readers think critically about how central ideas are connected across a text, including the ways they connect back to the title. After reading *My Pen*, help students reflect on the varied interpretations of a pen, how it can "tap-dance on the sky" and how these descriptions add to the overall message of the book. Suggest students revisit other lines that resonated with them and share how they enhanced their understanding of its theme.	**Exploring Figurative Language** Writers use symbols and figurative language to create images for their reader. Through personification, Christopher Myers uses his pen to represent bigger ideas about empowering oneself through art and creativity. Suggest students use personification as a figurative language device to refine a description in a piece they are working on.
Synthesizing Readers keep an eye out for the messages and big ideas an author wants them to learn. Explore the ways that Christopher Myers uses wide-ranging ideas and images to help students consider the power of the pen.	**Writing Opinions** Writers share their opinions citing examples to support their reasoning. Students might use writing to process strong feelings or personal opinions that emerge after considering Christopher Myers's sentiments on the power of words and writing.

LITERACY SNAPSHOTS IDEAS TO ADOPT OR ADAPT

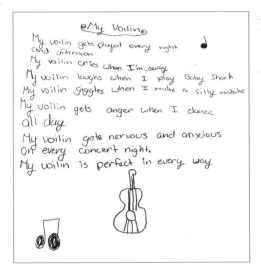

After reading *My Pen*, study personification as a way to share details about a variety of ideas. This fifth grader wrote about her violin using structure borrowed from Christopher Myers.

People robbed of their
Elegant past. Trying to
Evolve into the new
Law of the land. Forever
Enduring the pain that once was.

As we try to emulate patterns found in mentor texts, it's important to demonstrate our own writing lives. Mr. Peele models writing acrostic poems that go beyond initial letters to explore deeper meaning.

CONTINUING CONVERSATIONS 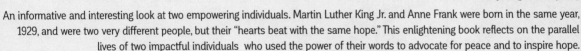 ADDITIONAL HEARTPRINT CONNECTIONS

Rise! From Caged Bird to Poet of the People, Maya Angelou by Bethany Hegedus, illustrated by Tonya Engel

In this engaging picture book biography of Maya Angelou, readers will learn about this powerful humanitarian, writer, activist, dancer, mother, and gift to our world whose poetry and life continue to inspire. This tribute to the Angelou's successes and the challenges she overcame will support discussions about finding courage and strength in the written word.

Martin & Anne: The Kindred Spirits of Dr. Martin Luther King, Jr. and Anne Frank by Nancy Churnin, illustrated by Yevgenia Nayberg

An informative and interesting look at two empowering individuals. Martin Luther King Jr. and Anne Frank were born in the same year, 1929, and were two very different people, but their "hearts beat with the same hope." This enlightening book reflects on the parallel lives of two impactful individuals who used the power of their words to advocate for peace and to inspire hope.

Malala Yousafzai: Warrior with Words by Karen Leggett Abouraya, illustrated by Susan Roth

Share this biography of the brave, determined girl who's empowered millions of children all over the world. Filled with quotes from her speeches and glimpses at her accomplishments, this exploration of Malala Yousafzai's young, impactful life focuses on the role literacy and education played in empowering her to be an agent of change.

CONTINUING CONNECTIONS MORE LAYERS FOR LEARNING TOGETHER

We're stronger writing teachers when we spend time writing regularly. In your next staff meeting, invite your colleagues to consider the role writing plays in our personal lives and how we can share our writing selves with our students. *Are we keeping our own writer's notebooks? Are we sharing our process as a model for students?* Bring your notebooks, share your ideas, do some free writing, and brainstorm how we can use our personal writing experiences to illustrate instructional principles for our students.

BEING TRUE TO ONESELF with *ANNIE'S PLAID SHIRT*

HEARTPRINT BOOK: *Annie's Plaid Shirt* by Stacy B. Davids, illustrated by Rachael Balsaitis

ABOUT THE BOOK: Annie loves her plaid shirt and wears it with pride every day. *Annie's Plaid Shirt* is about a comfortable, confident child who gets really uncomfortable when her mom insists she should wear a dress to her uncle's wedding.

LIFE LAYERS ♥ INVITATIONS TO SHARE CONNECTIONS, CARES, AND CONCERNS

Annie's Plaid Shirt addresses expectations and conforming to societal views. As readers explore Annie's plight, her story can be a vehicle to think about problem solving with others when there's a difference of opinions while honoring our own individuality.

Discussion Possibilities

- Encourage students to discuss some of their special things and why they are as important to them as Annie's feelings about her favorite plaid shirt.
- Share opinions about Annie's mom, Annie's brother, and Annie. Discuss how Annie was supported and how she was made to feel uncomfortable.
- Facilitate discussions as students share their thoughts about how Annie's dilemma was addressed and how they would have handled a similar situation.
- Help learners think about the concepts of originality, conformity, and independence and how they connect to individuality and honoring our preferences and sense of self.
- Discuss the ways Annie could inspire others.

LITERACY CONNECTIONS POSSIBILITIES FOR NURTURING OUR READERS AND WRITERS

Based on the needs of your students and their instructional goals, consider the following possibilities for layering in reading and writing connections to complement your workshop, small-group, or individual conversations.

As a Reader	As a Writer
Making Connections	**Writing Narratives**
Readers make connections from texts and express new understandings that result from similar experiences. Students could select examples from Annie's experience and reflect on how similar circumstances from their own lives support their understanding of her dilemma.	Writers use specific events to show significance or provide information in narratives in the same way Stacy B. Davids elaborates using Annie's different experiences with her mom and brother. As your students write about a personal memory, model how to brainstorm a list of possible events that can be included to add specific detail to a moment.
Analyzing Texts	**Elaborating**
Readers analyze texts in ways that affirm, challenge, or change their thoughts. Invite students to reflect on themes about tolerance and self-esteem in *Annie's Plaid Shirt* and discuss ways their thoughts about these themes were affirmed or challenged.	Writers reveal more about their characters by showing how they respond in certain situations. Invite writers to revisit a piece and try developing a character by adding detail through their actions, dialogue, or thinking in response to an event.
Critiquing Texts	**Writing in Response to Reading**
Readers consider specific decisions authors make and how those decisions affect their interpretation of the story. Help your students think about the ways the author shares multiple character perspectives in *Annie's Plaid Shirt*, why she chose to do this, and how it affects their understandings of the characters and their feelings and actions.	Writers get ideas about life lessons from stories and expand on those stories after looking at mentor texts. Consider ways students could use *Annie's Plaid Shirt* as a springboard to a written reflection or as inspiration to write about a significant occurrence from their own lives.

LITERACY SNAPSHOTS IDEAS TO ADOPT OR ADAPT

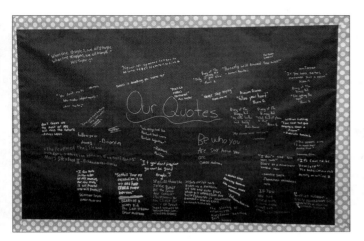

Invite your students to investigate specific issues of empowerment in books they are reading. These fifth graders explore titles from their classroom library and add quotes and original ideas that inspire deeper thinking.

For a closer look at empowered individuals, students used *Annie's Plaid Shirt* to reflect on characters critically, considering who has power and how this influences the characters, their relationships, or the events in the text.

CONTINUING CONVERSATIONS 📖 ADDITIONAL HEARTPRINT CONNECTIONS

Want to Play Trucks? by Ann Stott, illustrated by Bob Graham

Readers meet two friends playing together in the school sandbox. Jack likes trucks and Alex likes dolls. No problem. They can play with dolls that drive trucks! With connections to important messages about friendships and compromise, this book will spark conversations about recognizing we have control in our play spaces and choices about who and what we interact with.

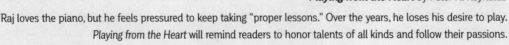

Playing from the Heart by Peter H. Reynolds

Raj loves the piano, but he feels pressured to keep taking "proper lessons." Over the years, he loses his desire to play. *Playing from the Heart* will remind readers to honor talents of all kinds and follow their passions.

Teddy's Favorite Toy by Christian Trimmer, illustrated by Madeline Valentine

Teddy's Favorite Toy is a sweet book that challenges gender norms in a nondidactic way. The main character, Teddy, has a treasured toy—a pink warrior princess with fierce style. When mom accidentally throws away his favorite toy, she goes to great lengths to retrieve it. In addition to validating the power of play and strong family relationships, the real message in the story is about the unconditional love between Teddy and his mom.

CONTINUING CONNECTIONS MORE LAYERS FOR LEARNING TOGETHER

To explore connections between learning, play, and social-emotional learning, gather a group of colleagues to read and study *Purposeful Play: A Teacher's Guide to Igniting Deep and Joyful Learning Across the Day* (Mraz, Porcelli, and Tyler 2016). In this engaging professional resource, the authors share research-driven methods for making playful interactions an integral part of your day.

PERSONALITY AND STYLE with *UNDER MY HIJAB*

HEARTPRINT BOOK: *Under My Hijab* by Hena Khan, illustrated by Aaliya Jaleel

ABOUT THE BOOK: A young girl narrates the story and introduces readers to important women in her family and community —each one unique and independent with her own personality and style. This informative, rhyming text explores powerful, independent women, while also giving a glimpse into the world of a proud Muslim American girl.

LIFE LAYERS ♥ INVITATIONS TO SHARE CONNECTIONS, CARES, AND CONCERNS

Books help us get to know more about cultures, communities, and characters. *Under My Hijab* is a discovery and celebration of self-expression and beauty, inside and out. Hena Khan includes bonus endnotes that teach about the cultural and religious significance of the hijab, while sharing an empowering story about strong women who have the confidence to meet their goals.

Discussion Possibilities

- Ask students to share their thoughts about the importance of being proud of items of ritual or cultural significance.
- Discuss Hena Khan's universal message and consider why she chose to showcase it through women from her culture and background.
- Invite students to discuss individuals who have influenced or inspired them in their lives.
- Ask students to reflect on what it means to have an individual style and why it is important to honor individuality in others.
- Take time to discuss the author's note and consider how it might confirm, challenge, or reinforce students' thinking about the content and messages in the book.

LITERACY CONNECTIONS POSSIBILITIES FOR NURTURING OUR READERS AND WRITERS

Based on the needs of your students and their instructional goals, consider the following possibilities for layering in reading and writing connections to complement your workshop, small-group, or individual conversations.

As a Reader	As a Writer
Thinking Beyond the Text Readers reflect on an illustrator's use of colors and symbols to support inferences. Ask students to consider the effectiveness of Aaliya Jaleel's artwork to explore social justice and equality. Remind students to support their ideas with evidence from the text.	**Developing Ideas** Writers develop ideas using multiple examples to communicate relevant, interesting information. Hena Khan uses scenes from women's lives to illustrate her message. Invite your writers to consider descriptive examples they could add using settings and scenarios to strengthen the message they are writing about.
Synthesizing Readers summarize and synthesize to connect information to new understandings. Invite your students to consider messages from *Under My Hijab*, and discuss how an author's experiences can influence our interpretations of a book.	**Analyzing Craft and Dialogue** Writers share details in their writing that provide deeper insights into their characters' motivations and emotions. Students could revisit the text and look for places where dialogue reveals more about the relationships and the various characters introduced in *Under My Hijab*. Then they could try this while adding dialogue to their own pieces.
Writing About Reading Readers write in response to reading to show evidence of their thinking. After sharing *Under My Hijab*, invite your students to record their own interpretations of the story, perhaps discussing connections to new or previous understandings.	**Revising Texts and Titles** Writers reflect on titles and how they connect to a book's message. Consider Hena Khan's title choice—*Under My Hijab*. Writers can share opinions about why she chose this title and then consider revising titles in their own writing to give their reader a hint to the big idea of their story.

LITERACY SNAPSHOTS IDEAS TO ADOPT OR ADAPT

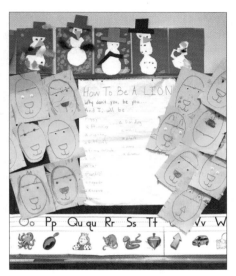

After discussing the empowering message to be whatever you want to be in *How to Be a Lion,* prekindergarten students shared animals they wish they could be and the powerful traits they admire.

As you explore themes of personality and individuality, writers might discuss their unique writing styles and some of their favorite pieces. Create a display where students can celebrate and reflect on what they have done as empowered writers.

CONTINUING CONVERSATIONS ADDITIONAL HEARTPRINT CONNECTIONS

How to Be a Lion by Ed Vere

This tale of unlikely friends, Marianne the duck and Leonard the lion, is charming. Leonard is ostracized for not being more like a lion. Leonard likes poetry, speaks softly, and is best friends with a duck. His pride of lions can't understand why he isn't fierce and frightening and why he wouldn't eat his friend, Marianne. After all, she is a duck. Share this with readers to explore the meaning of true friendship and the importance of being yourself.

Where Oliver Fits by Cale Atkinson

This charming story looks at Oliver, a puzzle piece who has always dreamed about where he will fit. Through trial and error and learning to be himself, Oliver learns that he doesn't have to try so hard to fit in.

A Moon for Moe and Mo by Jane Breskin Zalben, illustrated by Mehrdokht Amini

Readers are invited to take a look at the parallels and ensuing friendship of Moe and Mo, two boys with the same name who live in the same neighborhood and often get mistaken for twins. As their friendship grows, so does their understanding for their traditions, cultures, and celebrations. Readers will find endnotes with further explorations of Ramadan and Rosh Hashanah and learn about the ways the boys are even more alike than they think.

CONTINUING CONNECTIONS MORE LAYERS FOR LEARNING TOGETHER

 As a professional community, consider studying *Empowered Schools, Empowered Students: Creating Connected and Invested Learners* by Pernille Ripp (2015) to think about ways to engage all learners, give students a voice, and foster the individual talents and expertise of your colleagues.

POWER AND PRIDE with *YO SOY MUSLIM*

HEARTPRINT BOOK: *Yo Soy Muslim: A Father's Letter to His Daughter* by Mark Gonzales, illustrated by Mehrdokht Amini

ABOUT THE BOOK: Written as letter from a father to his daughter, Mark Gonzales dedicated *Yo Soy Muslim* to all children, so they would "know that they are loved." In his empowering messages, he shares advice and a promise as a parent to all children: to promote equity, to value others, and to celebrate all aspects of their multicultural origin and identity with pride. His story highlights the Muslim community as well as his Indigenous identity, with a message for all children.

LIFE LAYERS ♥ INVITATIONS TO SHARE CONNECTIONS, CARES, AND CONCERNS

Mark Gonzales's poetic verse can stimulate conversation in celebration of diversity, community, and individuality. Share this book as a vehicle to discuss the joy and power that come from having pride in one's identity, heritage, and faith. The elegant verse and rich illustrations in *Yo Soy Muslim* will inspire your readers and writers on their own journeys in life.

Discussion Possibilities

- ■ Invite your students to reflect on the author's decision to write in letter form to his daughter.
- ■ Consider the messages shared in this letter. Have students discuss what resonated with them the most.
- ■ Reflect with students on how we could use our words as a gift to our family or friends.
- ■ Invite children to discuss possibilities for creating something like the letter in the book to leave an inspiring message or demonstrate love for another person.
- ■ Lead a conversation about what messages students might want to share to empower others and how might they go about that.

LITERACY CONNECTIONS 👥 POSSIBILITIES FOR NURTURING OUR READERS AND WRITERS

Based on the needs of your students and their instructional goals, consider the following possibilities for layering in reading and writing connections to complement your workshop, small-group, or individual conversations.

As a Reader	As a Writer
Inferring Readers use words to create images. After exploring *Yo Soy Muslim*, suggest students examine how the figurative descriptions influence their inferences. Students could share specific examples to support their interpretations of the lines "Your smile will touch the sky" and you will "learn to count the stars like dreams."	**Exploring Language** Writers use second person when they want to engage readers more intimately. Mark Gonzales uses emotive messages as he gives advice to his daughter, addressing her directly in his letter. Students may elect to include text and language that speaks directly to their readers to inform or advise them about a topic.
Analyzing Word Choice Readers reflect on word choice and titles and think about how they connect to a book's message. Mark Gonzales repeats the phrase "Yo soy Muslim" throughout the text. Ask students to share their opinions and discuss the ways a repeated line reinforces an empowering message.	**Exploring Figurative Language** Writers use figurative language to create images and give readers new insights about ideas. Invite your students to revisit the empowering similes Mark Gonzales uses, such as his message to "learn to count the stars like dreams" and to consider ways they can use similes to describe comparisons.
Analyzing Book and Print Features Consider sharing the dedication with your students: "To all children—may you know you are loved." Prompt students to reflect on how this message echoes the central theme of the book.	**Analyzing Craft Choices** Inspired by Mark Gonzales, prompt your students to consider letters they could write to themselves or to other individuals to provide advice, to share their beliefs, or to amplify their voice and message.

LITERACY SNAPSHOTS IDEAS TO ADOPT OR ADAPT

Encourage your community members to craft a letter, draw a picture, or write a poem to share advice and empower others. Using a line from *Yo Soy Muslim*, this student created a message for a classmate—"Know You Are Wondrous."

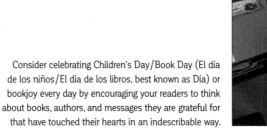

Consider celebrating Children's Day/Book Day (El día de los niños/El día de los libros, best known as Día) or bookjoy every day by encouraging your readers to think about books, authors, and messages they are grateful for that have touched their hearts in an indescribable way.

CONTINUING CONVERSATIONS 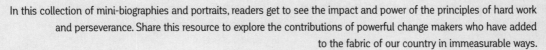 ADDITIONAL HEARTPRINT CONNECTIONS

The Very Last Castle by Travis Jonker, illustrated by Mark Pett

Written by school librarian Travis Jonker, this is a story about a young girl named Ibb who is brave and curious. Ibb lives in a town with the very last castle and a very ominous guard. The people in her town are quite content not knowing what is on the other side of the castle but not Ibb. Each day Ibb passes the guard, she tries to catch his eye because she really needs to know what is behind that gate. Jonker's *The Very Last Castle* speaks to empowerment in a variety of ways and can spark conversations about taking risks and being brave.

First Generation: 36 Trailblazing Immigrants and Refugees Who Make America Great by Sandra Neil Wallace and Rich Wallace, illustrated by Agata Nowicka

In this collection of mini-biographies and portraits, readers get to see the impact and power of the principles of hard work and perseverance. Share this resource to explore the contributions of powerful change makers who have added to the fabric of our country in immeasurable ways.

The Undefeated by Kwame Alexander, illustrated by Kadir Nelson

Kwame Alexander wrote and originally performed this poem for ESPN's The Undefeated (its premier social media platform), which explores the intersection of race, sports, and culture. Alexander's poem and performance represents an ode to the resilience of black American life. Now paired with Kadir Nelson's art, the text and images show powerful portraits.

CONTINUING CONNECTIONS MORE LAYERS FOR LEARNING TOGETHER

Children's book author Pat Mora is the founder of Children's Day/Book Day (El día de los niños/El día de los libros [Día]), which is celebrated April 30 (and every day of the year) to encourage bookjoy and the power of literacy in our lives. Check out her website to find more information and resources about how to get involved in this celebration and continue conversations about her mission to motivate children and their families to be readers.

FINDING STRENGTH AND RESILIENCY with *MANGO MOON*

HEARTPRINT BOOK: *Mango Moon* by Diane de Anda, illustrated by Sue Cornelison

ABOUT THE BOOK: In this timely and emotive book about a family torn apart by deportation, a young girl, Maricela, tells the story in flashback about how everything changes after the day her papi is taken away. The story reveals the strength, love, and resilience it takes for families to overcome challenging situations but also sends the message that it is all right to cry.

LIFE LAYERS INVITATIONS TO SHARE CONNECTIONS, CARES, AND CONCERNS

This resilient story will resonate with children as they consider themes of love, loss, or challenges of any kind and will build understanding and empathy for those experiences. Share this story to help all students gain appreciation for issues that might be out of their control, with an emphasis on finding hope. Reflect with your readers on the ways love stays strong "under the same mango moon."

Discussion Possibilities

- Reflect with your students on the impact of the emotions and feelings represented in the illustrations.
- Guide students to consider the meaning and applications of love being shared under the same (mango) moon.
- Encourage readers to ask questions and make connections to current events while being sensitive to the real concerns and fears that many students may have about deportation, loss, or separation of any kind.
- Talk about the message that love can exist no matter where you are.

LITERACY CONNECTIONS 👥 POSSIBILITIES FOR NURTURING OUR READERS AND WRITERS

Based on the needs of your students and their instructional goals, consider the following possibilities for layering in reading and writing connections to complement your workshop, small-group, or individual conversations.

As a Reader	As a Writer
Analyzing Inferring Illustrations Readers use information found in the text and images to enhance their understanding about an idea. Invite your students to reflect on the messages revealed through the careful placement of the mango moon throughout the story. Prompt your students to discuss the significance of the moon and how it adds to the feeling or the mood of this story.	**Writing Narratives to Develop Real or Imagined Ideas** Writers choose images and ideas to express meaning. Think about the ways that Diane de Anda includes the mango moon as a focal point of the story. Invite your students to revise a piece or start something new using a symbol, through illustrations or words, as an important part of a story they are telling or to extend an idea.
Reading to Grow Ideas Readers are often inspired to continue learning about a topic after reading about it. After sharing *Mango Moon*, invite readers to research and read across texts (using articles, speeches, videos, and images) to deepen their understanding of issues presented in *Mango Moon*.	**Writing Informational Texts** Writers gather information from a variety of sources to research a topic and look more closely through a specific lens of an idea. Students might be motivated to research facts, statistics, or quotes to write about topics presented in *Mango Moon*.
Analyzing Book and Print Features Readers explore additional information from text features to gain insight before and after reading a text. Ask your students to reflect on the dedication from author Diane de Anda—"To all the families who suffer forced separation, whose love reaches beyond borders"—and how this resonates in the message of the text.	**Writing in Response to Reading** Writers use different formats to communicate, such as emails, texts, letters, and social media. Inspired by the letter writing in *Mango Moon*, invite your writers to consider drafting a letter to someone they miss or appreciate.

LITERACY SNAPSHOTS IDEAS TO ADOPT OR ADAPT

To extend the conversation and connect the ways we can develop our understanding using symbols, images, and messages, students reflected on the dandelions in *Carmela Full of Wishes*. Inspired by the text students discussed their own wishes for all families.

Students can connect their learning to real-world issues by studying additional resources about current events. Maria Fabrizio's Wordless News (wordlessnews.com) provides images without text and connects those images to a news article to encourage readers to reflect on what's happening in the world. Reflect on her thought-provoking imagery to add to conversations about immigration, deportation, and the rights of all individuals.

CONTINUING CONVERSATIONS ADDITIONAL HEARTPRINT CONNECTIONS

Carmela Full of Wishes by Matt de la Peña, illustrated by Christian Robinson

With messages of hope, belonging, and caring, readers meet a little girl out celebrating her birthday with her sibling when she makes a special wish for her father because he's not able to be with her to celebrate. Author Matt de la Peña wrote this story to illustrate that "immigration is an American issue" and to celebrate love, loyalty, and the reality that we are not alone. Readers of all ages will appreciate illustrator Christian Robinson's engaging artwork with its nod to traditional Mexican culture with cut paper designs (*papel picado*).

Adrian Simcox Does NOT Have a Horse by Marcy Campbell, illustrated by Corinna Luyken

Share this more complex story as a vehicle for conversations about respect, kindness, and the dangers of judging others. Readers hear about Adrian Simcox, who no one believes has a horse. Sadly, Adrian is bullied because of his poverty. Read to spark reflections on empathy, respect for others, and the power of one's imagination.

Let's Go See Papá! by Lawrence Schimel, illustrated by Alba Marina Rivera

This story is told from the perspective of a young girl who is also separated from her dad when he leaves to work in the United States to save money to bring her family over with him. Share this book to explore a different point of view and connections to the things families do for love.

CONTINUING CONNECTIONS MORE LAYERS FOR LEARNING TOGETHER

 Share this inspirational video where author and illustrator Christian Robinson talks about the story behind the story in *Carmela Full of Wishes* and discusses the importance of appreciating and sharing all stories.

MAKING YOUR MARK with *THE DOT*

HEARTPRINT BOOK: *The Dot* by Peter H. Reynolds

ABOUT THE BOOK: The messages in Peter H. Reynolds's books will no doubt leave imprints on your heart. Vashti is upset and thinks she isn't a very good artist. At the end of art class, she leaves her paper blank. Thanks to the support of a caring teacher, Vashti is encouraged to sign it, make a mark, and celebrate her work. That message has ripple effects as Vashti is empowered to express herself and grow her talents.

LIFE LAYERS ♥ INVITATIONS TO SHARE CONNECTIONS, CARES, AND CONCERNS

With powerful lessons in art and in life, *The Dot* encourages an appreciation of our individual talents, empowering readers to view themselves as amazing creators. Share this book with children to spark conversations about expressing themselves and connecting with others.

Discussion Possibilities

- Aid students in discussing their own difficult times, how they felt, and how they reacted.
- Discuss with learners how they felt about what Vashti's teacher did. Ask them to talk about individuals in their lives who celebrate students' talents or help students see their hidden strengths.
- Ask students to reflect on the ending of the book and to consider advice they might also give to friends who, like Vashti, need to be lifted up.
- Extend the conversation to discuss situations in which we can lift ourselves up and how we might do that.

LITERACY CONNECTIONS 👥 POSSIBILITIES FOR NURTURING OUR READERS AND WRITERS

Based on the needs of your students and their instructional goals, consider the following possibilities for layering in reading and writing connections to complement your workshop, small-group, or individual conversations.

As a Reader	As a Writer
Inferring Character Traits	**Analyzing Ideas and Information**
Readers pay attention to actions of the characters and how they respond to situations to make inferences about those characters. In *The Dot*, Vashti's teacher refers to her as an artist, even with a blank page. Readers can explore what this says about her and can discuss their inferences about her influence on her students.	Writers borrow from models found in texts such as craft moves, word choice, and style to lift the level of their own writing. Peter H. Reynolds intentionally includes inner dialogue to reflect Vashti's emotions. Work with students to brainstorm possible ways to craft dialogue to describe a character's feelings.
Writing About Reading	**Analyzing Conclusions**
Readers can express their thinking about the texts and cite text evidence to support their ideas. After reading *The Dot*, students might respond in writing to show their understanding about what it means to make one's mark. Suggest students write about scenes or lines from the book that reveal more about the theme.	Writers think about the ending of their texts and consider ways they might leave messages for their readers, such as to end with an impactful thought or inspirational idea. Students might discuss the effectiveness of Peter H. Reynolds's decision to conclude with a circular ending (the story ends the way it began) and how they might use this technique in their own writing.
Analyzing Illustrations	**Exploring Craft Lessons**
Readers infer how writers and illustrators use specific words and images to communicate a message. Consider the ways that the art in *The Dot* provides meaning and adds to the story. Prompt readers to go back and look for evidence about the messages those images reveal.	Writers use a range of words, sketches, and/or colors to convey a mood or an effect for their readers. Highlight the deliberate use of colors as you share the artwork with young writers and help them consider ways to include images or graphics to complement the text in a piece of their own writing.

LITERACY SNAPSHOTS IDEAS TO ADOPT OR ADAPT

Invite your students to participate in Dot Day. Encourage them to share their talents. As part of the celebration of self-discovery, study simple dots that—depending on perspective—can be so much more.

To extend the theme of empowerment from *The Dot*, suggest students incorporate dots into messages such as images, poetry, or other forms of expression. Here, a student shares a message about using your voice for power.

CONTINUING CONVERSATIONS 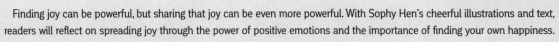 ADDITIONAL HEARTPRINT CONNECTIONS

Two by Kathryn Otoshi

Like Peter H. Reynolds, Kathryn Otoshi's picture books capture powerful messages with simple, yet big ideas. In *Two*, readers see numbers personified, displaying social-emotional and cognitive behaviors. The numbers all "count on each other" and are in harmony until two becomes the odd one out. Share this book to discuss how we all have the power within ourselves to speak up and the importance of surrounding ourselves with friends who will help us be our very best selves.

Pass It On by Sophy Henn

Finding joy can be powerful, but sharing that joy can be even more powerful. With Sophy Hen's cheerful illustrations and text, readers will reflect on spreading joy through the power of positive emotions and the importance of finding your own happiness.

Gracias/Thanks by Pat Mora, illustrated by John Parra

This bilingual (Spanish and English) text explores a young boy's expression of gratitude and encourages readers to be mindful of the little things that bring us joy. When we express gratitude, we strengthen our hearts and our minds, as well as the hearts and minds of others.

CONTINUING CONNECTIONS MORE LAYERS FOR LEARNING TOGETHER

Peter H. Reynolds's influence has touched the hearts, minds, and hands of educators and children all over the world. His work inspired an international movement, Dot Day, which is celebrated around September 15-ish (which is a nod to another Reynolds well-loved title) where people promise to express themselves, celebrate creativity, build community, and share their gifts. Visit the Dot Club website to learn more about how you and your students can participate in the festivities!

A VISION FOR A BETTER WORLD with *IMAGINE*

HEARTPRINT BOOK: *Imagine* by John Lennon, illustrated by Jean Jullien

ABOUT THE BOOK: In partnership with Amnesty International, French artist Jean Jullien released a picture book version of John Lennon's iconic song, "Imagine." With the same messages of love, peace, and harmony, Jullien's interpretation includes vibrant artwork and readers to illustrate a bird spreading the allegorical message of peace and kindness to birds of every size, shape, and color.

LIFE LAYERS ♥ INVITATIONS TO SHARE CONNECTIONS, CARES, AND CONCERNS

Pairing qualities of the CARE elements—*community, agency, respect,* and *empowerment*—with stories extends our shared, collaborative community experiences and reinforces powerful message for learners in literacy and in life. Read *Imagine* to invite your students to share their interpretations of the lyrics expressed in this song, and suggest they create their own anthem to acknowledge that we all have the power to imagine a better world.

Discussion Possibilities

- Consider sharing the original song, "Imagine," before and after reading to support inferences with the lyrics and the texts.
- Invite students to reflect on big ideas associated with *Imagine*, such as *What can we do to make the world, our school, our class a better place?*
- Suggest learners curate a list to describe and discuss the qualities of a better world they might be imagining.
- Encourage students to talk about one thing that they are hopeful for as they share what they imagine.

LITERACY CONNECTIONS 👥 POSSIBILITIES FOR NURTURING OUR READERS AND WRITERS

Based on the needs of your students and their instructional goals, consider the following possibilities for layering in reading and writing connections to complement your workshop, small-group, or individual conversations.

As a Reader	As a Writer
Inferring from Illustrations Readers pay attention to the influence of design elements, images, colors, and symbols that an artist uses to communicate meaning. After reading *Imagine*, invite your students to reflect on how the connected images help them develop further theories about the book's central message.	**Analyzing Craft Lessons** Illustrators select images and symbols to enhance meaning for readers. Ask students to share their thoughts about how Jean Jullien uses a bird as a symbol or a recurring idea and to consider using these techniques with words or illustrations in a piece they are working on.
Analyzing Texts Readers analyze texts to develop ideas and interpretations about what they have read. As your students reflect on the messages and lyrics in *Imagine*, discuss the ideas they agree or disagree with and encourage them to reflect on specific words as evidence to explain their thinking further.	**Finding Ideas** Writers find inspiration for writing as they make personal connections to the text and images they encounter in the books they read. As your students examine lyrics, word choice, phrases, and illustrations found in Jean Jullien's *Imagine*, invite them to use connections as a stimulus for writing.
Writing About Reading Readers write to show their thinking about reading texts and images. Together, use a T-chart to chart out lines from *Imagine* and the inferences they prompt. Suggest students use this method to stop and jot when they want to process inferences they're making in response to other texts as well.	**Writing for Change** John Lennon's song is seen as an anthem for peace. Artists often serve as role models for activism and may include messages in their works (fiction, informational texts, art, music, or poetry) to inspire others. Suggest students create their own expression of an idea that might invite discussions and action from other readers.

LITERACY SNAPSHOTS IDEAS TO ADOPT OR ADAPT

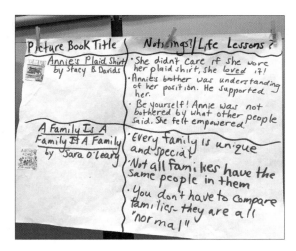

Invite students to collect and display titles and noticings that reflect important messages that impact their lives.

Consider creating a collage—a mural of hands coming together to commit to making your class and our community a better place. These students were inspired by Pink's "A Million Dreams" to create an image of their individual handprints as a pledge: "However big. However small. Let me be part of it all!"

CONTINUING CONVERSATIONS 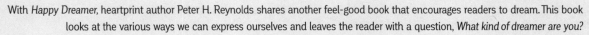 ADDITIONAL HEARTPRINT CONNECTIONS

Listen by Holly M. McGhee, illustrated by Pascal Lemaître

Holly M. McGhee and Pascal Lemaître collaborated on *Come with Me*, another heartprint book that demonstrates the power of what's possible when we care. Share this lyrical picture book as a vehicle to discuss listening with our hearts to nurture empathy and compassion.

Happy Dreamer by Peter H. Reynolds

With *Happy Dreamer*, heartprint author Peter H. Reynolds shares another feel-good book that encourages readers to dream. This book looks at the various ways we can express ourselves and leaves the reader with a question, *What kind of dreamer are you?*

Just Read! by Lori Degman, illustrated by Victoria Tentler-Krylov

Lori Degman's *Just Read!* is a tribute to books and reading. Through uplifting rhyming texts and joyful illustrations, readers encounter other readers to learn where and what they read. Share this book to reiterate connections to the power of books and stories.

CONTINUING CONNECTIONS MORE LAYERS FOR LEARNING TOGETHER

To encourage more reflective thinking about social issues, you might try showcasing one inspirational quote a day. Set aside time for students to share their connections or respond to the quote in writing. Visit the PassItOn website for resources that include motivational quotes that can spark conversations.

PROFESSIONAL BIBLIOGRAPHY

Adichie, Chimamanda Ngozi. 2009. "The Danger of a Single Story" Ted Talk. https://www.ted.com /talks/chimamanda_ngozi_adichie_the_danger_of_a_single_story/up-next

———. 2018. "Opening General Session." National Council Teachers of English NCTE Annual Convention.November. Houston, Texas.

Alexander, Kwame. 2015. "Newbery Medal Acceptance Speech." Speech presented at the American Library Association Annual Conference, San Francisco, CA, June 28, 2015. https://alair.ala.org/bitstream/handle/11213/7974/2015-newbery-speechpdf?sequence =1&isAllowed=y.

Allington, Richard L. and Rachel E. Gabriel. 2012. "Every Child, Every Day." *Journal of Educational Leadership* 69 (6): 10–15. http://www.ascd.org/publications/educational-leadership/mar12 /vol69/num06/Every-Child,-Every-Day.aspx.

Atwell, Nancie. 2014. *In the Middle: New Understanding About Writing, Reading, and Learning,* Third Edition. Portsmouth, NH: Heinemann.

Atwell, Nancie, and Anne Atwell Merkel. 2016. *The Reading Zone: How to Help Kids Become Passionate, Skilled, Habitual, Critical Readers.* 2nd ed. New York: Scholastic.

Banks, James A. 2007. *Educating Citizens in a Multicultural Society.* New York: Teachers College Press.

Banks, James A. and Michelle Tucker. 1998. "Multiculturalism's Five Dimensions." *NEA Today Online*: https://learning.educatetogether.ie/pluginfile.php/17421/mod_resource/content/1/Five Dimensions.pdf. Accessed March 2020.

Barrett, Peter, Fay Davies, Yufan Zhang, and Lucinda Barrett. 2015. "The Impact of Classroom Design on Pupils' Learning." Summary of Report: https://core.ac.uk/downloadpdf/42587797.pdf.

Beck, Isabel L., and Margaret G. McKeown. 2001. "Text Talk: Capturing the Benefits of Read-Aloud Experiences for Young Children." *The Reading Teacher* 55 (1) : 10–20.

Bennett-Armistead, V. Susan, and Nell Duke. 2003. *Reading and Writing Informational Text in the Primary Grades.* New York: Scholastic.

Bennett-Armistead, V. Susan, Nell Duke, and Annie M. Moses. 2007. *Beyond Bedtime Stories*. New York: Scholastic.

Bishop, Rudine Sims. 1990. "Mirrors, Windows, and Sliding Glass Doors." *Perspectives, Choosing an Using Books for the Classroom* 6 (3).

Boogren, Tina. 2018. *Take Time for You: Self-Care Action Plans for Educators.* Bloomington, IN: Solution Tree Press.

Bowie, Liz. 2018. "7 Ways to Use StickTogether Mosaic Posters in Your Library." Ideas + Inspiration. January 11. https://ideas.demco.com/blog/7-ways-sticktogether-posters-library/.

Burkins, Jan Miller, and Melody M. Croft. 2017. *Preventing Misguided Reading: Next Generation Guided Reading Strategies.* Portland, ME: Stenhouse.

Cassetta, Gianna, and Brook Sawyer. 2013. *No More Taking Away Recess: And Other Problematic Discipline Practices.* Portsmouth, NH: Heinemann.

Calkins, Lucy. 2000. *The Art of Teaching Reading.* New York: Pearson.

Charney, Ruth. 1992. *Teaching Children to Care: Management in the Responsive Classroom.* Greenfield, MA: Northeast Foundation for Children.

Christensen, Linda. 2009. *Teaching for Joy and Justice: Re-imagining the Language Arts Classroom.* Milwaukee, WI: Rethinking Schools Publication.

Clay, Marie M. 1991. *Becoming Literate: The Construction of Inner Control.* Portsmouth, NH: Heinemann.

Collaborative for Academic, Social and Emotional Learning (CASEL). 2013. Yale Center for Emotional Intelligence, New Haven, CT. https://casel.org/.

Cooperative Children's Book Center. 2018. "Publishing Statistics on Children's/YA Books About People of Color and First/Native Nations and by People of Color and First/Native Nations Authors and Illustrators." CCBC. Updated November 21.   http://ccbc.education.wisc.edu /books/pcstats.asp.

Corrie, Jalissa, "The Diveristy Gap in Children's Book Publishing," *The Open Book (blog)*, Lee and Low Books, May 10, 2018. https://blog.leeandlow.com/2018/05/10/the-diversity-gap -in-childrens-book-publishing-2018/.

Curby, Timothy W., Sara E. Rimm-Kaufman, and Tashia Abry. 2013. "Do Emotional Support and Classroom Organization Earlier in the Year Set the Stage for Higher Quality Instruction?" *Journal of School Psychology* 51 (5): 557–569. https://www.ncbi.nlm.nih.gov/pubmed/24060059.

Daniels, Harvey, and Sara K. Ahmed. 2015. *Upstanders: How to Engage Middle School Hearts and Minds with Inquiry.* Portsmouth, NH: Heinemann.

de la Peña, Matt. 2018a. "Finding Truths in Fiction." Penguin panel. National Council Teachers of English, Baltimore, MD. NCTE November 17, 2018.

——. 2018b. "Why We Shouldn't Shield Children from Darkness." *Time,* January 9.

Diller, Debbie. 2008. *Spaces & Places: Designing Classrooms for Literacy.* Portland, ME: Stenhouse.

Dweck, Carol. 2016. *Mindset: The New Psychology of Success.* New York: Ballantine Books.

Fountas, Irene C., and Gay Su Pinnell. 2006. *Teaching for Comprehending and Fluency: Thinking, Talking, and Writing About Reading*, K–8. Portsmouth, NH: Heinemann.

———. 2012. "Guided Reading: The Romance and the Reality." *The Reading Teacher* 66 (4): 268–284.

Gallagher, Kelly. 2011. *Write Like This: Teaching Real-World Writing Through Modeling & Mentor Texts*. Portland, ME: Stenhouse.

Gay, Geneva. 2010. *Culturally Responsive Teaching: Theory, Research, and Practice*, Second Edition. New York: Teachers College Press.

Graves, Donald H. 2001. *The Energy to Teach*. Portsmouth, NH: Heinemann.

Harwayne, Shelley. 1999. *Going Public: Priorities and Practices at the Manhattan New School*. Portsmouth, NH: Heinemann.

Heard, Georgia. 2013. *Finding the Heart of Nonfiction: Teaching 7 Essential Craft Tools with Mentor Texts*. Portsmouth, NH: Heinemann.

———. 2016. *Heart Maps: Helping Students Create and Craft Authentic Writing*. Portsmouth, NH: Heinemann.

Henderson, Anne T., Karen L. Mapp, Vivian R. Jonson, and Don Davies. 2007. *Beyond the Bake Sale: The Essential Guide to Family/School Partnerships*. New York: New Press.

Hertz, Christine, and Kristine Mraz. 2015. *A Mindset for Learning: Teaching the Traits of Joyful, Independent Growth*. Portsmouth, NH: Heinemann.

———. 2018. *Kids First from Day One: A Teacher's Guide to Today's Classroom*. Portsmouth, NH: Heinemann.

Huyck, David, and Sarah Park Dahlen. 2019. "Diversity in Children's Books." *sarahpark.com* (blog). June 19. https://readingspark.wordpress.com/2019/06/19/picture-this-diversity-in-childrens -books-2018-infographic/.

Immordino-Yang, Mary Helen, and Antonio Damasio. 2007. "We Feel, Therefore We Learn: The Relevance of Affective and Social Neuroscience to Education." *Mind Brain Education* (1): 3–10.

Ivey, Gay, and Peter H. Johnston. 2015. "Engaged Reading as a Collaborative Transformative Practice." *Journal of Literacy Research* 47 (3): 297–327. https://doi.org/10.1177 /1086296x15619731.

Johnston, Peter H. 2004. *Choice Words: How Our Language Affects Children's Learning*. Portland, ME: Stenhouse.

———. 2012. *Opening Minds: Using Language to Change Lives*. Portland, ME: Stenhouse.

Johnston, Peter, Gay Ivey, and Amy Faulkner. 2012. "Talking in Class: Remembering What Is Important About Classroom Talk." *The Reading Teacher* 65 (4): 232–237.

Keene, Ellin Oliver. 2012. *Talk About Understanding: Rethinking Classroom Talk to Enhance Comprehension*. Portsmouth, NH: Heinemann.

Klass, Perry. 2018. "Reading Aloud to Young Children Has Benefits for Behavior and Attention." *New York Times*, April 16.

Ladson-Billings, Gloria. 1995. "But That's Just Good Teaching! The Case for Culturally Relevant Pedagogy." *Theory into Practice* 34 (3): 159–165. http://www.jstor.org/stable/1476635.

Layne, Steven L. 2015. *In Defense of Read-Aloud: Sustaining Best Practice*. Portland, ME: Stenhouse.

Lesesne, Teri. 2006. *Naked Reading: Uncovering What Tweens Need to Become Lifelong Readers*. Portland, ME: Stenhouse.

Lickona, Thomas. 1991. *Educating for Character: How Our Schools Can Teach Respect and Responsibility*. New York: Bantam.

Mar, Raymond A. 2018. "Stories and the Promotion of Social Cognition." *Associations for Psychological Science*" 27 (4): 257–262.

Maunders, Kathryn and Paul Montgomery. 2015. "The Effectiveness of Creative Bibliotherapy for Internalizing, Externalizing, and Prosocial Behaviors in Children: A Systematic Literature Review." *Children and Youth Services Review* 55: 37–47.

Miller, Debbie. 2016. *Reading with Meaning: Teaching Comprehension in the Primary Grades*. 2nd ed. Portland, ME: Stenhouse.

Miller, Donalyn. 2009. *The Book Whisperer: Awakening the Inner Reader in Every Child*. San Francisco: Jossey-Bass.

Mraz, Kristine, Alison Porcelli, and Cheryl Tyler. 2016. *Purposeful Play: A Teacher's Guide to Igniting Deep and Joyful Learning Across the Day*. Portsmouth, NH: Heinemann.

Nel, Philip. 2017. *Was the Cat in the Hat Black? The Hidden Racism of Children's Literature, and the Need for Diverse Books*. Oxford: Oxford University Press.

Noddings, Nel. 1984. *Caring a Feminine Approach to Ethics and Education*. Berkley and Los Angeles: University of California Press.

——. 2005. *The Challenge to Care in Schools: An Alternative Approach to Education*. New York: Teachers College Press.

Noddings, Nel, and Laurie Brooks. 2017. *Teaching Controversial Issues: The Case for Critical Thinking and Moral Commitment in the Classroom*. New York: Teachers College Press.

Nora, Julie, and Jana Echevarría. 2016. *No More Low Expectations for English Learners*. Portsmouth, NH: Heinemann.

Oatley, Keith. 2011. *Such Stuff as Dreams: The Psychology of Fiction*. West Sussex, United Kingdom: Wiley-Blackwell.

Obama, Michelle. 2018. *Becoming*. New York: Viking.

Paris, Django, and H. Samy Alim. 2017. *Culturally Sustaining Pedagogies: Teaching and Learning for Justice in a Changing World*. New York: Teachers College Press.

"Peck Publishing Statistics on Children's/YA Books about People of Color and First/Native Nations and by People of Color and First/Native Nations Authors and Illustrators." n.d. Children's Books by and About People of Color. http://ccbc.education.wisc.edu/books/pcstats.asp.

Peck, M. Scott. 1998. *The Different Drum: Community Making and Peace.* New York: Touchstone.

Peterson, Ralph. 1992. *Life in a Crowded Place: Making a Learning Community.* Portsmouth, NH: Heinemann.

Ray, Katie Wood. 2006. *Study Driven: A Framework for Planning Units of Study in the Writing Workshop.* Portsmouth, NH: Heinemann.

Rief, Linda. 2006. *Read Write Teach: Choice and Challenge in the Reading-Writing Workshop.* Portsmouth, NH: Heinemann.

Ripp, Pernille. 2015. *Empowered Schools, Empowered Students: Creating Connected and Invested Learners.* Thousand Oaks, CA: Corwin.

Roberts, Frederika, and Elizabeth Wright. 2018. *Character Toolkit for Teachers.* London: Jessica Kingsley.

Rochman, Hazel. 1993. *Against Borders: Promoting Books for a Multicultural World.* Chicago: American Library Association.

Rosenblatt, Louise, M. 1978. *The Reader, The Text, The Poem: The Transactional Theory of the Literary Work,* Carbondale, IL: Southern Illinois University Press.

———. 1988. *Writing and Reading: The Transactional Theory.* Champaign, IL: University of Illinois at Urbana-Champaign.

———. 2005. *Making Meaning with Texts: Selected Essays.* Portsmouth, NH: Heinemann.

Routman, Regie. 2018. *Literacy Essentials: Engagement, Excellence, and Equity for All Learners.* Portland, ME: Stenhouse.

Rowling, J.K. 2008. "Harvard Commencement Speech" June. Cambridge, MA.

Ryan, James E. 2017. *Wait, What? And Life's Other Essential Questions.* New York: HarperOne.

Serafini, Frank. 2015. *Reading Workshop 2.0: Supporting Readers in the Digital Age.* Portsmouth, NH: Heinemann.

Souto-Manning, Mariana, Carmen Lugo Llerena, Jessica Martell, Abigail Salas, and Alicia Arce-Boardman. 2018. *No More Culturally Irrelevant Teaching.* Portsmouth, NH: Heinemann.

Souto-Manning, Mariana, and Jessica Martell. 2016. *Reading, Writing, and Talk: Inclusive Teaching Strategies for Diverse Learners, K–2.* New York: Teachers College Press.

Stewart, Melissa, and Nancy Chesley. 2014. *Perfect Pairs: Using Fiction & Nonfiction Picture Books to Teach Life Science, K–2.* Portland, ME: Stenhouse.

———. 2016. *Perfect Pairs: Using Fiction & Nonfiction Picture Books to Teach Life Science, Grades 3–5.* Portland, ME: Stenhouse.

Teaching Tolerance. 2016. *Let's Talk! Discussing Race, Racism and Other Difficulties with Students.* Montgomery, AL: Teaching Tolerance, A Project of the Southern Poverty Law Center.

Tovani, Cris. 2004. *Do I Really Have to Teach Reading? Content Comprehension, Grades 6–12.* Portland, ME: Stenhouse.

Trelease, Jim. 2019. *Previews of Jim Trelease Free Reading Posters.* "Oral Vaccine for Literacy" Poster. http://www.trelease-on-reading.com/poster-previews.pdf (page 5).

University of Salford. 2015. "Well-Designed Classrooms Can Boost Learning Progress in Primary School Pupils by Up to 16% in a Single Year, Research Reveals." *ScienceDaily.* April 1. https://www.sciencedaily.com/releases/2015/04/150401084453.htm.

Verden, Claire E. 2012. "Reading Culturally Relevant Literature Aloud to Urban Youths with Behavioral Challenges." *Journal of Adolescent & Adult Literacy* 55 (7): 619–628. https://doi.org/10.1002/jaal.00073.

Weissberg, Roger P. CASEL 2013a, 2013b. https://www.casel.org/wp-content/uploads/2016/08/PDF-19-weissberg-cascarino-phi-delta-kappan.pdf.

———. 2016. *Edutopia.* George Lucas Educational Foundation, February 15, 2016. https://www.edutopia.org/blog/why-sel-essential-for-students-weissberg-durlak-domitrovich-gullotta.

Whitehurst, Grover J. 2002. "Dialogic Reading: An Effective Way to Read Aloud with Young Children." *Reading Rockets: Launching Young Readers.* https://www.readingrockets.org/article/dialogic-reading-effective-way-read-aloud-young-children

Willingham, Daniel. 2018. "Just How Polarized Are We About Reading Instruction?" *Daniel Willingham—Science & Education* (blog). October 29. http://www.danielwillingham.com/daniel-willingham-science-and-education-blog/just-how-polarized-are-we-about-reading-instruction.

Zemelman, Steven. 2016. *From Inquiry to Action: Civic Engagement with Project-Based Learning in All Content Areas.* Portsmouth, NH: Heinemann.

Zins, Joseph E., Michelle R. Bloodworth, Roger P. Weissberg, and Herbert J. Walberg. 2007. "The Scientific Base Linking Social and Emotional Learning to School Success." *Journal of Educational and Psychological Consultation* 17: 2–3, 191–210. DOI: 10.1080/10474410701413145.

CHILDREN'S LITERATURE BIBLIOGRAPHY

Abouraya, Karen Leggett. 2019. *Malala Yousafzai: Warrior with Words*. New York: Lee & Low Books.

Alarcón, Francisco X. 2011. *Poems to Dream Together/Poemas Para Soñar Juntos*. New York: Lee & Low Books.

Alexander, Kwame. 2017. *Out of Wonder: Poems Celebrating Poets*. Somerville, MA: Candlewick.

——. 2017. *The Playbook: 52 Rules to Aim, Shoot, and Score*. New York: HMH Books for Young Readers.

——. 2019. *The Undefeated*. New York: Versify.

Amnesty International. 2016. *We Are All Born Free: The Universal Declaration of Human Rights in Pictures*. London: Frances Lincoln Children's Books.

Archer, Micha. 2016. *Daniel Finds a Poem*. New York: Nancy Paulsen Books.

——. 2019. *Daniel's Good Day*. New York: Nancy Paulsen Books.

Arnold, Marsha Diane. 2018. *Galápagos Girl/Galapagueña*. New York: Lee & Low Books.

Atkinson, Cale. 2018. *Where Oliver Fits*. New York: Penguin.

Bajaj, Varsha. 2019. *The Home Builders*. New York: Nancy Paulsen Books.

Balasubramaniam, Saumiya. 2019. *When I Found Grandma*. Toronto: House of Anansi Press.

Barnes, Derrick. 2017. *Crown: An Ode to the Fresh Cut*. Chicago: Agate.

——. 2019. *The King of Kindergarten*. New York: Nancy Paulsen Books.

Bates, Amy June. 2018. *The Big Umbrella*. New York: Simon and Schuster.

Beaumont, Karen. 2010. *I Like Myself!* New York: HMH Books for Young Readers.

Berger, Samantha. 2018. *What If . . .* New York: Little, Brown Books for Young Readers.

Birdsong, Bea. 2019. *I Will Be Fierce!* New York: Roaring Book Press.

Birtha, Becky. 2017. *Far Apart, Close in Heart: Being a Family When a Loved One Is Incarcerated*. Chicago: Albert Whitman.

Borden, Louise. 2004. *The A+ Custodian*. New York: Simon and Schuster.

Britt, Paige. 2017. *Why Am I Me?* New York: Scholastic.

Brown, Margaret Wise. 2006. *Another Important Book*. New York: HarperCollins.

Brown, Monica. 2011. *Marisol McDonald Doesn't Match/Marisol McDonald no combina*. New York: Children's Book Press.

Brown, Tameka Fryer. 2013. *My Cold Plum Lemon Pie Bluesy Mood*. New York: Viking Books for Young Readers.

Brozo, Patty. 2019. *The Buddy Bench*. Thomaston, ME: Tilbury House.

Bunting, Eve. 1993. *Fly Away Home*. Boston: Clarion Books.

———. 2006. *One Green Apple*. Boston: Clarion Books.

Button, Lana. 2014. *Willow's Whispers*. Toronto: Kids Can Press.

Byers, Grace. 2018. *I Am Enough*. New York: Balzer and Bray.

Calabrese, Keith. 2018. *Lena's Shoes Are Nervous: A First-Day-of-School Dilemma*. New York: Atheneum Books for Young Readers.

Campbell, Marcy. 2018. *Adrian Simcox Does NOT Have a Horse*. New York: Dial Books.

Campoy, Isabel, F. and Teresa Howell. 2016. *Maybe Something Beautiful: How Art Transformed a Neighborhood*. New York: HMH Books for Young Readers.

Carlson, Nancy. 1988. *I Like Me!* New York: Penguin.

Catalanotto, Peter. 2005. *Matthew A.B.C.* New York: Atheneum Books for Young Readers.

———. 2006. *Emily's Art*. New York: Atheneum Books for Young Readers.

Cherry, Matthew. *2019. Hair Love*. New York: Kokila.

Chung, Arree. 2018. *Mixed: A Colorful Story*. New York: Henry Holt.

Churnin, Nancy. 2018. *Martin & Anne: The Kindred Spirits of Dr. Martin Luther King, Jr. and Anne Frank*. San Francisco: Creston Books.

———. 2020. *Beautiful Shades of Brown: The Art of Laura Wheeler Waring*. San Francisco: Creston Books.

Clayton, Dallas. 2014. *A Is for Awesome*. Somerville, MA: Candlewick.

Cline-Ransome, Lesa. 2018. *Game Changers: The Story of Venus and Serena Williams*. New York: Simon and Schuster.

Cornwall, Gaia. 2017. *Jabari Jumps*. Somerville, MA: Candlewick.

Cottin, Menena. 2008. *The Black Book of Colors*. Toronto: Groundwood Books.

Cousteau, Philippe, and Deborah Hopkinson. 2016. *Follow the Moon Home: A Tale of One Idea, Twenty Kids, and a Hundred Sea Turtles*. San Francisco: Chronicle Books.

Crimi, Carolyn. 2017. *There Might Be Lobsters*. Somerville, MA: Candlewick.

Davids, Stacy B. 2015. *Annie's Plaid Shirt*. Austin, TX: Upswing Press.

de Anda, Diane. 2019. *Mango Moon*. Park Ridge, IL: Albert Whitman.

de la Peña, Matt. 2015. *Last Stop on Market Street*. New York: Penguin.

———. 2019. *Carmela Full of Wishes*. New York: Penguin.

Dean, James. 2015, *Pete the Cat's Groovy Guide to Life*. New York: HarperCollins.

Deedy, Carmen Agra. 2017. *The Rooster Who Would Not Be Quiet!* New York: Scholastic.

Degman, Lori. 2019. *Just Read!* New York: Sterling Children's Books.

Denise, Anika Aldamuy. 2019. *Planting Stories: The Life of Librarian and Storyteller Pura Belpré*. New York: HarperCollins.

Denos, Julia. 2017. *Windows*. Somerville, MA: Candlewick.

Doerrfeld, Cori. 2018. *The Rabbit Listened*. New York: Dial Books.

Downey, Roma. 2010. *Love Is a Family*. New York: HarperCollins.

Durango, Julia. 2017. *The One Day House*. Watertown, MA: Charlesbridge.

Editors and illustrators of Pajama Press. 2018. *A World of Kindness*. Toronto: Pajama Press.

Eggers, Dave. 2018. *What Can a Citizen Do?* San Francisco: Chronicle Books.

Elliott, Zetta. 2017. *Benny Doesn't Like to Be Hugged*. Scotts Valley, CA: CreateSpace Independent Publishing Platform.

———. 2017. *A Hand to Hold*. Scotts Valley, CA: CreateSpace Independent Publishing Platform.

Ellis, Carson. 2015. *Home*. Somerville, MA: Candlewick.

Engle, Margarita. 2017. *Bravo! Poems About Amazing Hispanics*. New York: Henry Holt.

Ewald, Wendy. 2002. *The Best Part of Me: Children Talk About Their Bodies in Pictures and Words*. Boston: Little, Brown Books for Young Readers.

Fanelli, Sara. 2001. *My Map Book*. New York: HarperCollins.

Faruqi, Reem. 2015. *Lailah's Lunchbox: A Ramadan Story*. Thomaston, ME: Tilbury House.

Foreman, Jack, and Michael Foreman. 2012. *Say Hello*. Somerville, MA: Candlewick.

Frame, Jeron Ashford. 2008. *Yesterday I Had the Blues*. Berkeley, CA: Tricycle Press.

Frank, John. 2014. *Lend a Hand: Poems About Giving*. New York: Lee & Low Books.

Freedman, Deborah. 2019. *Carl and the Meaning of Life*. New York: Viking Books for Young Readers.

Furst, Joshua. 2019. *The Little Red Stroller*. New York: Penguin Young Readers Group.

Gillard, Denise. 2011. *Music from the Sky*. Toronto: Groundwood Books.

Glenn, Sharlee. 2018. *Library on Wheels: Mary Lemist Titcomb and America's First Bookmobile*. New York: Harry N. Abrams.

Goldberg, Dana. 2012. *On My Block: Stories and Paintings by Fifteen Artists*. New York: Lee & Low Books.

Gonzales, Mark. 2017. *Yo Soy Muslim: A Father's Letter to His Daughter*. New York: Salaam Reads/ Simon and Schuster Books for Young Readers.

Gonzalez, Maya Christina. 2014. *Call Me Tree*. New York: Lee & Low Books.

Gonzalez, Xelena. 2017. *All Around Us*. El Paso, TX: Cinco Puntos Press.

Graham, Bob. 2012. *A Bus Called Heaven*. Somerville, MA: Candlewick.

Greven, Alec. 2010. *Rules for School*. New York: HarperCollins.

Gundersheimer, Ben. 2019. *Señorita Mariposa*. New York: Nancy Paulsen Books.

Hall, Michael. 2015. *Red: A Crayon's Story*. New York: Greenwillow Books.

Hegedus, Bethany. 2019. *Rise! From Caged Bird to Poet of the People, Maya Angelou*. New York: Lee & Low Books.

Heling, Kathryn, and Deborah Hembrook. 2019. *There's Only One You*. New York: Sterling Children's Books.

Henn, Sophy. 2017. *Pass It On*. New York: Penguin.

Herrera, Juan Felipe. 2018. *Imagine*. Somerville, MA: Candlewick.

Hoffman, Sarah, and Ian Hoffman. 2019. *Jacob's Room to Choose*. Washington, DC: Magination Press.

Hong, Jess. 2017. *Lovely*. San Francisco: Creston Books.

Hood, Susan. 2018. *Shaking Things Up: 14 Young Women Who Changed the World*. New York: HarperCollins.

Hopkins, Lee Bennett. 2015. *Amazing Places*. New York: Lee & Low Books.

Hopkinson, Deborah. 2017. *A Letter to My Teacher*. New York: Random House Children's Books.

Hunt, Lynda Mullaly. 2015. *Fish in a Tree*. New York: Penguin Random House.

Ikegami, Aiko. 2019. *Hello*. San Francisco: Creston Books.

Jenkins, Steve. 1997. *Biggest, Strongest, Fastest*. Boston: Houghton Mifflin Harcourt.

John, Jory. 2016. *Quit Calling Me a Monster*. New York: Random House Children's Books.

———. 2019. *The Good Egg*. New York: HarperCollins.

Jonker, Travis. 2018. *The Very Last Castle*. New York: Harry N. Abrams.

Judge, Lita. 2014. *Flight School*. New York: Atheneum Books for Young Readers.

Katz, Karen. 2002. *The Colors of Us*. New York: Square Fish.

Keating, Jess. 2018. *Cute as an Axolotl: Discovering the World's Most Adorable Animals*. New York: Alfred A. Knopf.

Kelkar, Supriya. 2019. *The Many Colors of Harpreet Singh*. New York: Sterling Children's Books.

Kerascoët. 2018. *I Walk with Vanessa: A Story About a Simple Act of Kindness*. New York: Penguin Random House.

Khan, Hena. 2015. *Golden Domes and Silver Lanterns: A Muslim Book of Colors*. San Francisco: Chronicle Books.

———. 2018. *Under My Hijab*. New York: Lee & Low Books.

Kirkfield, Vivian. 2019. *Sweet Dreams, Sarah.* San Francisco: Creston Books.

Knudsen, Michelle. 2009. *Library Lion.* Somerville, MA: Candlewick.

Kranz, Linda. 2006. *Only One You.* Lanham, MD: Cooper Square.

Krishnaswami, Uma. 2008. *The Happiest Tree: A Yoga Story.* New York: Lee & Low Books.

———. 2015. *Bringing Asha Home.* New York: Lee & Low Books.

Krosoczka, Jarrett J. 2015. *It's Tough to Lose Your Balloon.* New York: Alfred A. Knopf.

Kyle, Tracey. 2018. *A Paintbrush for Paco.* New York: Little Bee Books.

Laditan, Bunmi. 2018. *The Big Bed.* New York: Farrar, Straus Giroux.

Lamba, Marie. 2019. *A Day So Gray.* Boston: Clarion Books.

Lambert, Megan Dowd. 2016. *Real Sisters Pretend.* Thomaston, ME: Tilbury House.

Lamothe, Matt. 2017. *This Is How We Do It: One Day in the Lives of Seven Kids from Around the World.* San Francisco: Chronicle Books.

Latham, Irene, and Charles Waters. 2018. *Can I Touch Your Hair? Poems of Race, Mistakes, and Friendship.* Minneapolis, MN: Lerner.

Latour, Francie. 2018. *Aunt Luce's Talking Paintings.* Toronto: Groundwood Books.

Lê, Minh. 2018. *Drawn Together.* White Plains, NY: Disney-Hyperion.

Leannah, Michael. 2017. *Most People.* Thomaston, ME: Tilbury House.

Lebeuf, Darren. 2019. *My Forest Is Green.* Toronto: Kids Can Press.

Ledyard, Stephanie Parsley. 2019. *Home Is a Window.* New York: Neal Porter Books / Holiday House.

Lee, Spike, and Tonya Lewis Lee. 2011. *Giant Steps to Change the World.* New York: Simon and Schuster.

Lennon, John. 2017. *Imagine.* Boston: Clarion Books.

Levy, Debbie. 2016. *I Dissent: Ruth Bader Ginsburg Makes Her Mark.* New York: Simon and Schuster.

Lewis, J. Patrick. 2005. *Heroes and She-roes: Poems of Amazing and Everyday Heroes.* New York: Dial Books.

Llenas, Anna. 2016. *The Color Monster.* London, United Kingdom: Templar.

Lovell, Patty. 2001. *Stand Tall, Molly Lou Melon.* New York: G. P. Putnam's Sons.

Ludwig, Trudy. 2008. *Trouble Talk.* New York: Tricycle Press.

———. 2010. *Confessions of a Former Bully.* New York: Tricycle Press.

———. 2011. *Better Than You.* New York: Knopf Books for Young Readers.

———. 2013. *The Invisible Boy.* New York: Knopf Books for Young Readers.

———. 2015. *My Secret Bully.* New York: Dragonfly Books.

———. 2018. *Quiet Please, Owen McPhee!* New York: Penguin Random House.

Lukoff, Aidan. 2019. *When Aidan Became a Brother*. New York: Lee & Low Books.

Luyken, Corinna. 2017. *The Book of Mistakes*. New York: Dial Books for Young Readers.

———. 2019. *My Heart*. New York: Dial Books for Young Readers.

Lyons, Kelly Starling. 2019. *Going Down Home with Daddy*. Atlanta, GA: Peachtree.

Mantchev, Lisa. 2015. *Strictly No Elephants*. New York: Simon and Schuster.

Marcero, Deborah. 2018. *My Heart Is a Compass*. Boston: Little, Brown.

Martinez-Neal, Juana. 2018. *Alma and How She Got Her Name*. Somerville, MA: Candlewick.

Mayeno, Laurin. 2016. *One of A Kind, Like Me / Único como yo*. Oakland, CA: Blood Orange Press.

McAnulty, Stacy. 2016. *Beautiful*. Philadelphia: Running Press Kids.

———. 2016. *Excellent Ed*. New York: Alfred A. Knopf.

———. 2017. *Brave*. Philadelphia: Running Press Kids.

McGhee, Holly M. 2017. *Come with Me*. New York: G. P. Putnam's Sons.

———. 2019. *Listen*. New York: Roaring Book Press.

McKissack, Patricia C. 2000. *The Honest-to-Goodness Truth*. New York: Scholastic.

———. 2019. *What Is Given from the Heart*. New York: Schwartz & Wade Books.

Medina, Meg. 2015. *Mango, Abuela, and Me*. New York: Candlewick.

Méndez, Yamile Saied. 2019. *Where Are You From?* New York: HarperCollins.

Miller, Pat Zietlow. 2018. *Be Kind*. London: Macmillan.

———. 2019. *Remarkably You*. New York: HarperCollins.

———. 2019. *When You Are Brave*. New York: Little, Brown Books for Young Readers.

Millner, Denene. 2017. *Early Sunday Morning*. Chicago: Agate.

Mora, Oge. 2018. *Thank You, Omu!* New York: Little, Brown Books for Young Readers.

Mora, Pat. 2001. *Love to Mamá: A Tribute to Mothers*. New York: Lee & Low Books.

———. 2009. *Gracias/Thanks*. New York: Lee & Low Books.

———. 2018. *Bookjoy, Wordjoy*. New York: Lee & Low Books.

Morrison, Toni, and Slade Morrison. 2014. *Please, Louise*. New York: Simon and Schuster.

Moss, Marissa. 2018. *Kate Warne: Pinkerton Detective*. San Francisco: Creston Books.

Mulder, Michelle. 2019. *Home Sweet Neighborhood: Transforming Cities One Block at a Time*. Victoria, BC: Orca Book.

Myers, Christopher. 2015. *My Pen*. White Plains, NY: Disney-Hyperion.

Naberhaus, Sarvinder. 2017. *Blue Sky White Stars*. New York: Penguin Young.

Nagara, Innosanto. 2013. *A Is for Activist*. New York: Triangle Square Seven Stories Press.

Nargi, Lela. 2018. *A Heart Just Like My Mother's*. Minneapolis, MN: Kar-Ben.

National Geographic Society. 2008. *Every Human Has Rights: A Photographic Declaration for Kids*. Washington, DC: National Geographic.

Neal, Christopher Silas. 2016. *Everyone . . .* New York: Candlewick.

Neal, Kate Jane. 2017. *Words and Your Heart*. New York: Macmillan.

Nelson, Kadir. 2015. *If You Plant a Seed*. New York: Balzer and Bray.

Newman, Lesléa. 2015. *My Name Is Aviva*. Minneapolis, MN: Kar-Ben.

———. 2017. *Sparkle Boy*. New York: Lee & Low Books.

Nikola-Lisa, W. 2009. *How We Are Smart*. New York: Lee & Low Books.

Nuño, Fran. 2017. *The Map of Good Memories*. Madrid, Spain: Cuento de Luz.

O'Leary, Sara. 2017. *A Family Is a Family Is a Family*. Toronto: Groundwood Books.

Orloff, Karen Kaufman. 2019. *Miles of Smiles*. New York: Sterling Children's Books.

Otheguy, Emma. 2017. *Martí's Song for Freedom*. New York: Lee & Low Books.

Otoshi, Kathryn. 2008. *One*. Novato, CA: KO Kids Books.

———. 2010. *Zero*. Novato, CA: KO Kids Books.

———. 2014. *Two*. Novato, CA: KO Books.

Otoshi, Kathryn, and Bret Baumgarten. 2015. *Beautiful Hands*. Novato, CA: KO Kids Books.

Palacio, R. J. 2014. *365 Days of Wonder*. New York: Alfred A. Knopf.

———. 2017. *We're All Wonders*. New York: Alfred A. Knopf.

Parr, Todd. 2017. *Love the World*. New York: Little, Brown Books for Young Readers.

Paul, Miranda. 2019. *Little Libraries, Big Heroes*. Boston: Clarion Books.

Penfold, Alexandra. 2018. *All Are Welcome*. New York: Random House Children's Books.

Pérez, Amada Irma. 2009. *My Diary from Here to There/Mi diario de aquí hasta allá*. New York: Lee & Low Books.

Pilutti, Deb. 2014. *Ten Rules of Being a Superhero*. New York: Henry Holt and Christy Ottaviano Books.

Pla, Sally J. 2019. *Benji, the Bad Day, and Me*. New York: Lee & Low Books.

Polacco, Patricia. 2012. *Thank You, Mr. Falker*. New York: Philomel Books.

Quintero, Isabel. 2019. *My Papi Has a Motorcycle*. New York: Kokila.

Ransome, James. 2012. *My Teacher*. New York: Penguin Young Readers Group.

Raschka, Chris. 2013. *Everyone Can Learn to Ride a Bicycle*. New York: Schwartz & Wade Books.

Rex, Adam. 2016. *School's First Day of School*. New York: Roaring Book Press.

Reynolds, Aaron. 2017. *Nerdy Birdy Tweets*. New York: Roaring Book Press.

Reynolds, Peter H. 2003. *The Dot.* Somerville, MA: Candlewick.

——. 2009. *The North Star.* Somerville, MA: Candlewick.

——. 2016. *Playing from the Heart.* Somerville, MA: Candlewick.

——. 2017. *Happy Dreamer.* New York: Orchard Books.

——. 2018. *The Word Collector.* New York: Orchard Books.

——. 2019. *Say Something!* New York: Scholastic.

Robinson, Christian. 2019. *Another.* New York: Atheneum Books for Young Readers.

Robinson, Sharon. 2014. *Under the Same Sun.* New York: Scholastic.

Rohmer, Harriet, ed. 2013. *Just Like Me: Stories and Self-Portraits by Fourteen Artists.* New York: Lee & Low Books.

Rosenthal, Amy Krouse. 2009. *Duck! Rabbit!* San Francisco: Chronicle Books.

——. 2015. *Plant a Kiss.* New York: HarperCollins.

Rubenstein, Lauren. 2014. *Visiting Feelings.* Washington, DC: Magination Press.

Rylant, Cynthia. 2017. *Life.* New York: Beach Lane Books.

Saltzberg, Barney. 2018. *Enough Is Enough!* San Francisco: Creston Books.

Sanders, Rob. 2018. *Peaceful Fights for Equal Rights.* New York: Simon and Schuster.

Sauer, Tammi. 2016. *Mary Had a Little Glam.* New York: Sterling Books.

Say, Allen. 2013. *The Favorite Daughter.* New York: Arthur A. Levine Books.

Schimel, Lawrence. 2011. *Let's Go See Papá!* Toronto: Groundwood Books.

Seeger, Laura Vaccaro. 2015. *I Used to Be Afraid.* New York: Roaring Book Press.

Serres, Allan. 2012. *I Have the Right to Be a Child.* Toronto: Groundwood Books.

Sheth, Sheetal. 2018. *Always Anjali.* New York: Bharat Babies.

Silvestro, Annie. 2019. *Butterflies on the First Day of School.* New York: Sterling Books.

Sima, Jessie. 2017. *Not Quite Narwhal.* New York: Simon and Schuster.

Simon, Seymour. 2002. *Animals Nobody Loves.* San Francisco: Chronicle Books.

Singer, Marilyn. 2019. *Every Month Is a New Year.* New York: Lee & Low Books.

Smith, Charles R., Jr. 2003. *I Am America.* New York: Scholastic.

Smith, Monique Gray. 2016. *My Heart Fills with Happiness.* Victoria, BC: Orca Books.

——. 2017. *You Hold Me Up.* Victoria, BC: Orca Books.

Sosin, Deborah. 2015. *Charlotte and the Quiet Place.* Berkeley, CA: Plum Blossom Books.

Sotomayor, Sonia. 2018. *Turning Pages: My Life Story.* New York: Philomel Books.

Spires, Ashley. 2014. *The Most Magnificent Thing.* Toronto: Kids Can Press.

Stead, Philip C. 2010. *A Sick Day for Amos McGee.* New York: Roaring Book Press.

Steptoe, Javaka. 2016. *Radiant Child: The Story of Young Artist Jean-Michel Basquiat.* New York: Little, Brown Books for Young Readers.

Stewart, Melissa. 2018. *Pipsqueaks, Slowpokes, and Stinkers: Celebrating Animal Underdogs.* Atlanta, GA: Peachtree.

Stott, Ann. 2018. *Want to Play Trucks?* Somerville, MA: Candlewick.

Sturgis, Brenda Reeves. 2017. *Still a Family: A Story About Homelessness.* Park Ridge, IL: Albert Whitman.

Tameki, Jillian. 2018. *They Say Blue.* New York: Harry N. Abrams.

Tarpley, Natasha Anastasia 2004. *Destiny's Gift.* New York: Lee & Low Books.

Tate, Nikki. 2018. *Better Together: Creating Community in an Uncertain World.* Victoria, BC: Orca Book.

Thompkins-Bigelow, Jamilah. 2018. *Mommy's Khimar.* New York: Simon and Schuster.

Tinari, Leah. 2018. *Limitless: 24 Remarkable American Women of Vision, Grit, and Guts.* New York: Simon and Schuster.

Tran, Truong. 2003. *Going Home, Coming Home/Về Nhàm, Thăm Quê Hu'o'ng* (Vietnamese). New York: Lee & Low Books.

Tregonning, Mel. 2018. *Small Things.* Toronto: Pajama Press.

Trimmer, Christian. 2018. *Teddy's Favorite Toy.* New York: Atheneum Books for Young Readers.

Vail, Rachel. 2005. *Sometimes I'm Bombaloo.* New York: Scholastic.

Van, Muon. 2015. *In a Village by the Sea.* San Francisco: Creston Books.

Vere, Ed. 2018. *How to Be a Lion.* New York: Penguin.

Verde, Susan. 2017. *I Am Peace: A Book of Mindfulness.* New York: Harry N. Abrams.

——. 2018. *Hey, Wall: A Story of Art and Community.* New York: Simon and Schuster.

Waber, Bernard. 2002. *Courage.* New York: HMH Books for Young Readers.

Wallace, Sandra Neil, and Rich Wallace. 2018. *First Generation: 36 Trailblazing Immigrants and Refugees Who Make America Great.* New York: Little, Brown for Young Readers.

Wallmark, Laurie. 2015. *Ada Byron Lovelace and the Thinking Machine.* San Francisco: Creston Books.

Weatherford, Carole Boston. 2017. *Schomburg: The Man Who Built a Library.* Somerville, MA: Candlewick.

Wenjen, Mia. 2019. *Sumo Joe.* New York: Lee & Low Books.

Wenzel, Brendan. 2016. *They All Saw a Cat.* San Francisco: Chronicle Books.

Wheeler, Eliza. 2013. *Miss Maple's Seeds.* New York: Nancy Paulsen Books.

Williams, Laura E. 2017. *The Can Man.* New York: Lee & Low Books.

Wimmer, Sonja. 2012. *The Word Collector.* Madrid, Spain: Cuento de Luz.

Witek, Jo. 2014. *In My Heart: A Book of Feelings.* New York: Harry N. Abrams.

———. 2016. *All My Treasures: A Book of Joy.* New York: Harry N. Abrams.

Woodson, Jacqueline. 2012. *Each Kindness.* New York: Nancy Paulsen Books.

———. 2014. *Brown Girl Dreaming.* New York: Nancy Paulsen Books.

———. 2018. *The Day You Begin.* New York: Nancy Paulsen Books.

———. 2018. *Harbor Me.* New York: Nancy Paulsen Books.

Yahgulanaas, Michael Nicoll. 2010. *The Little Hummingbird.* Vancouver, Canada: Greystone Books.

Yamada, Kobi. 2013. *What Do You Do with a Chance?* New York: Compendium.

———. 2016. *What Do You Do with a Problem?* New York: Compendium.

Yamasaki, Katie. 2018. *When the Cousins Came.* New York: Holiday House.

Young, Jessica. 2013. *My Blue Is Happy.* Somerville, MA: Candlewick.

Young, Timothy. 2013. *I Hate Picture Books!* Atglen, PA: Schiffer.

Zalben, Jane Breskin. 2018. *A Moon for Moe and Mo.* Minneapolis, MN: Lerner.

INDEX

CREDITS

Chapter 1:

From *Ten Rules of Being a Superhero* © 2014 by Deb Pilutti. Reprinted by permission from Henry Holt Books for Young Readers. All rights reserved.

Excerpt from *The Little Hummingbird* by Michael Yahgulanaas reprinted with permission from Greystone Books Ltd.

Each Kindness cover image used with permission from Penguin Random House.

my cold plum lemon pie bluesy mood cover image used with permission from Penguin Random House.

Chapter 2:

From *Duck! Rabbit!* © 2009 by Amy Krause Rosenthal. Used with permission of Chronicle Books, LLC, San Francisco. Visit ChronicleBooks.com.

My Secret Bully cover image used with permission from Penguin Random House.

Chapter 3:

Charlotte and the Quiet Place cover illustration copyright Sara Woolley.

Harbor Me cover image used with permission from Penguin Random House.

Chapter 5:

What Is Given from the Heart cover image used with permission from Penguin Random House.

From *School's First Day of School* © 2016 by Christian Robinson. Reprinted by permission from Roaring Brook Press, a division of Hotlzbrinck Publishing Holdings Limited Partnership. All rights reserved.

The Big Umbrella, Illustrations Copyright © 2018 by Amy June Bates.

My Papi Has a Motorcycle cover image used with permission from Penguin Random House.

Cute as an Axolotl cover image used with permission from Penguin Random House.

All Are Welcome cover image used with permission from Penguin Random House.

Blue Sky White Stars cover image used with permission from Penguin Random House.

From *A Sick Day for Amos McGee* © 2010 by Erin E. Stead. Reprinted by permission from Roaring Brook Press, a division of Holtzbrinck Publishing Holdings Limited Partnership. All rights reserved.

My Name Is Aviva by Lesléa Newman, illustrated by Ag Jatkowska. Text copyright © 2015 by Lesléa Newman. Illustration copyright © 2015 by Aj Jatkowska. Reprinted with the permission of Kar-Ben Publishing, Inc., a division of Lerner Publishing Group, Inc. All rights reserved. No part of this excerpt may be used or reproduced in any manner whatsoever without the prior written permission of Lerner Publishing Group, Inc.

First published in the United States under the title *Pipsqueaks, Slowpokes, and Stinkers* by Melissa Stewart, illustrated by Stephanie Laberis. Text copyright © 2018 by Melissa Stewart. Illustrations copyright © 2018 by Stephanie Laberis. Published by arrangement with Peachtree Publishing Company, Inc.

A Letter to My Teacher cover image used with permission from Penguin Random House.

Little Red Stroller cover image used with permission from Penguin Random House.

Stand Tall Molly Lou Melon cover image used with permission from Penguin Random House.

Thank You, Mr. Falker cover image used with permission from Penguin Random House.

I Am Peace by Susan Verde; art by Peter H. Reynolds. Text copyright © 2017 Susan Verde. Illustrations copyright © 2017 Peter H. Reynolds. Used by permission of Abrams Books for Young Readers, an imprint of Harry N. Abrams, Inc., New York. All rights reserved.

Chapter 6:

Libraries on Wheels by Sharlee Glenn. Text copyright © 2018 Sharlee Glenn. Used by permission of Abrams Books for Young Readers, an imprint of Harry N. Abrams, Inc., New York. All rights reserved.

Strictly No Elephants. Illustrations copyright © 2015 by Taeeun Yoo.

Hey Wall. Illustrations copyright © 2018 by John Parra.

Giant Steps to Change the World. Illustrations copyright © 2011 by Sean Qualls.

Peaceful Fights for Equal Rights. Illustrations copyright © 2018 Jared Andrew Schorr.

From *Be Kind* © 2018 by Jen Hill. Reprinted by permission from Roaring Brook Press, a division of Holtzbrinck Publishing Holdings Limited Partnership. All rights reserved.

From *Bravo!* © 2017 by Rafael López. Reprinted by permission from Henry Holt Books for Young Readers. All rights reserved.

From *Words and Your Heart* © 2017 by Kate Jane Neal. Reprinted by permission from Feiwel & Friends. All rights reserved.

Planting Stories cover image used with permission from HarperCollins Publishers.

Rules for School cover image used with permission from HarperCollins Publishers.

Shaking Things Up cover image used with permission from HarperCollins Publishers.

A Is for Activist cover image used with permission from Seven Stories Press.

Out of Wonder. Text copyright © 2017 by Kwame Alexander. Illustrations copyright © 2017 by Ekua Holmes. Reproduced by permission of the publisher, Candlewick Press, Somerville, MA.

Library Lion. Text copyright © 2006 by Michelle Knudson. Illustrations copyright © 2006 by Kevin Hawkes. Reproduced by permission of the publisher, Candlewick Press, Somerville, MA.

Schomburg: The Man Who Built a Library. Text copyright © 2017 by Carole Boston Weatherford. Illustrations copyright © 2017 by Eric Velasquez. Reproduced by permission of the publisher, Candlewick Press, Somerville, MA.

Rooster Who Wouldn't Keep Quiet cover image used with permission from Scholastic, Inc.

Say Something cover image used with permission from Scholastic, Inc.

Word Collector cover image used with permission from Scholastic, Inc.

Images from *Auntie Luce's Talking Paintings* Text copyright © 2018 by Francie Latour and illustrations copyright © 2017 by Qin LengLeng Ken Daley. Reproduced with permission from Groundwood Books Limited, Toronto. www.groundwoodbooks.com.

Book Joy, Word Joy cover image used with permission from the publisher, Lee & Low Books, Inc.

Call Me Tree cover image used with permission from the publisher, Lee & Low Books, Inc.

Can Man cover image used with permission from the publisher, Lee & Low Books, Inc.

Destiny's Gift cover image used with permission from the publisher, Lee & Low Books, Inc.

Galapagos Girls cover image used with permission from the publisher, Lee & Low Books, Inc.

Just Like Me cover image used with permission from the publisher, Lee & Low Books, Inc.

Lend a Hand cover image used with permission from the publisher, Lee & Low Books, Inc.

Marti's Song for Freedom cover image used with permission from the publisher, Lee & Low Books, Inc.

The One Day House. Text copyright © 2017 by Julia Durango. Illustrations copyright © 2017 by Bianca Diaz. Used with permission by Charlesbridge Publishing.

Ada Byron Lovelace and the Thinking Machine cover image used with permission from Creston Publishing.

Hello cover image used with permission from Creston Publishing.

Sweet Dreams, Sarah cover image used with permission from Creston Publishing.

Kate Warne: Pinkerton Detective cover image used with permission from Creston Publishing.

Limitless. Illustrations copyright © 2018 by Leah Tinari.

Miles of Smiles cover image used with permission from Sterling Publishing.

Little Libraries, Big Heroes cover image used with permission from Houghton Mifflin Harcourt.

Maybe Something Beautiful cover image used with permission from Houghton Mifflin Harcourt.

Daniel Finds a Poem cover image used with permission from Penguin Random House.

Home Sweet Neighborhood used with permission from Orca Books.

I Walk with Vanessa cover image used with permission from Penguin Random House.

Last Stop on Market Street cover image used with permission from Penguin Random House.

Quiet Please, Owen McPhee cover image used with permission from Penguin Random House.

Turning Pages cover image used with permission from Penguin Random House.

Cover image from *My Forest Is Green* written by Darren Lebeuf and illustrated by Ashley Barron is used by permission of Kids Can Press Ltd., Toronto. Cover illustration © 2019 Ashley Barron.

Chapter 7:

We're All Wonders cover image used with permission from Penguin Random House.

Yesterday I Had the Blues cover image used with permission from Penguin Random House.

Not Quite Narwhal. Illustrations copyright © 2017 by Jessie Sima.

Life. Illustrations copyright © 2017 by Brendan Wenzel.

Another. Illustrations copyright © 2019 by Christian Robinson.

Matthew ABC, Illustrations copyright © 2002 by Peter Catalanotto.

Emily's Art. Illustrations copyright © 2001 by Peter Catalanotto.

Say Hello cover image used with permission from Penguin Random House.

The Invisible Boy cover image used with permission from Penguin Random House.

First published in the United States under the title *Going Down Home with Daddy* by Kelly Starling Lyons, illustrated by Daniel Minter. Text copyright © 2019 by Kelly Starling Lyons. Illustrations copyright © 2019 by Daniel Minter. Published by arrangement with Peachtree Publishing Company, Inc.

Sparkle Boy cover image used with permission from the publisher, Lee & Low Books, Inc.

A World of Kindness cover image used with permission from Pajama Press.

Lovely cover image used with permission from Creston Publishing.

Enough Is Enough! cover image used with permission from Creston Publishing.

In a Village by the Sea cover image used with permission from Creston Publishing.

A Day So Gray cover image used with permission from Houghton Mifflin Harcourt.

Courage cover image used with permission from Houghton Mifflin Harcourt.

Home Builders cover image used with permission from Penguin Random House.

Miss Maple's Seeds cover image used with permission from Penguin Random House.

Senorita Mariposa cover image used with permission from Penguin Random House.

Lailah's Lunchbox cover image used with permission from Tilbury House.

The Buddy Beach cover image used with permission from Tilbury House.

Trouble Talk cover image used with permission from Penguin Random House.

I Like Myself cover image used with permission from Houghton Mifflin Harcourt.

The Honest-to-Goodness Truth illustrations copyright © 2000 by Giselle Potter.

Please Louise illustrations copyright © 2014 by Shadra Strickland.

Chapter 8:

From *The Big Bed* © 2018 by Tom Knight. Reprinted by permission from Farrar, Straus, Giroux Brooks for Young Readers. All rights reserved.

From *I Used to Be Afraid* © 2015 by Laura Vaccaro Seeger. Reprinted by permission from Roaring Brook Press, a division of Holtzbrinck Publishing Holdings Limited Partnership. All rights reserved.

From *Listen* © 2019 by Holly M. McGhee, illustrations 2010 by Pascal Lemaitre. Reprinted by permission of Roaring Brook Press, a division of Holtzbrinck Publishing Holdings Limited Partnership. All rights reserved.

From *I Will Be Fierce* © 2019 by Bea Birdsong and Nidhi Chanani. Reprinted by permission from Roaring Brook Press, a division of Holtzbrinck Publishing Holdings Limited Partnership. All rights reserved.

Crown cover image used with permission from Agate Publishing.

I Am Enough cover image used with permission from HarperCollins Publishers.

In My Heart: A Book of Feelings Copyright © 2014 De La Martiniere Jeunesse, a division of La Martiniere Europe, Paris. Text copyright © 2014 Jo Witek. Illustrations copyright © 2014 Christine Roussey. English translation © 2016 Harry N. Abrams, Inc.

There Might Be Lobsters. Text copyright © 2017 by Carolyn Crimi. Illustrations copyright © 2017 by Laurel Molk. Reproduced by permission of the publisher, Candlewick Press, Somerville, MA.

Jabari Jumps. Copyright © 2017 by Gaia Cornwall. Reproduced by permission of the publisher, Candlewick Press, Somerville, MA.

Imagine. Text copyright © 2017 by Juan Felipe Herrera. Illustrations copyright © 2017 by Lauren Castillo. Reproduced by permission of the publisher, Candlewick Press, Somerville, MA.

Where Oliver Fits cover image used with permission from Penguin Random House.

Happy Dreamer cover image used with permission from Scholastic, Inc.